Advance Praise for *The Snowflakes' Revolt*

"Colleges don't teach journalism. As this book reveals, students are instead taught to cry about micro-aggressions and then take that victimhood mentality to media outlets across America. This progressive outlook is a cancer rotting our institutions from within, from the military to newsrooms."

—**Lisa Boothe**, Host of *The Truth with Lisa Boothe*

"This book is a must read for anyone seeking a deeper understanding of the destructive effects of totalitarian cancel culture. It walks you through how it happened, and what will happen if we don't stop it."

—**Dan Bongino**, Author and Host of *The Dan Bongino Show*

"Conservatives are no longer engaged in a battle over ideas—we are engaged in an existential war over whether our ideas will even be allowed to be heard. Wonder how we got here? Amber Athey knows. She has been on the frontlines of the 'cancel wars' for her entire career and has even been in the crosshairs. I saw firsthand how her courage, tenacity, and spirit inspired so many to stand up and refuse to be silenced. Hers is a vital voice going forward in this new, Orwellian era in American public discourse."

—**Larry O'Connor**, Host of
O'Connor & Company on WMAL
and Columnist at *Townhall*

"Amber Athey combines her impressive guts with intelligent writing to reveal the inner workings of the corrupt corporate media in America. I hope and expect that her excellent book will accelerate the trend of sending these legacy platforms toward total irrelevance."

—**Steve Cortes**, Former Senior
Advisor to former President Trump

THE SNOWFLAKES' REVOLT

HOW WOKE MILLENNIALS HIJACKED AMERICAN MEDIA

AMBER ATHEY

Published by Bombardier Books
An Imprint of Post Hill Press
ISBN: 978-1-63758-354-8
ISBN (eBook): 978-1-63758-355-5

The Snowflakes' Revolt:
How Woke Millennials Hijacked American Media
© 2023 by Amber Athey
All Rights Reserved

Cover Design by Matt Margolis

This is a work of nonfiction. All people, locations, events, and situation are portrayed to the best of the author's memory.

Post Hill Press
New York • Nashville
posthillpress.com

Published in the United States of America
1 2 3 4 5 6 7 8 9 10

To Dad. I hope I made you proud.

CONTENTS

INTRO

"**E** very girl is bi. You just have to figure out if it's polar or sexual."

That was the joke that set off a firestorm at the *Washington Post*, leading to the suspension of one reporter and the termination of another.

Comedian Cam Harless tweeted this wisecrack just before midnight on June 1, 2022,[1] unintentionally setting up the very public destruction of the *Post*'s last remaining shreds of dignity.

Two days later, politics reporter Dave Weigel retweeted Harless. Weigel, who started his second stint with the *Post* in 2015 (he worked there briefly in 2010 but was canned over some unsavory leaked emails) was somehow blissfully unaware that corporate newsrooms are no longer receptive to attempts at comedy.

Sure enough, one of Weigel's humorless colleagues took umbrage with his retweet. Felicia Sonmez, also on the politics desk, initially privately chastised Weigel for retweeting the joke on a company Slack channel, but then, two minutes later, blasted

---

[1] Harless, Cam. "Every Girl Is Bi. You Just Have to Figure out If It's Polar or Sexual." Twitter. Twitter, June 2, 2022. https://twitter.com/hamcarless/status/1532209116134920192.

him publicly on her Twitter account.[2] It seems she was the "polar" half of Harless's equation.

"Fantastic to work at a news outlet where retweets like this are allowed!" Sonmez sarcastically exclaimed.

Weigel did what you should never do in the face of an angry mob, particularly when you've done nothing wrong: He apologized.

"I just removed a retweet of an offensive joke. I apologize and did not mean to cause any harm," Weigel said.

The *Post* also released a statement: "Editors have made clear to the staff that the tweet was reprehensible and demanding language or actions like that will not be tolerated."[3]

Weigel's apology did little to calm the storm. Sonmez continued to angrily tweet, now directing her ire at another *Post* colleague, Jose A. Del Real, who argued it was inappropriate for Sonmez to air her grievances publicly and that she had behaved cruelly by encouraging the internet to pounce on Weigel. Sonmez wouldn't accept that she might be the aggressor in this situation. Instead, she cried that *she* was the victim of a targeted online harassment campaign. Sonmez publicly urged *Washington Post* editor Sally Buzbee to *do something!* Left-wing journos rallied behind their champion, declaring Sonmez a hero for fearlessly taking on sexism.

---

[2] Klein, Charlotte. "'Clusterf--k': Inside the Washington Post's Social Media Meltdown." *Vanity Fair*, June 8, 2022. https://www.vanityfair.com/news/2022/06/inside-the-washington-posts-social-media-meltdown.

[3] Gonzalez, Umberto. "Washington Post Writer Apologizes for Retweet of Sexist Tweet Claiming 'Every Girl Is Bi.'" TheWrap, June 4, 2022. https://www.thewrap.com/washington-post-david-weigel-apologizes-retweet-sexist-tweet/.

The next day, CNN reported that Weigel was suspended from his job for a month without pay.[4]

Victory! Sonmez got her scalp. Except she wasn't finished. Sonmez had made clear in her days-long tweet storm that her problem wasn't just with Weigel, but also with an allegedly toxic workplace at the *Post* and an uneven enforcement of newsroom policies. It turned out that pretending to be wildly offended by the joke about women being either bipolar or bisexual was just a pretense for Sonmez to bring up a professional grievance she had been stewing over for the past two years.

In 2020, Sonmez had been placed on paid administrative leave by the *Washington Post* for tweeting a story about rape allegations against Kobe Bryant shortly after the basketball star perished alongside his daughter in a gruesome helicopter crash. Over 200 of Sonmez's colleagues signed a letter criticizing *Post* leadership for the move, Weigel included. He clearly received zero goodwill for his efforts.

Sonmez insisted in a long tweet thread after the Weigel incident that white men in the newsroom were able to "get away with murder" on social media while women and minorities faced unfairly harsh punishments when they seemingly broke company social media policy. It's worth pointing out that Sonmez received a paid suspension for spitting on a dead man's grave, while Weigel received an unpaid suspension for making a dumb joke. To whom was the social media policy applied more harshly? The white man or the woman?

Finally, the *Post* fired Sonmez after a full week of nonstop tweets trashing the company's leadership. It was a rare moment in

---

4   Darcy, Oliver. "The Washington Post Suspends Reporter David Weigel over Sexist Retweet | CNN Business." CNN. Cable News Network, June 6, 2022. https://www.cnn.com/2022/06/06/media/dave-weigel-washington-post-suspended/index.html.

which an unhinged liberal reporter actually faced consequences for her actions.[5]

But why was Sonmez so eager to risk her reporting job by publicly trashing her colleagues and employer?

Sonmez's lawsuit against the Post might have something to do with it, but we'll get into more details about that in a later chapter.

Most important is that corporate media companies like the *Washington Post* and the *New York Times* have incentivized this kind of reckless sociopathy.

Over the past decade, a crisis of poor decision-making and an abdication of leadership have accelerated the decline of these once-prestigious media outlets. Rather than invest in talented, professional, and objective reporters, major outlets have instead staffed their newsrooms with young woke activists who prefer advancing progressive political causes over adhering to journalistic ethics.

Take Taylor Lorenz, a tech reporter for the *Post*, formerly with the *New York Times*. At the same time Sonmez was publicly tarnishing the *Post*, Lorenz was trying to explain why her latest piece of shoddy reporting required multiple edits and why the *Post* chose not to initially disclose those edits publicly.

In Lorenz's piece, she attacked commentators who said that the Johnny Depp vs. Amber Heard trial demonstrated the excesses of the #MeToo movement. Problem was, multiple subjects in the story said Lorenz had lied about reaching out to them for comment. Lorenz blamed this on a "miscommunication" with her editor and insisted the criticism was merely part of a "bad faith campaign" to tarnish her reputation. She even had the

---

5   Darcy, Oliver. "The Washington Post Fires Felicia Sonmez after a Week of Feuding Publicly with Her Colleagues." CNN. Cable News Network, June 10, 2022. https://www.cnn.com/2022/06/09/media/felicia-sonmez-washington-post/index.html.

gall to say that she hoped *others* would "learn from this experience.[6] Lorenz frequently uses her poor excuse for journalistic ethics to advance the woke cause du jour—whether that's calling out office air conditioning for being "sexist," trying to harass an anonymous right-wing Twitter account into hiding for reposting deranged left-wing TikTok videos, or chastising a COVID victim for daring to joke about his illness. In any serious industry, Lorenz would be unemployable. In corporate media, she is celebrated and compensated accordingly.

It's no secret that journalists have been mostly card-carrying Democrats for a long time, but this new generation of reporters is a different beast entirely. They are not only radically left-wing, but they demand 100 percent ideological purity and unconditional support from everyone around them. Like Sonmez and Lorenz, many of them have learned that "journalism" can be a very powerful tool for activism. In addition to advancing their own pet causes, they can use the platforms afforded to them by major corporate outlets to pressure and shame anyone who dissents from left-wing orthodoxy.

Media outlets were all too happy to go along with this at first. They leaned left anyway, so what was the big deal about bringing in a few radicals? Sure, the woke kids might get involved in controversy from time to time, but that only helped generate digital buzz for the paper and prove to mostly liberal audiences that they were down for the cause.

What media outlets failed to recognize is that these young Bolsheviks wouldn't be satisfied with turning their rage outward. Eventually, newsroom leaders would become the targets, too.

---

6   Wulfsohn, Joseph A. "Questions Remain as Taylor Lorenz Blames Editor, 'Bad Faith Campaign' over Erroneous Wapo Report." Fox News. FOX News Network. Accessed September 2, 2022. https://www.foxnews.com/media/washington-post-silent-taylor-lorenz-blames-editor-miscommunication.

This was entirely predictable if you were paying attention at all to what the young progressives had been doing on college campuses over the past decade. Conservatives sounded the alarm bells, but the media was too busy mocking their concerns as unfounded hysteria. Even the right didn't fully get it. They were convinced these whiny students—condescendingly dubbed the "snowflakes"—would melt once exposed to the "real world."

Unfortunately, I saw firsthand how influential these activists could be—and why they wouldn't just go away after graduation. During my time as an undergraduate at Georgetown University I was the campus left's favorite villain. I experienced every tactic and heard every argument the woke mob used to wrestle their opponents into submission. Through my eyes, you'll see how these malignant narcissists manage to play the victim in every scenario, why they reframe every political debate as a matter of life and death, how words became "violence," and why political civility is dead.

The woke left operates with a different playbook than your average political activist. Their worldview allows them to justify stamping out dissent by any means possible, whether through riotous protest, relentless character attacks and public shaming, or outright lies. They create a culture of fear in which everyone—including the adults who are supposed to be in charge—is terrified of stepping out of line and becoming a target of the bullies. The supposed authority figures hand over the keys to the kingdom, fearing the reputational damage that could occur if they don't comply.

The campus left learned they could successfully bully their professors and campus administrators into acquiescing to all of their demands, from campus diversity requirements to shutting down conservative speakers. Why stop there? As I left college and entered the media, so did my left-wing peers. They used the same moblike behavior to take over their newsrooms, pushing media coverage further to the left than ever, scalping their non-woke colleagues, abandoning journalistic principles, and sending the corporate media into chaos.

As former President Donald Trump once said, "Everything woke turns to shit."

Newsroom leadership, which was wholly unprepared for the revolution, ran for cover in the hopes they wouldn't find themselves under the guillotine. Even right-leaning media outlets who purport to believe in free speech and objective reporting were guilty of this abdication of leadership. Apparently no one is courageous enough to stand athwart the young bullies and yell *stop!*

The woke mob has attempted to cancel me on numerous occasions, but I'm still here. Here is my story, from how wokeness migrated from campus to the corporate media, to why this volatile ideology will decimate an already struggling industry, and how conservatives can fight back.

CHAPTER 1

GETTING STARTED

I strolled into my sociology class my senior year of high school in Walkersville, Maryland, and was greeted by a row of scrumptious-looking pies: apple, cherry, pumpkin. My teacher had a smirk on his face. I was immediately suspicious. What was he up to?

My teacher was an outspoken leftist. My friend Hannah and I, who quickly bonded over our shared conservativism, were always ganging up on him during class. He seemed to relish getting our friends to turn on one another by forcing us to debate divisive topics. He would lounge smugly in his corner desk as he pushed us to argue about whether DREAMers should get in-state tuition at US colleges or if abortion should be legal.

As the rest of the students filed into class that day, there were murmurs of excitement over the pies. My teacher finally stood up at the front of the class and revealed the true intentions behind his treats. The pies would be distributed based on the hierarchy of grades in the class. The person with the top grade in the course would get three slices of pie. The next five people with the highest grades would get two slices, the next ten would get one slice, and the bottom tier with the lowest grades would get no pie. But! We were told that we could "redistribute" our slices of pie however we wanted.

It just so happened that I had the highest grade in the class. I swear my teacher had a gleam in his eye when he announced my name to be the first to get pie. Unfortunately for him, I knew exactly what he was up to. I walked over to the pies and took my three hefty slices. The class watched with bated breath to see who would get the extras. Instead, I stopped briefly at the front of the class, said "sucks to suck!" and sat down to eat every last bite of my pie. There were audible gasps around the room.

Of course, I didn't really want three slices of pie, but it seemed obvious to me that my teacher dreamed up this twisted little social experiment to make a point about income inequality. The teacher wanted to convince people that they should redistribute their income because "nobody needs" a lot of money—or, in this case, three slices of pie.

I was annoyed that he tried to trick my classmates with his poor analogy, so I blew up his plan. After all of the pie was handed out, he explained to the rest of the class the purpose of the exercise. He stared daggers at me as he explained that usually people give away their extra pie, the same way wealthy people should give away their money to the less fortunate. Giving away the pie, he suggested, was the right thing to do.

Of course, ask any of those high school kids if they'd give away two-thirds or half of their hard-earned income to people who didn't work, and he'd get a much different response. It would have been fair to point out as well that, unlike income, the pie was not our primary reward for getting a good grade. The pie was a bonus we weren't depending on or even expecting and was thus easier to give away. The exercise wasn't meant to be fair though. It was propaganda.

I was lucky to catch what was going on that day. Unlike a lot of my classmates, I was already pretty obsessed with politics. My interest started way back in my eighth grade government class. President Barack Obama had just started his first term in office, and my teacher was *obsessed* with the administration. We watched the daily White House and State Department press briefings whenever they fell during our class time. Otherwise, we had to watch daily headlines from CNN. My teacher especially loved Secretary of the Treasury Timothy Geithner, who he would always call a "bright young man." We'd have to listen to unending monologues about how the stimulus package was going to save the country.

My dad, a lifelong union member, was a registered Democrat at the time, and my mom was and still is a registered Independent. However, I think that the way they raised me made it almost inevitable that I would be a conservative. I was taught the value of hard work. Keep your head down and don't complain. Fifteen minutes early is on time, on time is late. Take responsibility for your actions and show respect to authority. Have pride in your country, and put your faith in God. I learned to shoot, hunt, and fish at a young age. I killed my first deer when I was seven and was always taught to have respect for the outdoors and for the animal.

I am also naturally skeptical, a trait I got from my mother. When my government teacher started making declarative statements about the Obama administration that I couldn't find in a textbook, I had questions. I'd go home to my parents and get their opinion on what I learned in government class that day. It was also around this time that I started watching Fox News. The analysis I heard from Fox's hosts and pundits comported with my sense of the world more than anything my government teacher was saying, so I would challenge him in class. When he talked about how many jobs the stimulus package was going to create, I pointed out that most of the infrastructure-related jobs would be seasonal or temporary. I questioned how the stimulus package would help women, whose unemployment rate was rising just as fast as men's but who are also reluctant to work in construction or green energy. More generally, I wondered if the government was actually any good at creating jobs and how we would know that the more than $800 billion spent would be used efficiently and effectively.

These might have seemed like overly mature questions for a fourteen-year-old girl, but politics were more than a hobby for me—they were a necessity. The 2008 recession deeply affected my family. The things we were talking about in my government class were real life, not just a lesson in school.

Neither of my parents went to college. My dad went to trade school and worked as a master plumber and pipefitter his entire life. He was a member of the Plumbers and Gasfitters Local 5 Union in Washington, DC. My mom was a manager at a video store until I was born in 1994 and then she stayed at home with the kids. My dad was laid off multiple times during the 2008 recession and was suffering from a debilitating, life-threatening illness. My parents did their best to shield me and my brother from everything that was going on at the time, but we knew something was wrong. Dad would usually be gone for work well before sunrise, but there were months-long periods where he was in the living room watching TV when my brother and I got up for school. It was hard to tell when he was not at work because he had been laid off, and when he was not at work because he was too sick.

I remember visiting him at the hospital on one occasion when he developed a severe staph infection. He lied to me about how good the hospital food was. When he was at home, we spent a lot of time coloring or working on puzzles because he was too weak to do much else. Financially, I know my mom was severely stressed about the medical bills that were racking up and the lack of a steady household income. My brother and I started getting free lunches at school. We couldn't just go out and buy something without really needing it and finding the best coupons and sales. We didn't take fancy beach vacations to Florida like I saw other families doing. I remember feeling a deep sense of anxiety when my friends convinced me to spend my entire mall budget one weekend on a fifteen dollar pair of sunglasses from Nordstrom so we could take MySpace selfies in the bathroom. I don't know that I ever felt poor, but I did think that people who lived in homes with multiple floors must be really rich.

I'd always wanted to go to a prestigious college. Our financial struggles throughout the recession and its aftermath only made my dream seem more urgent. I wanted to graduate and get a good job to be able to provide for my future family and give back to my parents, who sacrificed so much. I wanted them to be proud of me so that they knew it was all worth it. I also understood that paying the tuition at a highfalutin school wouldn't be easy. Still, my parents never discouraged me from aiming high with my college goals. They saved up money so that I could go on college tours up and down the East Coast. We drove up to Boston for a long weekend so I could attend a field hockey camp at Harvard and tour Boston College. Then we went on to Philadelphia to see UPenn and Villanova and to North Carolina to see Duke and UNC Chapel Hill. I liked most of the colleges I visited, but I knew before even setting foot on campus that I wanted to go to Georgetown. As we drove along the George Washington Parkway, I looked across the Potomac River to the left and saw Healy Hall peeking through the trees. It was glorious.

My guidance counselor told me and my mom that I was getting my hopes too high. She recommended paring down my applications and focusing on safety schools because there was no way a little ol' Walkersville girl would get into a prestigious college, and I was just wasting my money. Four years earlier, the same guidance counselor assumed in a college preparation meeting that my brother, who also had an excellent GPA and extracurriculars, wouldn't be going to college.

I applied Early Acceptance at Georgetown and heard while I was at an indoor track meet in December 2011 that my letter had arrived in the mail. The meet didn't end until close to ten that evening and I was doing everything I could to distract myself from the thought of that letter. When I finally got home, I saw my family waiting with the envelope. It was small—the size of a normal envelope, unlike the big packets that some other schools sent. My mom assured me that the college blogs she spent all day reading said that Georgetown sends both acceptance and rejection letters in the same size envelopes.

I opened the letter in the kitchen as my parents watched with wide eyes. We cried and hugged when I announced I had been accepted.

There was still no guarantee I would be able to go. Tuition plus room and board was $70,000 a year! My parents warned me that it was a bad idea to take on too much student debt just to go to my dream school, and they were right. I was prepared to save money and go to a local state school. Luckily, I didn't have to make that choice because Georgetown offered me an incredibly generous financial package. I guess we were considered pretty low-income by Georgetown's standards. They offered membership in the Georgetown Scholarship Program (GSP), a group for first-generation and low-income college students. GSP pays for a portion of federal student loans and provides numerous resources to help its members adjust to college life. I visited the campus for Admitted Students Weekend and purchased a little plush Jack the Bulldog to bring back to my guidance counselor to thank her for her "help."

With a combination of financial aid, GSP, scholarships, working through school, and my parent's modest savings, I was able to go to Georgetown and graduated with just $10,000 in student loans. It completely changed the course of my life.

CHAPTER 2

THE OL' COLLEGE TRY

I was so excited to start school at Georgetown. Move-in day was fun and frustrating, pushing moving carts up and down the hill from the parking garage to my dorm in the oppressive heat of late August. When it was time to finally say goodbye, it was hard to tell whether we were all crying or just sweating.

As I settled in, I was nervous about making friends. Despite being a three-sport athlete in high school, I wasn't the most popular kid and I've always been rather introverted. At Georgetown, I was worried about my working-class background and my politics. My classmates wore T-shirts that cost more than some of my nicest outfits. Strolling around in cowboy boots and carrying a flip phone next to business majors with Gucci loafers and the newest iPhone was pretty jarring. Still, the wealth difference had nothing on the political chasm between me and most of my classmates. I couldn't have prepared for how willing my peers were to demean and abuse me for daring to disagree with them.

My first semester at Georgetown was in the midst of the 2012 presidential election between Barack Obama and Mitt

Romney. The trouble started when I met someone on my floor who, despite being a California liberal, loved guns. (We are still really good friends and see each other a few times a year.) We talked about starting an official university gun club, which would focus on firearm safety and education but maybe would eventually become a competitive team. The process for starting any new club at Georgetown was quite onerous, let alone one with so many legal restrictions, but the first step was to demonstrate interest from at least thirty potential members. An easy start, I thought, was to recruit other freshmen living on my floor. I drew up a flier of sorts on the white board on my dorm room door, which was conveniently located smack in the middle of a long, carpeted hallway. We named the club the "Georgetown University Firearms Association (GUFA)" and my flier featured a rudimentary drawing of an AR-15.

I soon received an email from my RA telling me that some of my neighbors had submitted complaints about feeling "unsafe" around my white board. Indeed, few things are scarier than a cartoon firearm drawn with a dry-erase marker. My RA requested I take down the GUFA ad or at least remove the gun to make other residents feel more comfortable.

I showed a couple of friends the email and we all agreed it was a ridiculous request. Some pointed out that there were tons of other messages on white boards throughout the dorm that could be considered offensive. Those residents were presumably never asked to remove them because, well, they didn't run afoul of the unspoken rule that all political content must be liberal. That was when we stumbled upon a rather genius idea.

I took a trip around the entire dorm building and snapped pictures of every crass white board drawing: drawings of penises, curse words, slurs. The real kicker was when we found an especially horrible cartoon that depicted the male and female RA

9

from my floor engaged in a sexual act, with their names clearly labeled. The cherry on top of my dossier.

I attached all of the photos I gathered to an email and sent them to my RA. I informed him that my white board would be erased as soon as he sent similar email requests to every other resident who had white board messages and images that I deemed inappropriate. Until then, I would consider removal of the contents of my white board a violation of the university's free speech policy.

"Touché," the RA replied, and I never heard another complaint about the gun club.

Unfortunately, that wasn't the last of the harassment from my neighbors. I was getting annoyed at all of the Obama signs on my neighbors' doors and the literature constantly being slid under my own, so I drew up a Romney sign. Oftentimes I would come home from class to find the sign defaced or scribbled over with profane messages, including poorly drawn penises, curse words, and the ever-poetic "I love to suck Obama's dick." Sometimes, when I was studying or watching TV in my room, I would hear giggling outside of my door and the faint sound of scribbling from dry-erase markers. Of course, when I finally would go to check, new messages had appeared. I still wish that I had been brave enough to swing open the door and confront the perpetrators face to face.

I got to experience some of the venom in person when watching the vice-presidential debate between Joe Biden and Paul Ryan in our common room. One of my neighbors, Makaiah, almost couldn't help herself from blurting out digs in my direction. When the debate moved to gun control, Makaiah sneered, "Well, we know Amber loves guns." The rest of the room chuckled. You have to be a liberal to get the joke, I guess. What's funny about supporting a God-given right enshrined in our Constitution? Maybe it was just their way of calling me a redneck.

Makaiah had no other reason to be catty toward me besides politics. In fact, I went out of my way to try to be a friend to her. During new student orientation that year, Makaiah's mom told my mom that her daughter was stressed and worried about making friends at Georgetown. I was surprised by this because Makaiah was a pretty, trendy, hippie California girl, but I sympathized with her fears. I decided to drop by Makaiah's dorm room later that day, introduce myself, and offer to attend any new student events with her or grab a bite to eat so that she didn't feel alone. She seemed grateful at the time, but Makaiah treated me like a pariah the rest of the year and was the source of spiteful rumors about me to the rest of the dorm floor. This "nasty woman" would go on to work for the Hillary Clinton presidential campaign in 2016. How fitting.

Unfortunately for me, Obama won re-election that November. I originally planned on walking to the White House since it was my first election cycle while living in DC, but I came down with a fever that evening and decided to stay in, tucked under my covers. My neighbors yelled and banged on my door on their way out in celebration. My RA stopped by and knocked too; when I answered, he gleefully rubbed the results in my face. He must've still been stinging from my victory over the gun club advertisement.

CHAPTER 3

BEATING A DEAD HORSE

After being harassed and bullied for two semesters of my college career, I was acutely aware that I needed to find some more conservative friends. I ran into some College Republican members early on in the fall semester of my sophomore year, and they convinced me to come help out with the club's tabling efforts in "Red Square"—the appropriately named center of campus activity. Tabling quickly became one of my favorite activities at Georgetown. We set up beautiful custom-made cornhole boards with our club logo, blasted country music, and got to hang out with fellow Republicans and bring in new members. Since tabling took place on Friday afternoons, we also would sometimes sneak some beer or mimosas (shh!). I immediately thought that social events like this should be the main focus of the CRs. On a campus as hostile as Georgetown, we had to destigmatize being conservative. I wanted shy Republicans to feel comfortable being open about their political views and know that they had an army of like-minded individuals ready to back them up. What better way to draw them in than by simply having a good time?

It was with this goal in mind that I ran for and won Director of Campus Affairs at the end of my fall sophomore semester.

Campus activists became even more aggressive around this time because of the police shooting of Michael Brown in Ferguson, Missouri, in the summer of 2014. A group of student activists actually organized a trip to Ferguson so that they could join the protests with Black Lives Matter. I infuriated them by condemning the violence wrought by BLM, which saw arson, looting, destruction, and assaults on police officers. The city of Ferguson had become what our former president would call a "shithole" for weeks, and my classmates contributed to the nightmare with the warped idea that they actually were doing good.

It wasn't enough for these Georgetown students to ruin someone else's city. They had to ruin Christmas too. Every year after Thanksgiving break, Georgetown splashes the campus with beautiful Christmas decorations and puts up a huge tree in the square outside of Dahlgren Chapel. The tree-lighting ceremony was one of my favorite events at Georgetown. Campus volunteers passed out hot chocolate and treats, we sang Christmas carols, and we had a countdown until President John DeGioia lit the tree. It was one of the few events at Georgetown that unapologetically celebrated Christianity (how sad, at a Catholic school) and was apolitical.

Alas, the campus left doesn't believe we get to have nice things. At the 2014 Christmas tree lighting, a group of students staged a "die-in" to protest the Michael Brown shooting. When President DeGioia lit the tree, the students dropped to the ground and played dead for four and a half minutes, in reference to the four and a half hours Michael Brown lay on the street after he was killed. Then, the group stood up and chanted "Black Lives Matter" and "No Justice, No Peace," before walking away from the tree lighting. It blew my mind that anyone thought an event celebrating the birth of Jesus Christ was an appropriate venue to protest on behalf of a man who beat a police officer and tried to take his gun.

These students were clearly miserable, and they wanted to make everyone else miserable too.

They were also blissfully unaware of and indifferent to facts. Ballistic evidence from the shooting found that "Hands Up, Don't Shoot" narrative was a lie—Brown did not have his hands up to surrender when he was shot, nor did he have his back to Officer Darren Wilson. He was charging the officer at the time he was shot and had previously beat him through the window of his police cruiser. Wilson was hardly harassing an innocent black man, either. He was aware that Brown matched the description of a suspect who was reported stealing cigarillos from a local convenience store. The Georgetown Grinches wouldn't apologize for ruining the Christmas tree lighting, though, nor would they stop using Michael Brown as a martyr for their campus activism. Any criticism of the campus left was met with cries that you cannot be mean to or criticize black people because of police brutality… or something.

In the summer of 2014, I wrote a piece for the GUCR blog called "No Climate for Conservatives" about some of my casual observations on how left-wing students react to conservative speech on campus.

"Liberal students at Georgetown University have created a toxic and hostile environment for conservatives. The attitudes expressed by militant, left-wing Hoyas are incredibly dangerous to a productive university atmosphere, one that is supposed to champion free speech and diversity of opinion," I wrote at the time.

I was never expecting that many people to read it, but the piece went semi-viral. An editor at my hometown newspaper saw the piece and offered me a monthly political column. It was my first professional writing gig.

It also elevated me from casual conservative to right-wing campus pariah. Scores of Georgetown leftists proved the point of my piece by bashing me on social media and treating me like dirt when I returned to campus for the fall semester. I learned about their organizing tactics from friends of mine who leaned left but were disturbed at the way I was being treated. The main planning tool was what was known colloquially as the "Black GroupMe". GroupMe was the communications app of choice for Georgetown student groups. The "Black GroupMe" was where members of the various minority-based political groups on campus gathered digitally to plan protests, complain about campus policies, organize parties, and talk a lot of smack about conservatives like me. Georgetown is a relatively small campus—a little over seven thousand undergraduate students—and I can tell you that having a couple hundred of them on one messaging app gabbing about how much they hate you can make campus feel awfully lonely.

I would have been well within my rights to retreat into a victim mindset—lord knows that's what leftist students did when anyone challenged them. Instead, I leaned into my status as Georgetown's resident conservative loudmouth. I was already "canceled," so to speak, so what more harm could I do by doing and saying the things that other campus conservatives were too scared to do or say?

The "Black GroupMe" wasn't the only organizing tool of the left. Left-wing campus activists loved Twitter, at least partially because it was easier to be anonymous than on Facebook. The Twitter activists also used a type of code language to avoid being busted for their most radical thoughts. They didn't want future employers or campus administrators to be able to search their accounts for inflammatory language. Instead of using "white people" in tweets, for example, they would use "yt people" or "yt ppl." "Blk" would be used instead of "black." Sometimes letters or words were replaced by emojis.

The Twitter activists had been using a hashtag campaign #BBGU, or Being Black at Georgetown University, since early 2014 to document their alleged experiences with campus racism. The purpose was to slime the university so they could gin up support for a series of policy proposals, most notably the addition of a diversity requirement in the academic curriculum. The diversity requirement would mandate students take two classes that focused primarily on issues of diversity and equity before graduating from the university. Aya Waller-Bey, the creator of the hashtag, admitted that she leaned on the effectiveness of a public tarring campaign to get Georgetown to take the diversity requirement seriously.

"Hey, this public shaming thing works," Waller-Bey told the *Washington Post*.[7] "When the university is embarrassed or when things are just not held within a community of students, they're forced to respond because it looks bad PR-wise."

The #BBGU hashtag consisted primarily of students complaining about perceived microaggressions. One student tweeted that being black at Georgetown meant having an adviser tell you that taking certain classes might be "too much," suggesting that the adviser was underestimating her due to her skin color. Another student complained that she believed guys didn't want to hook up with her at parties because of her race. One student

---

[7]   Butler, Bethonie. "Being Black at Georgetown Founder Hopes Conversation Continues after School Year Ends." *Washington Post*. WP Company, May 15, 2014. https://www.washingtonpost.com/lifestyle/style/being-black-at-georgetown-founder-hopes-conversation-continues-after-school-year-ends/2014/05/15/50749264-d219-11e3-937f-d3026234b51c_story.html.

said being black at Georgetown meant not knowing how to react to "You went to Georgetown, wow!" because it could mean that they were surprised a black person could be smart enough to go to school there. All assumptions, no evidence. According to Waller-Bey, however, these small instances of alleged racism made living on campus like being on a "battlefield." Uh, the Greatest Generation would like a word.

Shavonnia Corbin-Johnson tweeted that being black at Georgetown meant "having an academic advisor who acts really surprised when you excel in your classes." She is now the political director for the Pennsylvania Democratic Party.

"Having to defend why I am part of student organizations that are predominately white," was a tweet from Jimmy Ramirez, who worked for Google after graduation. Ever wonder why Google executives felt the need to comfort their traumatized employees[8] after Trump won the 2016 election, or why Google's algorithm seems biased against conservative websites? It's because they hire lots of people who think like Ramirez.

The Georgetown administration was filled with liberals, as is most of academia, but it at least gave lip service to the ideas of political heterodoxy and free speech. As I'll share during my story about bringing Dr. Christina Hoff Sommers to campus later on in this book, administrators mostly had my back against people who wanted to shut down her speech. However, you're concocting a dangerous brew when university leadership either agrees with the campus left or is deathly afraid of them. If you take a look back at campus protests of the last ten years, you'll see a common theme: the administrators give the protesters some, if

---

8   Bokhari, Allum. "Leaked Video: Google Leadership's Dismayed Reaction to Trump Election." Breitbart, September 13, 2018. https://www.breitbart.com/tech/2018/09/12/leaked-video-google-leaderships-dismayed-reaction-to-trump-election/.

not all, of what they want. They express a desire to work with the students. They praise their ideas. They talk about how proud they are to see students standing up to make a change. They think that if they give these students a pat on the head, they'll be free from accusations of racism and the students will just happily go back to class. What they don't understand is that every time they give in, they incentivize the students' behavior. Imagine a child throwing a temper tantrum because he wants an extra lollipop at the doctor's office. If the parent eventually gives the child the extra lollipop, what happens? The child is satisfied for a short while but learns that the tantrum yields results. The campus left is actually worse than this, because they are never satisfied, even temporarily. They should've gotten the lollipop sooner, or it should've been bigger, or they should get three lollipops because they shouldn't have even had to throw the tantrum in the first place! Giving them the extra lollipop was the right thing to do from the beginning and the administration failed, dammit! Reparations now!

I assure you I am not exaggerating. Let's get back to the #BBGU campaign.

The official university Facebook page and Georgetown administrators endorsed the campaign and shamelessly cheered on the public smearing of their employer.

"Check out #BBGU. An important conversation—voices of students, alumni, faculty, and staff—we all need to listen and engage," Vice President for Student Affairs Todd Olson tweeted.

"#BBGU: a powerful reminder that acknowledging privilege and striving for justice is a lifelong endeavor. Never over," Center for Student Engagement Director Erika Cohen Derr tweeted.

Their words weren't enough. Waller-Bey said Georgetown needed to "step up" and do more beyond just expressing support on social media. Georgetown officials started quietly working with the activists involved in the #BBGU movement and other campus advocacy groups. In the spring of 2014, Georgetown President John DeGioia sat down for dinner with residents of the Black House (no, this is not racial segregation because of historical oppression or something), where they presented him with an eight-point proposal regarding diversity on campus. By December 2015, the Provost's Office's Diversity Working Group was drafting an official proposal for the addition of a diversity requirement in the Georgetown undergraduate curriculum. The working group was formalized[9] two months later as the Provost's Committee for Diversity, a permanent addition to the Georgetown administration. Provost Groves admitted the idea was borne out of the #BBGU movement and DeGioia's sit-down with activists:

> *"Due to the leadership of some undergraduate students last year, a set of concerns and proposals with regard to activities in and out of class, curricular ideas and alumni ideas that would enrich the experience of students from minority racial and ethnic status was proposed. Those issues came to the forefront and were presented to President DeGioia for discussion and resolution. This was also linked to larger national concerns that manifested themselves in the Twitter campaign of #BBGU—Being Black at Georgetown University—last year."*

The diversity requirement proposal was the culmination of over a decade of campus organizing and was hotly debated among students. The idea had been rejected by the College Curriculum

---

9   Puri, Ashwin. "Committee To Address Diversity." *The Hoya*. February 3, 2015. https://thehoya.com/committee-address-diversity/.

Committee in the past. The CCC claimed[10]—correctly, in my experience—that the classes currently required for undergraduate students already covered issues related to diversity.

"It would be almost impossible to obtain a Georgetown degree without having engaged in at least some classes which explicitly dealt with issues of pluralism," the CCC said in 2002.

About 60.5 percent of students either agreed or strongly agreed that a required diversity class is a necessary part of the Georgetown curriculum, according to a political values survey by the *Georgetown Voice*. I was surprised that it wasn't more popular. For context, 85.3 percent of students opposed defunding Planned Parenthood, 64.7 percent believed Georgetown should have gender-neutral restrooms, and 83.7 percent think "rape culture" exists on college campuses.

Even though the diversity requirement wasn't as hugely popular as some other political pet causes, the campus left acted like you were committing a mortal sin if you didn't support the proposal. Friends of mine who served on the Georgetown University Student Association (GUSA), the student government body, were publicly accused of racism because they didn't want to vote for the diversity requirement in a proposed referendum.

Maybe the Georgetown administrators who worked with these students really believed that they were asking for good campus policy. I'm a bit more cynical, so I think they were probably trying to combat the public allegations of racism. Either way, the university's commitment to working with student activists to advance their social justice projects probably should've been enough to quell the idea that Georgetown was systemically racist.

---

[10] "The Final Push: An Ongoing Struggle for an Academic Diversity Requirement." *Georgetown Voice*, August 3, 2015. https://georgetownvoice.com/2015/03/19/the-final-push-an-ongoing-struggle-for-an-academic-diversity-requirement/.

Not so. The student activists were so desperate to cling to the racism narrative that they made an innocent political cartoonist out to be the face of evil. His name is Dylan Cutler, and what happened to him was one of the most appalling things I saw during my time on campus.

Student government is a huge deal at Georgetown. Conde Nast, President Bill Clinton, Oklahoma Governor Frank Keating, and other notable alumni built their resumes on student government. Every year, disgustingly ambitious students who think they are destined to be a future president of the United States run for student body president to flex their political prowess. The 2015 election cycle was unique, though, because two campus comedians decided to throw their hats in the ring. Joe Luther and Connor Rohan, both members of the Georgetown Improv Association, ran something of a mock campaign[11] satirizing the insane things students would promise to get elected as well as the general ineffectiveness of student government.

"A Luther-Rohan administration would end this living nightmare that we call home," Rohan deadpanned in the pair's first campaign video. "We're going to make Georgetown perfect, and you'll never ever have a problem again. Ever."

Students ate it up, and the Luther-Rohan ticket rocketed to the top of the polls.

One casualty of the Luther-Rohan campaign was the uber-serious Christopher Wadibia and Meredith Cheney ticket. Wadibia was extremely well-liked at Georgetown, but the Wadibia-Cheney

---

[11] Sen, Mallika. "Ticket Profile: Joe Luther and Connor Rohan." The Hoya, February 19, 2015. https://thehoya.com/ticket-profile-joe-luther-connor-rohan/.

campaign fell victim to trying to appeal to everyone with vague[12] and poorly thought out proposals. It was the student government version of Kamala Harris's 2020 presidential campaign. During the annual GUSA debate, Wadibia practically came unglued as it became clear he hadn't automatically won the support of the student body with his natural charisma. He declared that it was a "bad sign" for Georgetown if he didn't win the presidency, and accused his opponents of being untalented, elitist, and of bad character. The Wadibia-Cheney campaign lost any legitimacy in the eyes of students and the Luther-Rohan campaign only got more popular after the debate.

After Luther and Rohan won the election, The *Georgetown Voice* published a political cartoon by Dylan Cutler satirizing the downfall of the Wadibia-Cheney campaign. The cartoon, titled "Beating The Dead Horse", showed Luther and Rohan clubbing a dead Wadibia and Cheney inside a horse costume. It was a pretty innocuous play on the idiom, or so I thought, but a group of Georgetown students deemed the cartoon racist and sexist.

Students claimed the cartoon was racist because it depicted violence against Wadibia, who is black. The cartoon was also sexist because Cheney is a woman.

"The white patriarchal message this image sends is insensitive and incredibly racist given the history of black men and women being lynched and beaten at the hands of white people in this nation's past and present," the Black Leadership Forum posted on its Facebook page. "It is also concerning that a woman is being depicted as the ass of the horse, reminiscent of the misogynistic and socially inferior treatment women have suffered for centuries."

---

[12] Maness, Haley, Maddy Moore, Alum, Mo Schmo, Hoya '15, Hoyalum, et al. "Sexual Assault Platform Lacks Dignity." The Hoya, May 21, 2015. https://thehoya.com/sexual-assault-platform-lacks-dignity.

Humorless much?

The *Voice* caved to the criticism immediately, publishing an apology on their Facebook page and removing the cartoon. Student activists (including Cheney, who now works for Facebook and puts her pronouns in her LinkedIn bio) organized a town hall in St. Williams Chapel. The town hall meeting was attended by over one hundred people, including Cutler. Black students took the podium and said the cartoon "threw salt on wounds that are really deep for some people in our community" and claimed it was especially insensitive given the alleged rise in police brutality against the black community. Others said that even if the intent of the cartoon wasn't racist or sexist, that only proved that the *Voice* and Cutler lacked cultural sensitivity.

After the students were mostly done—excuse my language— beating the dead horse, Cutler approached the podium to grovel for forgiveness.

"I made a mistake," he said with tears in his eyes. "My privilege is that I have the ability to look past…the possible damage that that image could cause. And I'm sorry. I stand with you. I want to help silence the message of hate."

Students gave him a standing ovation, but they weren't done getting their pound of flesh. They held a second protest called "Beating Ignorance, Raising Consciousness" in Red Square the day after the town hall. Students and staff held a ten-minute moment of silence with their fists raised. After again eviscerating the *Voice* and Cutler for the publication of the cartoon, students immediately pivoted to their fight for the diversity requirement on campus. They insisted that requiring students to take diversity courses would prevent a similar incident in the future.

Esther Owolabi, who now works as a Diversity & Inclusion Officer for Google, tried to rally support from professors to sign the proposal for a diversity requirement.

"How are you supposed to be 'men and women for others' when you don't know who the others are?" Kimberley Blair, one of the rally organizers, asserted.

I was used to Georgetown student activists trying to destroy conservatives, but what happened to Cutler was so shocking and horrific because he was ostensibly on their side. Cutler's other cartoons and social media posts expressed support for leftist causes. It didn't matter. He was expendable to the left because he could be used to advance their political priorities. They nearly ruined this young man's college career to rally support for a diversity requirement. This was the first time I had seen such a poignant real-life example of the left eating its own. Most people value personal loyalty, but not the progressive left. They value ideological purity and devotion to the cause du jour above all else. No matter how much you concede or declare yourself an ally, you are never safe.

The student activists' tactics worked. The Main Campus Executive Faculty voted in April of 2015 to adopt the diversity requirement with "overwhelming support." The MCEF did not seek the input of the wider student body and did not address the logistical concerns of implementing a new two-course require-ment for students with already packed schedules.

The university, by implementing the diversity requirement, sent the signal to leftist students that as long as they cried loud and long enough, laid on a massive guilt trip, shamed their oppo-nents as racist, and threw their allies under the bus, they could get whatever they wanted. Think about the precedent that it set for all future campus activism. Is it any surprise that by May

2021, campus newspapers already were reporting that students were unsatisfied with the diversity requirement?[13]

"The requirement has come under criticism from many students for not appropriately engaging with issues of diversity, especially racial diversity, leading some to feel the requirement is only a nominal commitment to diversity and inclusion on campus. In response to these concerns, and with a mandated deadline to reevaluate the five-year-old requirement fast approaching, representatives from different academic councils and student groups have worked to compile research on what a revamped requirement could look like," the *Georgetown Voice* reported.

Still not convinced that history repeats itself? Michael Brown's death was the impetus for a large chunk of campus activism on the diversity requirement when I was on campus. This time around, students are citing George Floyd's death as a reason to revisit the classes offered under the requirement.

It's never enough for the campus left. Oh, and the *Voice* is *still* apologizing for that "Beating the Dead Horse" cartoon.

---

[13] "Is It Enough? Georgetown's Diversity Requirement Comes under Scrutiny." *Georgetown Voice*, May 3, 2021. https://georgetownvoice.com/2021/05/02/is-it-enough-georgetowns-diversity-requirement-comes-under-scrutiny/.

CHAPTER 4

CRUEL SOMMERS

Just before Cutler was censored for his "racist" cartoon, I ran for chair of Georgetown College Republicans and won. One of the duties of the CR chair is to invite speakers and organize events. When I was still serving as Director of Campus Affairs, our club brought former speaker Dennis Hastert—yikes!—Rep. Mick Mulvaney, and then-House majority whip Kevin McCarthy.

McCarthy was protested[14] by leftist students who accused him of not supporting immigration reform. Despite everything I had been through, I still believed that there was the possibility of open debate and reconciliation with the left and appreciated McCarthy's attempts to placate his detractors. Now, being stripped of all naivety, I view his appeasement of mere college students as weak and sad.

McCarthy declined to unapologetically defend conservatism, instead seeking areas of agreement with the mob. He

---

14 Verhovek, Johnny. "McCarthy Speech Faces Protests." The Hoya, June 19, 2014. https://thehoya.com/mccarthy-speech-faces-protests/.

mistakenly believed that the protesters were logical actors who could be convinced with reason. McCarthy insisted that he supports immigration reform, telling the protesters that it is too hard to become a citizen: "We have a system today, where 42 percent of everyone that's here illegally came here legally but overstayed a visa." McCarthy now sends out statements[15] decrying amnesty for visa overstays.

McCarthy said he would not vote for the Employment Non-Discrimination Act, a bill that would prohibit employers from discriminating in hiring based on sexual orientation and/or gender identity, but noted, "I don't think anyone should be discriminated against for any reason…I don't care what your sexuality is—you shouldn't be discriminated against."

This is exactly what the protesters wanted. They surely knew that a sitting Republican congressperson wasn't going to change their views on the spot due to some pressure from college students. But if they could chip away and make him just uncomfortable enough to concede some of their premises, the entire Overton window would shift toward their conclusions. The "slippery slope" argument is a fallacy until the slope is pretty damn real. Just look at where we are on "nondiscrimination" policy a few years later. The left didn't even need McCarthy's vote on the Employment Non-Discrimination Act because the conservative-majority Supreme Court decided in Bostock vs. Clayton County to amend the Civil Rights Act to include sexual orientation and gender identity as categories protected from

---

15 McCarthy, Kevin. "This Socialist Spending Scam Provides Amnesty for Millions of Illegal Immigrants and Visa Overstays-in the Middle of the Worst Border Crisis in Recorded History. If Democrats Jam This Thing through, a Billion Dollars of Your Taxes Will Be given to Illegal Immigrants." Pic. twitter.com/txw8i2bszd. Twitter. November 19, 2021. https://twitter.com/GOPLeader/status/1461513708342026240.

discrimination. This threatened the ability of religious organizations to only hire people who live in accordance with their faith traditions and the feasibility of women's sports leagues to exclude biological men. Now the left is trying to pass the Equality Act, which would further enshrine special protections on the basis of gender identity. Members of the Republican Party responded by once again seeking a "compromise" through the Fairness for All Act. McCarthy didn't take a position on that legislation, but his soft and conciliatory tone on the issue years ago is exactly how we got into the position to be called "bigots" for standing up for religious freedom and biological truths.

If McCarthy was an example of what *not* to do when dealing with a hostile reception at a college campus, then Dr. Christina Hoff Sommers was the model for how it should be done.

My friend Mallory first approached me about bringing Hoff Sommers to campus in the spring semester of my junior year. I didn't know much about Hoff Sommers at the time, but I learned that she called herself an "equality feminist" because she was disturbed by the radicalism and antimen sentiment inherent in modern feminism. That was good enough for me. Mallory promised to take care of most of the planning for the event alongside the Clare Boothe Luce Policy Institute (now known as the Clare Boothe Luce Center for Conservative Women). Hoff Sommers's speech was scheduled for April 2015 and I excitedly set up a Facebook event. That was when all hell broke loose.

The Facebook event page was quickly spammed with comments from students claiming that "the equality feminist's" presence on campus would make them feel "unsafe" and that her speech would actively harm survivors of sexual assault. Hoff Sommers's speech was not even supposed to be about sexual assault—the title was "What's Right (And Badly Wrong) with Feminism"—but left-wing students latched onto previous comments she'd made about the "one in five" (now amended to one in four!) campus rape statistic. Questioning that statistic, the students argued, made Hoff Sommers a rape apologist.

The "one in five" statistic is indeed very flimsy. Per reporting from Ashe Schow at the *Washington Examiner*,[16] one of the sources for that number was a 2007 Department of Justice (DOJ) study on campus sexual assault. The study surveyed more than five thousand women across two college campuses. Except, it did not ask them directly if they were sexually assaulted or raped. Instead, it walked them through a series of leading questions that seemed designed to elicit a high response rate. For example, the survey makes the assumption that all drunken sexual contact is nonconsensual. It also asks the women about events that they "think" happened, not just events they are sure happened. A 2010 Center for Disease Control (CDC) study took a similar approach to measuring sexual assault in the United States more generally and, naturally, produced similar results. The CDC survey, for example, asks women if they have ever had vaginal sex while "drunk or high," which easily could be interpreted by respondents to include consensual encounters or to reinterpret encounters to be nonconsensual.

Hoff Sommers addressed this in her criticisms of the study in a *YouTube* video for the American Enterprise Institute:[17]

> *"Now, 61.5 percent of the women the CDC projected as rape victims in 2010 experienced what*

---

[16] Schow, Ashe. "No, 1 in 5 Women Have Not Been Raped on College Campuses." *Washington Examiner*. August 13, 2014. https://www.washingtonexaminer. com/no-1-in-5-women-have-not-been-raped-on-college-campuses.

[17] American Enterprise Institute, "Sexual assault in America: Do we know the true numbers?" Factual Feminist, April 28, 2014, https://www.youtube. com/watch?v=lNsJ1DhqQ-s&list=PLytTJqkSQqtr7BqC1Jf4nv3g2yDfu7X-md&index=12

> the CDC called quote 'alcohol and drug-facili-
> tated penetration'. If a woman was unconscious or
> incapacitated, then every civilized person would
> call it rape. But what about sex while inebriated?
> I mean, few people would say that intoxicated sex
> alone constitutes rape."

Concluding that a woman cannot consent to sex when drunk is rather sexist. It denies agency to women, who are perfectly capable of making decisions after a few cocktails. It also creates an unreasonable standard for men. People can seem in control even when they are very drunk. It is not right to expect a man to be able to tell when an otherwise functioning woman has become too drunk to consent, unless she is incapacitated. Aaron White, a researcher with the National Institute on Alcohol Abuse and Alcoholism says that even people who get "blackout" drunk can "look quite sober" to bystanders.[18] And what happens if both parties involved in the encounter are intoxicated? The CDC methodology seems to assume that in a heterosexual drunken sexual encounter, the man is the aggressor and the woman is the victim. Left-wing feminists somehow simultaneously believe that women are strong and independent but that we also bear no responsibility for our actions with a slightly elevated blood alcohol content. It is a completely incoherent ideology.

The CDC survey also counts as rape sexual activity that occurs through coercive tactics, such as a partner making promises about the future they knew were untrue, telling lies, or guilt tripping. While this is immoral, it is questionable whether it should count as "rape".

---

[18] "Why Do Only Some People Get Blackout Drunk?" BBC Future. BBC. Accessed September 4, 2022. https://www.bbc.com/future/article/20180613-why-do-only-some-people-get-blackout-drunk.

Glenn Kessler, the infamous *Washington Post* fact checker who presides over the "Pinocchio" system, fact checked the one in five statistic in 2014.[19] President Barack Obama and Vice President Joe Biden put together a task force at the time to investigate the issue based on the CDC and DOJ studies. Kessler opted not to provide a verdict on the claim, noting that the sample size across two universities was just too small to be representative.

Despite all of these issues with the research, the Obama administration implemented new guidelines demanding that universities use the lowest standard of proof in determining the guilt of those accused of sexual assault—a "preponderance of the evidence." This means the event was "more likely than not" to have occurred. It is a much weaker standard than that of the American judicial system, which requires prosecutors to prove that a defendant committed a crime "beyond a reasonable doubt." Students who are found "guilty" by their university under the "preponderance of the evidence" standard are subject to suspension or expulsion.

Stories about accused young men who received no due process during university investigations became plentiful during this time period. Many colleges did not offer the men the chance to face their accuser, allowed victim advocates to simultaneously serve on the committees deciding guilt or innocence, allowed the same group of people on these committees to play judge and jury, did not permit the men to see the evidence presented against them, and did not allow the men to have a lawyer present during proceedings.

---

[19]   Kessler, Glenn. "One in Five Women in College Sexually Assaulted: The Source of This Statistic." *Washington Post*. WP Company, December 7, 2021. https://www.washingtonpost.com/news/fact-checker/wp/2014/05/01/one-in-five-women-in-college-sexually-assaulted-the-source-of-this-statistic/.

Emily Yoffe of the *Atlantic* reported the following in 2017 after observing how the changes in campus sexual assault guidance were affecting young men:[20]

> *"Over the past several years of reporting and writing on this subject, the people I've spoken with who deal closely with campus sexual assault—school administrators, lawyers, higher-education-policy consultants, even investigators for the Office for Civil Rights—do not typically describe campuses filled with sociopathic predators. They mostly paint a picture of students, many of them freshmen, who begin a late-night consensual sexual encounter, well lubricated by alcohol, and end up with divergent views of what happened."*

All of that is to say that Hoff Sommers wasn't spouting anything outrageous or unfounded about campus rape statistics that would warrant her being deemed a rape apologist. Just like during the Ferguson protests, facts didn't matter to the leftists on campus. Students planned protests and "safe spaces" for Hoff Sommers's appearance. Georgetown's Sexual Assault Peer Education program sent an email to its members warning that "an extremist anti-feminist speaker that dismisses and denies survivors of sexual assault" was coming to campus and insisted[21] that the event needed "trigger warnings."

---

20 Yoffe, Emily. "The Uncomfortable Truth about Campus Rape Policy." *The Atlantic.* Atlantic Media Company, September 29, 2017. https://www.theatlantic.com/education/archive/2017/09/the-uncomfortable-truth-about-campus-rape-policy/538974/.

21 Carr, Mallory, Moderate Anon, Really?, Tony Host, Rodger, Jason, Veronika, et al. "America's Failing Feminism." America's Failing Feminism, April 24, 2015. https://thehoya.com/americas-failing-feminism/.

I released a statement from the official College Republicans page rejecting the idea of trigger warnings. It was not up to us to tell other adults whether or not they could handle the content of Hoff Sommers' lecture. Survivors of sexual assault could do their own research and decide whether or not they were mentally equipped for the event. I also denounced the idea of setting up a safe space, noting that if any student really felt "unsafe" due to Hoff Sommers' speech, they could simply not attend.

At one point during the lead-up to the event, I was called into the office of the student activities coordinator for Georgetown. She expressed concerns that Hoff Sommers's visit could get out of hand because of the potential for rowdy protesters, but she supported our club's right to continue with the event. She also helped coordinate for plain-clothes campus police officers to be in attendance to make sure that anyone who tried to interrupt the author would be removed. Many college conservatives had to fight their administrations in addition to their fellow students, so I was grateful for her support.

The few days prior to the speech were some of the hardest of my college career. I was constantly defending myself and the College Republicans. Every day there seemed to be another threat to our ability to hold the event. There was hardly any time for school work or my normal social activities because of the constant harassment. Some members of the club's executive board wondered if we were better off just canceling the event so we didn't have to deal with it anymore. I refused to reward the protesters, but I certainly understood the impulse. This is why I am always sympathetic to college conservatives going through similar experiences. It is not easy. It is not fair that we have to work so much harder to have our views heard. But it is important to carry on fighting. If we do not persevere, many college students would never hear anything but leftist drivel and the campuses would be thrown to the wolves.

Hoff Sommers made it to campus and stood up bravely against a line of protesters who stood at the back of the room declaring her a rape apologist, a participant in rape culture, and a misogynist. I gave the introduction to her speech, during which I was instructed by the university to reiterate the campus free speech policy prohibiting attendees from disrupting invited speakers.

Luckily, no one interrupted Hoff Sommers and she addressed their criticism head on.[22] She even took questions from a number of hostile protesters, offering them a dialogue that, frankly, they didn't deserve. Some of the students spent their question time lecturing her about domestic abuse and sexual assault survivors they had volunteered with, as if a college student had identified a gap in the knowledge of a woman who spent her career studying feminism. It was patently ridiculous. Almost as ridiculous as the protesters snapping their fingers or using jazz hands to signal agreement with their peers, who provided commentary disguised as questions. It looked more like a Brooklyn poetry slam than a college lecture.

Several student activists spoke with the *Hoya*[23] about how horrified they were by the event.

"It was an extremely problematic talk. She was racist, ableist and her [statistics] on boys being suspended is extremely racialized," Queen Adesuyi said. "Her insensitivity to race was absolutely ridiculous."

---

[22] CBLucePolicyInst. "What's Right (and Badly Wrong) with Feminism?" YouTube. YouTube, April 18, 2015. https://www.youtube.com/watch?v= VbK1xeWJsOw&t=9s.

[23] Heftler, Margaret, Tyrone, Ha, A Student, The Dude, No Victim, A Parent, Wait a minute, and Facts. "Sommers Event Sparks Dialogue, Protest." The Hoya, April 22, 2015. https://thehoya.com/sommers-event-sparks-dialogue-protest/.

"We're here tonight to silently protest. [Sommers] has, in the past, made statements trivializing survivors of sexual assault and saying that survivors are not legitimate. We are here in solidarity with survivors," H*yas for Choice vice-president Michaela Lewis said.

Nonetheless, Hoff Sommers received a nice round of applause at the end of her speech while protesters cried in a safe space next door. Afterward, the College Republicans grabbed dinner with Hoff Sommers off campus. She seemed completely unbothered by the fact that she was the most hated woman on campus that day and handled the whole situation with grace. She was incredibly inspiring.

I thought that quiet, peaceful dinner would be the end of the ordeal. How wrong I was.

The same core group of leftist students tended to be behind most of the protests on campus, and they usually moved on to the next pet project pretty quickly. In this case, however, the student newspaper decided to join the mob a few days after the event.

The Hoya's editorial board published a piece called "No More Distractions" that chastised us for bringing Dr. Hoff Sommers to campus. The op-ed accused us of "knowingly endors[ing] a harmful conversation" and "imped[ing] the progress of the university's commitment to providing increased resources to survivors." But isn't it important to have accurate statistics around the problem so that resources can be distributed in the most efficient manner? In fact, it used to be the point of the university to encourage critical thinking skills. What could be more in line with the idea of "critical thinking" than using facts to evaluate a situation and then come up with solutions?

The piece went on to engage in one of the most magnificent displays of doublethink that I've ever encountered:

> *"It is necessary and valuable to promote the free expression of a plurality of views, but this back-and-forth about whether or not certain statistics are valid is not the conversation that students should be having. Students should engage in a dialogue that focuses on establishing a safe space for survivors while at the same time tackling the root causes of sexual assault."*

The editorial board believes in free expression, but only if it's the type of expression that they deem valuable? The truth is that the editorial board doesn't believe in free expression at all. They only claimed to value it because they thought it would save them from accusations of censorship. Unfortunately for them, no amount of political doublespeak could get past people who actually use their brains to evaluate arguments.

Dr. Hoff Sommers shared the censorious op-ed with her followers, who quickly filled the comment section with rebukes of its main arguments. It was beyond satisfying to see that, outside of our little campus bubble, there were scores of people who supported our right to host Dr. Hoff Sommers and saw through the leftist students' ridiculous arguments in favor of silencing us.

As the debate raged on amongst students, the once-helpful Georgetown administration began to turn on us as well. They discovered that the Clare Boothe Luce organization, our co-host for the event, had filmed Hoff Sommers's speech and put it on YouTube. I received an email from the student activities coordinator demanding I tell Clare Boothe Luce to take down the video because the student protesters caught on camera did not consent to being filmed. The email[24] suggested that the College Republicans and I would face consequences for breaking the campus videography policy if the video weren't removed immediately:

> *"What was the response from Clare Boothe Luce about the video? I see that it is still up online. Please let me know asap as an edited version needs to be released without students who did not give permission to be taped. If they are unwilling or unresponsive to the request, Georgetown will need to step in. Let me know!"*

To be honest, I was terrified. I never had any problem scrapping with my fellow students because I was already used to the social consequences. However, being disciplined by the university could mean consequences for my ability to remain on campus or even graduate. Perhaps I was being a bit dramatic, but was I really willing to put my future at stake for this speech?

Luckily, the organization was ready to fight.

Laurel Conrad, then the lecture director for CBL, wrote in *Legal Insurrection*, "While many Universities are accustomed to bullying students until they bend to a left wing point of view, a conservative women's organization named after the courageous Clare Boothe Luce is not impressed or moved by such bullying."

CBL sent a response to the student activities coordinator threatening legal action if they forced us to take down the video. They argued that the event was open to the public and thus the students in attendance had no reasonable expectation of

---

[24]   Conrad, Laurel. "Georgetown Demands Edits to Christina Hoff Sommers Video." Le·gal In·sur·rec·tion |, February 28, 2018. https://legalinsurrection.com/2015/04/georgetown-demands-edits-to-christina-hoff-sommers-video/?fbclid=IwAR22mb-9F234hWQSBGaN8yWmxS9v0gN9zkA5kvYg-4SwVVxyRzCTIR1PBCEA.

privacy. The university immediately dropped the issue, although I did receive a snarky email from the student activities coordinator complaining that her email had been passed along to Clare Boothe Luce. Too bad, so sad. The university didn't actually care about the video policy, anyway. They were just embarrassed that their students became the subject of national news for their idiotic protest.

Our event with Hoff Sommers started somewhat of a trend. The event received massive coverage, from Fox News, to *National Review*, *Independent Journal Review*, the *Daily Caller* and the *Daily Wire*. Just a week later, Dr. Hoff Sommers faced an even larger protest at Oberlin College. A group of students pre-empted her speech in the *Oberlin Review* with a piece titled "A Love Letter to Ourselves."[25]

Similar to *The Hoya* editorial board, which argued that Hoff Sommers's speech was a "distraction" and "not the conversation students should be having," the Oberlin students insisted it was a waste of time to even explain why they objected to Hoff Sommers or debate her ideas.

"We could spend all of our time and energy explaining all of the ways she's harmful. But why should we? Anger is productive, and critiques are necessary. At this point, though, why don't we stop spinning our wheels and burning ourselves out on conversations with Christina Hoff Sommers' Twitter followers?" the students whined.

It was around this time that professional pundits started pushing the narrative on Fox News and in other conservative outlets that the campus snowflakes were nothing to worry about.

---

[25] Oberlin community members. "In Response to Sommers' Talk: A Love Letter to Ourselves." *Oberlin Review*. Accessed September 5, 2022. https://oberlinreview.org/8032/opinions/in-response-to-sommers-talk-a-love-letter-to-ourselves/.

They would get to the real world, and their bosses wouldn't tolerate their behavior. Maybe, they surmised, these kids wouldn't even get hired anywhere. Signing a letter like this should've put students on an employment blacklist a la the Hollywood blacklist of the 1950s.

"The real world is not a safe space," Julie Roginsky said on Fox News' "The Five" in November 2015.[26] Her co-hosts readily agreed and stated they would not hire the architects of campus protests.

"How will today's college students function once they leave campus and find the world no giant "safe space" protecting them from things they don't want to hear?" the *New York Post*'s editorial board wondered in March 2016.[27]

Spoiler alert: the kids did just fine. The Oberlin letter's signatories landed jobs in various industries, including progressive activism, local government, law, nursing, and even teaching your kids. Some inevitably ended up in the media.

Madeline Peltz, one of the signatories and a staff writer at the *Oberlin Review*, has been working as a researcher at Media Matters for America since 2017. More on her later. Another signee, Anna Menta, writes woke film reviews for *Decider*. She encourages the uptick in Hollywood's production of progressive content and insufferably political award show speeches by writing articles like "Michelle Williams Delivered An Emotional, Pro-Choice Speech

---

[26] "Outrage Erupts on College Campuses Igniting Free Speech Debate." Fox News. FOX News Network. Accessed September 5, 2022. https://www.foxnews.com/transcript/outrage-erupts-on-college-campuses-igniting-free-speech-debate.

[27] Board, Post Editorial. "'Sensitivity' Fascists Are Turning Colleges into Day-Care Centers." *New York Post*. New York Post, March 8, 2016. https://nypost.com/2016/03/07/sensitivity-fascists-are-turning-colleges-into-day-care-centers/.

at the Golden Globes"[28] and tweets about films being "problematic."[29] Gracie Freeman Lifschutz recently completed the Columbia Publishing Course, a prestigious Columbia Journalism program that prepares its students to work in book publishing. Just what the industry needs—another censorious progressive deciding what Americans get to read.

Back at Georgetown, there were a few students who decided to do some real journalism. Kenneth Lee and Graham Piro—who coincidentally now reports for the *Washington Free Beacon*—reported about the state of free speech on campus for the *Georgetown Voice*, a campus newspaper rival to the *Hoya*. The piece, called "Safe Spaces or Echo Chambers? Understanding the Discourse Surrounding Georgetown's Political Climate"[30] included interviews with various members of the Georgetown community, including me, other members of the College Republicans, College Democrats, and some of the progressive activists who tried to prevent Hoff Sommers from speaking on campus.

The article provided some new insight about the pathology of the students who wanted to cancel Hoff Sommers and GUCR. Pepi-Lewis, the aforementioned vice-president of H*yas for Choice, told Lee and Piro, "H*yas for Choice, as a group, had a discussion about our feelings on the university bringing

---

[28] Menta, Anna. "Michelle Williams Delivered an Emotional, pro-Choice Speech at the Golden Globes." Decider. Decider, January 6, 2020. https://decider.com/2020/01/05/michelle-williams-golden-globes-speech/.

[29] Menta, Anna. "I Didn't Leave Knives out Feeling That the Movie Is Problematic but @Mcastimovies Helped Me See That's Because the Movie Was Speaking Solely from the POV of White Liberalism, despite the Fact That It Was Intended as a Critique." Twitter. Twitter, December 2, 2019. https://twitter.com/annalikestweets/status/1201629376527421441.

[30] "Safe Spaces or Echo Chambers? Political Discourse at Georgetown." *Georgetown Voice*, March 31, 2019. https://georgetownvoice.com/2015/10/22/safe-spaces-or-echo-chambers/.

Christina Hoff Sommers as a speaker, and [we] found some of her past work to be offensive. We did feel the need to make a note that we did not agree with the message that was being presented."

Um, why would H*yas for Choice need to tell people they didn't agree with the message? They weren't hosting the event. They weren't sponsors. None of their members were involved in the planning. They certainly weren't required to attend. They had literally nothing to do with the event at all! It takes a serious case of narcissism to believe that people need your opinion on something that has nothing to do with you or your club. Of course, campus leftists are experts at getting attention and making everything about them. If they can't make it personal, then they can't use their emotionally driven arguments to shut down their opponents.

The chair of the Georgetown College Democrats also dismissed my concerns that a certain segment of the Georgetown student body would happily shut down conservative speech, as if the entire Hoff Sommers fiasco hadn't just happened.

"When you're talking about your friends, your fellows, your classmates, and say that they are all 'hell-bent' on oppressing conservatives, it seems to me like an extreme exaggeration and it just doesn't seem…[like] something that you can really take that seriously," Matthew Gregory said.

And yet, Vincent DeLaurentis, a member of the Georgetown Solidarity Committee, confirmed that his goal is to disrupt and intimidate. Such tactics are justified, he claimed, because "These systems are killing people everyday [sic], these systems are actively working to oppress us and to stop us from doing this type of work."

> "Students are so concerned with this pre-professional culture and this faux-discourse of

> *respect and mutual exchange. The dominant system relies on conformity, it relies on quietness, it relies on maintenance of the status quo. For the majority of people who are not facing pretty explicit violence in their daily lives, it's pretty hard to understand that there's violence going on around us and violence happening in all of our interactions."*

DeLaurentis now works for the Worker Rights Consortium in Washington, DC.

My favorite comment from the *Georgetown Voice* article was from Josue Coronado, the Latinx Leadership Forum's media chair, who spoke about his efforts to start a "Casa Latina" on campus. Why not a Casa Latinx? Who knows.

"You feel emotions, because you have lived it, you've transferred into this fight for a house, a space for inclusivity on campus...These are issues that we feel and because we feel them then they are true."

Because we feel them then they are true! I couldn't encapsulate the social justice warrior ideology any perfectly if I spent ten years writing this book. Facts, reality, truth be damned. It's all about how you feel. Don't deny my lived experience!

CHAPTER 5

SLAVING AWAY

I mentioned before that Georgetown's adoption of the diversity requirement—despite activists publicly smearing the university and its students as a bunch of evil racists—wouldn't end well.

The next big racial debate on campus started in the summer of 2015 when resurfaced historical documents revealed Georgetown's ties to the slave trade. According to records, Georgetown benefited financially from the sale of 272 slaves owned by the Maryland Province of the Society of Jesus in 1838. The sale, worth about $3.3 million today, was facilitated by two of Georgetown's early presidents.

The timing of this news couldn't have been worse for the university. They were just about ready to reopen a residence hall named after one of those university presidents, Rev. Thomas F. Mulledy, after extensive renovations. DeGioia noted Mulledy's "difficult" past when announcing the reopening of the building to students. Mulledy was a member of the Maryland Jesuits that owned and sold the slaves. Mulledy supported the gradual freeing of the slaves but worried that it would not be accepted in

Maryland because its residents were already growing weary of the large number of freed men in the state. Mulledy's proposed compromise was that the slaves would be sold, and the Jesuits eventually agreed under the conditions that families remain intact and that the resulting funds be used only to advance Jesuit causes. Some of the money was used to keep Georgetown, which was struggling financially at the time, afloat. The Jesuit Society and Catholic Church later excoriated Mulledy for the sale and sent him into exile.

DeGioia addressed the controversy head on,[31] declaring that the reopening of Mulledy Hall would be an opportunity for students to learn from the bad parts of the university's history.

"Over the coming months, we will provide opportunities for our community to learn more about this history, and its legacy, in greater detail," he said. "This is what we do best as a university community: we come together to confront difficult events, learn from and with one another, and rely on the collective wisdom and resources of our extraordinary community to determine how we may best move forward toward justice and truth."

He should've known this nuanced approach wouldn't fly. Students immediately organized protests to rename the hall. The ensuing drama was the elite university version of the nation-wide statue debate. Over the coming years, activists would call for the removal of statues of Robert E. Lee, Junipero Serra, Christopher Columbus, Theodore Roosevelt, Thomas Jefferson, and Abraham Lincoln. Oddly enough, Georgetown students still haven't called for the removal of the Bishop John Carroll just inside the front gates, despite his history as a slave-owner, nor

---

[31] "A Message Regarding Mulledy Hall." President John J. DeGioia, December 5, 2018. https://president.georgetown.edu/mulledy-hall/.

have they advocated for changing the name of the entire university even though it is assumedly named after King George II.

That September, President DeGioia responded to the heat by putting together a "Working Group on Slavery, Memory, and Reconciliation" to determine how the university should address the sale of the 272 slaves. The working group discussed renaming Mulledy Hall and other reparation-based ideas with plans of releasing a report with recommendations the following year.

Remember Chris Wadibia, of failed GUSA presidential candidate fame? He was on the Working Group, alongside several other students, faculty, and historians. Crystal Walker, who was appointed to the group after complaints that there weren't enough black students on the committee, was the primary pot-stirrer. I lived just a couple of doors down from Crystal my freshman year and got along with her well. We bonded over our love for the *Pretty Little Liars* television show, music, and our small-town backgrounds. That fledgling friendship didn't last long once she became involved with the Black Leadership Forum, Black House, and other progressive campus groups that threw my name around like garbage in their group chats. Freshman year, Crystal had a bright and sunny disposition and could make anyone smile. By senior year, she read as perpetually angry and looking for revenge. I was grateful for my education at Georgetown, but for some it was almost a burden. Campus activists brutalized them with the idea that they were wronged by the system, that their communities were doomed from the start, and that everyone was out to get them. It seemed to make them very unhappy.

As I mentioned, Crystal was on the slavery working group. Great news, right? She could work directly with the university to determine the best course of action to reconciling Georgetown today with its slave-soaked history. Not so fast. As we learned during the kerfuffle over the diversity requirement, the campus left is not satisfied with working within the system to build relationships, make compromises, and achieve some goals. They need total and complete power. So, Crystal, along with her friends Candace Milner, Queen Adesuyi, Ayo Aruleba, and Stephanie Estevez organized a "solidarity demonstration."

Quite a few of these students were fresh off protesting Hoff Sommers, of course, and were some of the most vicious online harassers I encountered.

The students claimed that the "Demonstration of Solidarity" was to show support for student protesters at Mizzou and Yale. Mizzou students were protesting over claims that the administration wasn't appropriately responding to racial slurs being yelled at black students; activists responded by blocking the president's car and camping out on the quad, where journalism professor Melissa Click infamously asked[32] for some "muscle" to force out student reporters. Football players boycotted Mizzou's games that season. Yale students, meanwhile, were livid that some administrators pushed back[33] on a campuswide email urging students not to wear potentially offensive or culturally insensitive Halloween costumes.

"In these past couple weeks, students of color at Yale and specifically Black students at Mizzou have expressed their frustration at being ignored by the administrators of their various institutions of higher learning. We have seen the POWER we students have at creating lasting and impacting change. Yet, resignations aren't enough, especially when we still are targeted by

---

[32] Chappellet-Lanier, Tajha. "A Suspension for Mizzou Professor Melissa Click." *The Atlantic*. Atlantic Media Company, January 28, 2016. https://www.theatlantic.com/education/archive/2016/01/melissa-click-suspended-mizzou/432564/.

[33] Nelson, Libby. "Yale's Big Fight over Sensitivity and Free Speech, Explained." Vox, November 7, 2015. https://www.vox.com/2015/11/7/9689330/yale-halloween-email.

our racist and bigoted peers and professors," the organizers of Georgetown's solidarity demonstration said.

Hundreds of students gathered in Red Square for the event,[34] and the discussion turned quickly from Mizzou and Yale to allegations of racism at Georgetown.

"Anti-blackness is real. Anti-blackness is a thing," one student said.

Another asserted, "We will hold Georgetown responsible for the experiences of black students on this campus."

I walked by the demonstration that day and was immediately disturbed by chants of "fuck the police," but didn't stay because I didn't want my presence to be mistaken for support. Instead, I went back to my dorm and watched a livestream of the insane event.

After opening statements, a black football player who weighed probably 300 pounds grabbed the microphone and urged students to share their stories of racism on campus. He insisted that he felt "unsafe" walking on campus at night because of the "racially charged" atmosphere. In what bizarro world is a man his size at risk for violence? At Georgetown, of all places?

Students continued to share experiences of "racism," including a Physics major who complained that she was the only Latina in one of her classes, and another student who asserted that all white students are racist regardless of intent because they exist in a racist "system."

The real purpose of the event, though, was to promote a sit-in scheduled for the following morning at President DeGioia's office. Organizers announced that students would gather with

---

[34] "Student Activists Announce Sit-in in President Degioia's Office, Call for Name Change to Mulledy Hall." *Georgetown Voice*, November 14, 2015. https://georgetownvoice.com/2015/11/12/student-activists-announce-sit-in-in-president-degioias-office-call-for-name-change-to-mulledy-hall/.

a list of six demands for the university, including the renaming of Mulledy Hall. All of those "stories" and "experiences" shared by students were meant to prime the pump, so to speak, so that administrators were already feeling guilty when students arrived on their doorstep the following morning.

Here were the six demands: rename Mulledy Hall, install plaques on unmarked slave graves on campus, implement an annual program on slavery's legacy at Georgetown, revise campus tours to include information about the roles of black people in Georgetown's history, implement mandatory diversity training for professors, and create an endowment to recruit black professors.

I had no problem with the demand for a plaque on the graves, but mandatory diversity training? It's very well documented that diversity training simply doesn't work. Diversity training tends to make workplaces even more divisive[35] because it forces employees to see everything through the lens of race. Coercing employees into mandatory trainings can also activate feelings of resentment against the very groups the training seeks to protect.

The demand for an endowment for black professors was undoubtedly the dumbest idea, though. Activists demanded the endowment be "equivalent to the Net Present Value of the profit generated from the transaction in which 272 people were sold into bondage." Inflation would put the value of the $115,000 slave sale at $3 million today. But if you want to calculate net present value, you need to tack on the interest you would earn by investing that money. I'm not a financial expert, but some rudimentary math puts the resulting endowment at tens of billions of dollars.

---

[35] Redstone, Ilana. "This Is Why Diversity Programming Doesn't Work." *Forbes Magazine*, November 18, 2020. https://www.forbes.com/sites/ilanaredstone/2020/11/18/this-is-why-diversity-programming-doesnt-work/?sh=28a4d4eb66d5.

That's a hell of a lot of black professors. As of 2020, black professors were actually overrepresented at Georgetown. Twenty percent of Georgetown faculty are black compared to 13.4 percent of the US population.

I needed to do something to have my voice heard ahead of the sit-in, so I sent the following email to President DeGioia's chief of staff, Dr. Joseph Ferrara:

> *Hello Mr. Ferrara,*
>
> *I am not sure if this is the best way to get my message to President DeGioia, but hopefully you will pass it along.*
>
> *I am a student in the College, Class of 2016, and I am concerned for our university.*
>
> *Today, in Red Square, students gathered for a "Demonstration of Solidarity" to show support for the students at Mizzou and Yale University. What actually happened was much different. As I was walking past the demonstration, I heard protestors yelling, "fuck the police." I kept walking, as it was clear I wanted no part of such a movement. Watching videos later on tonight, I heard statements degrading white people and suggesting that all white people contribute to racism. I heard students claiming that the campus was racist because they happened to be the only person of color in one of their courses. I heard a 350-pound football player tell the attendees that he was scared to walk around campus at night because of the "racially charged" atmosphere on campus. I heard*

protestors chanting that if they did not get their demands, they would shut down the university, disrupting our education that we pay so much money for, but are also so privileged to have.

This is my 4th year on campus. These claims of racism are at best, highly exaggerated, and, at worst, completely false. While I do not want to deny the experiences of my peers, I feel that catering to people who bully those who disagree with them and threaten to disrupt the operation of the university is a huge mistake.

Students will be staging a sit-in tomorrow outside of President DeGioia's office. They have a list of 6 demands. I hope that you will refuse them. Administrators must stand up to these bullies, as our history and education are at stake.

I am not alone in my sentiments. There are many students just like me who are scared to publicly voice their opinion because they do not want to face the wrath of the protestors. Please consider the implications of giving in to these demands.

I received a response from Dr. Ferrara; he said he would pass my message along to President DeGioia. But a strongly worded email doesn't sway university administrators nearly as much as thirty smelly students slurping down pizza on the floor of their office. The sit-in started on November 13. President DeGioia approved the renaming of Mulledy Hall one day later.

"Friday morning, I met with a group of students who gathered in the President's Office. The students shared with me their opinions on the importance of changing the name of two build-ings. On Friday afternoon, the Working Group shared with me their recommendation to rename Mulledy Hall and McSherry Hall. I have reviewed the working group's recommendation with our Board of Directors and I have accepted the recommendation to remove these names," DeGioia said in a statement.[36]

I was still the College Republican's chair during all of this and my public opposition to the students' demands made me even more toxic than I already was, if that was possible. A good friend of mine, who I'll call J, decided to run an outsider campaign for the Georgetown University College Democrats (GUCD) and asked me to endorse him. We thought it'd be a nice example of bipartisanship.

"[J] clearly has experience to boot, and I am also proud to say he is a really great friend. I have discussed politics with him on many occasions, and always find him to be respectful, passionate, and rational. These qualities are so important for the head of a student organization, especially one with political ties," I wrote in my endorsement post on Facebook.

Less than three hours later, he messaged me asking me to take it down. The current board members of GUCD threatened to publicly endorse his opponent if I continued to support him.

---

[36] Hung, Toby, Bishop John Carroll, J, Beyond Yale: These other university buildings have ties to slavery and white supremacy says: Beyond Yale: These other university buildings have ties to slavery and white supremacy | Breaking News for College Students | CredHatch says: Beyond Yale: These other university buildings have ties to slavery and white supremacy | Breaking News for College Students says: Beyond Yale: These other university buildings have ties to slavery and white supremacy – HEOP.org says: and Beyond Yale: These other university buildings have ties to slavery and white suprem-acy – USA TODAY | Meek Voices says: "DeGioia Approves Renaming of Mulledy, Mcsherry Halls." The Hoya, November 14, 2015. https://thehoya.com/degioia-approves-renaming-of-mulledy-mcsherry-halls/.

CHAPTER 6

A HIGHER CLASS

Georgetown was unique from other colleges in that its left-ward shift seemed to occur almost entirely among students as opposed to the faculty or administration. Even in my Government major, the professors were generally center left and still believed deeply in free speech and open debate in the classroom. Most of my classes were devoid of intense bias, with a few exceptions.

I took a class in the Sociology department in the spring of my freshman year to fulfill a social sciences requirement. The course was called "Social Inequality" and the syllabus was filled with exactly the left-wing drivel you'd expect. This was the first time I read the Communist Manifesto in its entirety, and it was difficult to take the ideas within as seriously as my professor clearly did. The professor also decided to let the class choose how our grades would be weighted. We could opt for a normal merit-based system, or we could choose an "equitable" grading system wherein we all received the same letter grade no matter how well we performed individually. There was also the option of receiving grades under a reparations or affirmative action system, where minority students would receive bonuses based on how many oppression points they had. If you were black, a woman, gay, or some other "marginalized" group, your grade would receive a bump. Bonus points for intersectionality! Luckily, a majority of the class voted to use the merit-based system. The professor couldn't hide the look of disappointment on his face.

This was the first time in my college career that I felt the need to challenge the professor during our discussion periods. He would often spout off what I thought were uninformed opinions about blue collar manual laborers and unions. The professor insisted, for example, that unions could not be corrupt. My father spent his entire career as a union plumber and pipefitter, so I would often bring his experiences into the conversation to counter the professor's arguments. I did not consider that, unlike in high school, grades are much more subjective. Even though I never scored below a 95 percent on one of our many multiple-choice exams, I finished the course with a B. The professor had given me a C on my final paper, which was worth about half of our grade. I cannot prove that this was due to my outspokenness in class, but I did find it odd that he only wrote one small critical note on the entire paper.

Still, I loved that class because it gave me some great insight into the absurd propaganda that was being fed to students in the social sciences. I was also struck by how much dumber my classmates seemed compared to classes I took in the Mathematics, History, and even English departments. Perhaps they weren't as used to rigorous coursework. Or maybe Sociology, Gender Studies, and similar disciplines just attract idiots.

Many people do not know that I started my college career as a Math major. I did really well in Math classes in high school and scored a five on my AP Calculus I and II exam junior year and a five on my AP Statistics exam senior year. My goal heading into college was eventually to become an Actuarial Scientist, mostly because it paid well and had good job security. God had other plans for me. My first college Math course was Multivariable Calculus and to say it kicked my butt would be an understatement. I would study endlessly for exams, attend office hours with my professor, and form study groups with my classmates, but the material just wouldn't click. I believe I got a 34 percent on my first exam and didn't improve a whole lot from there. I finished the class with a C. It was pretty jarring since I'd received straight As my entire life. I didn't fare much better in my next few math classes, receiving no better than a C+ in any of them. My Intro to Proofs and Problem Solving class in the fall of my sophomore year was when I decided something needed to change. I was still working twice as hard to do half as well as my peers in the class, and my struggles were compounded by health issues that caused multiple trips to the student health center and the emergency room. That spring, I took a few exploratory classes in other disciplines and decided to change to a double major in Government and Economics. I took one more course in Math to finish out a minor and called it a day. What a relief! I was able to explore my love for politics in my Government courses, and the Economics major used a lot of applied mathematics, which was a breeze after the highly theoretical Math courses I was taking prior.

The spring semester of my senior year I was rounding out my Econ degree with an International Finance course. I was very surprised when the class received an email from our professor, Pedro Gete, telling us that we would be participating in Georgetown's "Let Freedom Ring" Initiative. This was an annual week-long event to celebrate Dr. Martin Luther King. According to Professor Gete's email, the initiative would "continue a conversation" on how the Georgetown community can "bring about social change". The MLK planning committee said the 2016 theme "Why We Can't Wait" would highlight "the importance of social justice activism, particularly for a university like Georgetown."[37] Professors were encouraged to "Teach the Speech" during the first month of their courses, so we were assigned Dr. King's 1964 Nobel Peace Prize acceptance speech. We also had a class discussion about the "Economics of Discrimination" by Gary Becker. Look, there's no doubt that Dr. King's contributions to society should be taught in schools. But at the college level? In an International Finance course? I couldn't help but feel we were wasting valuable instruction time on material I had been learning since elementary school.

Georgetown is known for having some pretty famous alumni: Bradley Cooper, Bill Clinton, Antonin Scalia, Allen Iverson, Paul Tagliabue, a few Jordanian princes, and the president of Colombia. I never got that close to any big names, but I did take my Social Inequality class with Maryland Governor Martin O'Malley's daughter, Grace. A couple of years later, O'Malley announced his intention to run for president. One of his chief campaign issues was the rising cost of higher education and how to tackle student debt. O'Malley talked incessantly about how his family had gone more than $300,000 into debt to send Grace to Georgetown and his other daughter Tara to the College of Charleston. Grace sent out a campaign email on her father's behalf:

> *"Do I go to the college we can afford or do I take out loans to go to the college of my dreams? At the age of 18, I made the decision to follow my*

---

[37]   Pongsajapan, Robert. "Georgetown Honors Martin Luther King Jr.. Legacy with Events." Georgetown University, January 13, 2016. https://www.georgetown.edu/news/georgetown-honors-martin-luther-king-jr-legacy-with-events/.

> *dreams. My family and I now face years of debt—*
> *and we know we're not the only ones."*

There were so many things wrong with this narrative. The average amount of debt per student in the United States is less than $30,000 a year, yet the O'Malleys somehow managed to be in the hole for TEN TIMES that figure. Why? Because of poor decision-making, plain and simple. After her graduation, Grace became a teacher in Baltimore.[38] Did she really need to spend all of that money to go to Georgetown to get a teaching degree? Meanwhile, her father was receiving free housing at the governor's mansion for eight years and a $150,000-a-year salary.[39]

What really burned me up, though, was remembering how Grace would stroll into Social Inequality class with all kinds of designer purses. When I was a senior in high school, I used to stop by the guidance counselor's office once a week to pick up a copy of every single scholarship application being offered to students. I spent hours applying to everything I was even remotely qualified for. My parents scrimped and saved for years to be able to afford tuition. I worked through college and took advantage of Georgetown's scholarship program for first generation and low-income students so that I could reduce my loan burden as much as possible. It was a slap in the face to see a family as privileged as the O'Malleys demand taxpayers foot the bill for their financial illiteracy.

---

[38] Millstein, Seth. "Who Is Grace O'Malley, Martin O'Malley's Daughter? the Baltimore Teacher Could Be One of the next 'First Kids.'" Bustle, October 13, 2015. https://www.bustle.com/articles/116350-who-is-grace-omalley-martin-omalleys-daughter-the-baltimore-teacher-could-be-one-of-the-next.

[39] Wagner, John. "Martin O'Malley: Little in Savings, Lots of Debt." *Washington Post.* WP Company, November 26, 2021. https://www.washingtonpost.com/news/post-politics/wp/2015/07/16/omalley-discloses-heavy-debt-paid-speeches-as-he-runs-for-president/.

In case you want some insight into how the DC political machine works, allow me an aside to discuss Father Kevin O'Brien. It is the perfect example of how 1. Everyone in DC knows each other and 2. Icky people get away with bad deeds for far too long.

Father O'Brien was one of the Jesuit professors at Georgetown and, arguably, the most popular. Georgetown freshmen constantly heard from peer advisors, alumni, faculty, and other people "in the know" that they shouldn't graduate without taking one of Father O'Brien's classes.

It is no secret that Jesuits tend to be liberal politically. O'Brien is a longtime friend and spiritual advisor to the Biden family, and served as a pastor at Holy Trinity in Georgetown, President Joe Biden's preferred Catholic Church while living in Washington, DC. In 2018, O'Brien recorded a viral video for Mic.com[40]—a progressive policy site that later rebranded to focus on pop culture and social justice—attacking the idea of a "war on Christmas" and even suggested people shouldn't say "Merry Christmas" if it's likely to offend people of other faiths:

"We have to be careful about the language we use in a pluralistic society…because, in it, we encounter people of different faith traditions."

I bring up Father O'Brien because he was the officiant at Grace O'Malley's wedding in Baltimore in 2016. O'Brien left Georgetown a few years later to serve as president of Santa Clara University in California. He hurried back to DC in January 2021 to lead an inaugural mass for President-elect Joe Biden.

---

[40] Ciesemier, Kendall. "A Jesuit Priest Reveals the Big Problem with the so-Called 'War on Christmas.'" Mic. Mic, December 5, 2017. https://www.mic.com/articles/186563/a-jesuit-priest-reveals-the-big-problem-with-the-so-called-war-on-christmas.

"O'Brien…has been friends with the Biden family for nearly 15 years, dating back to when O'Brien was serving at Georgetown University," a statement from Santa Clara University said back in January. "O'Brien accepted the invitation to celebrate Mass from President-elect Biden, as he did before in Biden's previous inaugurations."

In his homily, O'Brien compared Biden to Jesus, according to reporting by the *Washington Post*.

"Your public service is animated by the same conviction to help and protect people and to advance justice and reconciliation, especially for those who are too often looked over and left behind," O'Brien said.

Just a few months later, O'Brien was placed on leave from Santa Clara pending an investigation into alleged inappropriate conduct. O'Brien resigned[41] after the investigation found that he "engaged in behaviors, consisting primarily of conversations, during a series of informal dinners with Jesuit graduate students that were inconsistent with established Jesuit protocols and boundaries."

Curiously, no other details about O'Brien's behavior have been reported. Tom Deignan of *Irish Central* noted[42] how strange it was that the allegations seemed to just disappear.

"You would think claims made against a 'family friend' of the most powerful man in the land would grab lots of attention," Deignan wrote.

---

[41] Levenson, Michael. "Inappropriate Behavior Cited in Resignation of Santa Clara U. President." *New York Times*, May 13, 2021. https://www.nytimes.com/2021/05/12/us/priest-santa-clara-university.html.

[42] "The Mystery of Biden Family Friend Father Kevin O'Brien." IrishCentral.com, May 9, 2021. https://www.irishcentral.com/opinion/others/father-kevin-obrien-biden-mystery.

No kidding. I also found it odd that Georgetown University didn't announce its own investigation into O'Brien's conduct, considering he served as both a professor and the head of Campus Ministry for years. We know that men who engage in inappropriate conduct usually have a pattern of behavior. It is quite rare that they commit just one offense. Without knowing the details of O'Brien's behavior, could there be students at Georgetown who were "victims"? I reached out to Georgetown when Santa Clara announced its investigation, asking if they would launch its own. They did not reply to me.

Georgetown loves to talk about social justice in its promotional materials and when appeasing progressive student activists, but they are oddly silent when a longtime beloved Jesuit professor is the one in the crosshairs. Classic leftist hypocrisy.

By the way, Father O'Brien is also a friend of and former professor to one of our favorite White House reporters: Yamiche Alcindor, who hosts programming on PBS and covers the White House for NBC.

Grace O'Malley wasn't the only interesting run-in I had with a fellow student in one of my classes. I was required to take a seminar course my senior year for my Government major, and ended up in a class called "Politics of Social Welfare" taught by Father Matthew Carnes. The subject matter was inevitably slanted to the left; the course naturally spent a lot of time on the assumption that poverty could only be combated by expanding government-run social welfare programs. Still, the seminar format meant we only had about ten people in the entire class and focused heavily on discussion time. The discourse was some of the most enriching of my college career. I appreciated that the course challenged me and the conversations we had in that small group, to me, were what college was supposed to be. There was one student, though, who wasn't thrilled that conservatives were also allowed to have opinions in class.

The night before each class, we were supposed to log on to an online message board to share our thoughts about the latest reading. I was stunned when I logged on one evening to see that a female classmate had written a post stating that "Republicans don't recognize humanness." I responded with a rather impassioned paragraph. I told my classmate that her words were hurtful and untrue, and that her decision to stereotype people based on their political beliefs furthers the type of division she claims to be against. It was a bit nerve-racking going into class the next day, not knowing how, or if, my professor was going to respond. To my pleasant surprise, he addressed the issue at the top of the class and took my side!

Without addressing any of the students involved by name, the professor said that he saw a troubling post on the class message board. He warned the class about making sweeping generalizations about political parties or our fellow classmates, and noted that a small group discussion only works when everyone in the class feels comfortable sharing their opinions without backlash. The professor also praised my response as thoughtful and appropriate.

I have no way of proving that this incident was the catalyst, but the female student didn't show up to class the next week. Or the week after. I later learned that she had dropped the class entirely. The intolerant left loves to spout off when they don't believe there will be consequences. As soon as anyone challenges them or refuses to give in, they crumble.

This was a common theme throughout my years at Georgetown. The same people who talked crap about me in group chats behind my back or trolled me on social media had shockingly little to say when I saw them in person. It gave me more courage to keep sharing my views because it told me that these people used intimidation because they were unprepared to actually defend their positions. The more they went after me, the more I knew I was right.

The night before its commencement ceremony, Georgetown hosts a senior ball for graduating students and their families. I ran into Father Carnes at the ball, and he stopped me to thank me for speaking up in class. He told me that he often worries that his students don't hear enough conservative viewpoints on campus, and that he hoped my presence in class provided them with some much-needed perspective.

Father Carnes was correct. Jonathan Ladd, a professor in the Government department, told the *Georgetown Voice* that the out-spoken students inside and outside of his classroom tended to be liberal. Hans Noel, who teaches a class on political parties that I took my senior year, said that his in-class anonymous surveys on students' political affiliation confirm that the student body skews left. While many students identify on the survey as "extremely liberal," almost none identify as "extremely conservative." If I remember correctly, I was one of just two students who identified as "extremely conservative" in class.

"You've got both sides, but there are a chunk of conservatives who are just not there," Noel said.

My encounter with Father Carnes always stuck with me and reaffirmed that it was important for me to be a vocal advocate for conservative politics on campus and beyond.

CHAPTER 7

UNPLANNED PARENTHOOD

In April 2016, during my senior year at Georgetown, the "non-partisan" GU Lecture Fund invited Planned Parenthood president Cecile Richards to speak on campus. The announcement sparked cheers among the student body and dismay among the Catholic community in DC. Georgetown, the oldest Catholic and Jesuit university in the country, would be hosting the head of the United States' largest abortion provider.

The Archbishop of Washington, DC, Cardinal Donald Wuerl,[43] condemned Georgetown for providing a platform for Richards, stating that "it is neither authentically Catholic nor within the Catholic tradition for a university to provide a special platform to those voices that promote or support" issues that reject Catholic morality. Leftists, who had no problem demanding universities disinvite conservative speakers like Ben

---

[43] "Washington Cardinal Rebukes Georgetown for Inviting Planned Parenthood Chief." Religion News Service, March 8, 2016. https://religionnews.com/2016/03/08/cardinal-donald-wuerl-georgetown-university-planned-parenthood-abortion-cecile-richards/.

Shapiro,[44] Jeff Sessions,[45] Jason Riley,[46] and Condoleezza Rice,[47] suddenly extolled the virtues of free speech and insisted that any invocation of Georgetown's Catholic heritage to question Richards's invitation was blind censorship. I felt myself somewhat torn between my Catholic identity and belief that the university should advance the values of the Church and my political activism in favor of free speech. When the Richards event finally took place, however, it was clear that this event was not about "discourse" or "debate," but blatant pro-abortion propaganda.

GU Lecture Fund is a student-run organization and is supposed to be nonpartisan. In practice, the group is a Make-a-Wish foundation for left-wing college students. It is nonpartisan in the same way that Black Lives Matter, the Human Rights Campaign, NARAL, and Moms Demand Action are. The Lecture Fund rakes in tens of thousands of dollars[48] each year from "student activities fees," a mandatory semesterly fee to fund student activity groups on campus (this is in addition to the already exorbitant tuition and room and board).

[44] "Ben Shapiro Escorted by Police from Csula Due to Angry Protesters." ABC7 Los Angeles, February 26, 2016. https://abc7.com/ben-shapiro-csula-escorted-protest/1219358/.

[45] "Sign the Petition." Change.org. Accessed September 5, 2022. https://www.change.org/p/robert-altenkirch-uah-edu-honoring-jeff-sessions-a-challenge-to-uah-values.

[46] "I Was Disinvited on Campus." *The Wall Street Journal*. Dow Jones & Company, May 4, 2016. https://www.wsj.com/articles/i-was-disinvited-on-campus-1462313788.

[47] Kelly Heyboer | NJ Advance Media for NJ.com. "Condoleezza Rice Pulls out of Giving Rutgers Commencement Speech." nj, May 3, 2014. https://www.nj.com/education/2014/05/condoleezza_rice_pulls_out_of_giving_rutgers_commencement_speech.html.

[48] Nyantakyi, Afua. "Gusa Releases Draft Budget; Club Sports and CSJ Face Largest Cuts." The Hoya, March 13, 2019. https://thehoya.com/gusa-releases-draft-budget-club-sports-csj-face-greatest-cuts/.

The Lecture Fund is one of the most well-funded of these groups, receiving nearly 10 percent of the annual student activities budget. They use the allocated money for speaker honorariums and to partner with other student organizations who may bring guests to campus. The Lecture Fund's stated mission[49] is to "enrich the academic experience of the Georgetown community" and "to enlighten, educate and, occasionally, entertain." Given its claim to be "nonpartisan" and the fact that it is using student's money, one would expect the Lecture Fund to provide an equal platform to speakers of all political stripes. According to a breakdown by the *Georgetown Review*, however, the Lecture Fund's liberal guests far outnumber conservatives and moderates.[50] Between 2013 and 2017, 71 percent of the invited speakers were liberal or left-leaning, while just 18 percent were conservative or right-leaning and 12 percent were moderate. (I suspect some of these moderate speakers might be classified as liberal or left-leaning by my standards.) In my experience, the conservative speakers that ended up coming to campus through the support of the Lecture Fund were usually recommended by the College Republicans and coordinated as a partnership campaign between the two groups. It was certainly not uncommon for our requests for funding to be turned down entirely.

The Lecture Fund's commitment to "academic enrichment" and "dialogue" was on full display during the Cecile Richards event, which turned out to be a de facto abortion rally. The Lecture Fund's Associate Board declined a Jesuit request to have a pro-life activist speak alongside Richards. The president and vice-president of H*yas for Choice, a pro-choice student group

---

[49] The Lecture Fund. "Georgetown University Lecture Fund." 2022. https://www.lecturefund.com.

[50] "Alex Ives Archives." *The Georgetown Review*, September 2, 2022. https://gureview.org/byline/alex-ives/.

that cannot even use "Hoyas" in its name because it is neither officially recognized nor funded by the university, introduced Richards. It was clear that the Lecture Fund was officially hosting the event as a way to skirt the fact that H*yas for Choice is not allowed to bring speakers to campus.

Luckily for H*yas for Choice, the moderators for the event, the Lecture Fund President Helen Brosnan, and Vice Chair of Finance Elizabeth Rich, carried their pro-abortion message. Brosnan tweeted the morning of the event that she woke up feeling like it was "Christmas morning," and later confirmed that it was "unequivocally one of the best days of my life." The young women wore pink dresses to signal their support for Planned Parenthood and warmly embraced the H*yas for Choice leaders, declaring them fighters for the euphemistic "reproductive justice." These "nonpartisan" Lecture Fund representatives asked the audience to give a round of applause for abortion providers, celebrated the fact that Richards was heavily involved in Hillary Clinton's presidential campaign, and avoided asking Richards about any of the moral objections to abortion. Brosnan stunningly told the crowd that she is a "devout Catholic" but that she believes "God is pro-choice." Was future White House press secretary Jen Psaki taking notes?

Brosnan and Rich later told the student newspaper that Richards had been on their "dream list"[51] of Lecture Fund speakers since they were freshmen four years prior.

Richards, of course, did a wonderful job of carrying the pro-abortion mantle herself. She compared fighting for abortion

---

[51] Eagan, Owen, Matt Martin, COL '16, Anne Childs, and Chris Pilgrim. "Richards Event Sees Gu, DC Backlash." The Hoya, November 16, 2016. https://thehoya.com/richards-event-sees-gu-dc-backlash/.

access to the Civil Rights movement,[52] and unironically praised eugenicist Margaret Sanger moments later. The Lecture Fund events usually leave about thirty minutes for audience Q&A; Richards took just four questions from the audience, which were partially prescreened. Georgetown Right to Life, a student pro-life organization, were told only that one of its members would get a chance to ask a question. Julie Reiter took up the mantle, asking Richards about Guttmacher Institute statistics that show the vast majority of Planned Parenthood's pregnancy services are abortion-related. Despite citing the Guttmacher Institute in her lecture, Richards accused Reiter of using made-up statistics, prompting the crowd to laugh derisively.

"She got her first challenge and she laughed at it," Reiter said[53] of Richards's response to her question. "I don't think she took it seriously or that there was a dialogue."

I was also selected to ask a question because of my past affiliation with the College Republicans. I asked Richards about her assertions that being pro-life is an "extremist" position; polls show that a plurality of Americans believe that life begins at conception and that a majority believe that life begins sometime within the first three months, I noted. Why is being pro-life considered an extremist position, but believing, like Richards, that babies can be aborted up until the moment of birth is not? Richards predictably avoided answering the actual question, instead pivoting to

---

[52] Richards, Cecile. "Cecile Richards Spoke at Georgetown University for the First Time - Here's What She Said." Medium. Planned Parenthood Action Voices, June 10, 2016. https://medium.com/planned-parenthood-action-fund/cecile-richards-spoke-at-georgetown-university-for-the-first-time-here-s-what-she-said-5f408f1129ae#.vb3knfhdu.

[53] Cna. "A Rally, Not a Dialogue – Georgetown Students Spurn Cecile Richards' Talk." Catholic News Agency. Accessed September 5, 2022. https://www.catholicnewsagency.com/news/33775/a-rally-not-a-dialogue-%E2%80%93-georgetown-students-spurn-cecile-richards-talk.

how her organization is merely about giving people the "choice" of abortion. It was in the vein of other pro-choice activists who throw out the fallacious argument that if you don't want an abortion, you don't have to get one. If you don't like murder, just don't murder anyone! Problem solved!

The other two questions were given to adoring fans of Richards and Planned Parenthood.

An even more obvious indication that the Richards speech was a rally and not a "dialogue" is the way the Georgetown administration locked down the event. H*yas for Choice members freely sold club T-shirts and passed out condoms and Planned Parenthood brochures on campus, but Georgetown police told independent protesters they were not allowed[54] to hold signs displaying victims of abortions. Most disturbingly, media were not allowed inside the auditorium, and the university did not set up a taping of the event to share afterward.

When I heard this, I took it upon myself to live tweet the event under the hashtag #CecileAtGU. I thought it was important for alumni, community members, and Catholics to be aware of what was being preached at the oldest Jesuit university in the world. My tweets went "viral"—at least by my standards at the time—and were picked up by Students for Life, the *Daily Wire*, *Life Site News*, *Live Action*, and more. In retrospect, it was probably the first real act of journalism I ever did in my life. I had no idea at that time that I would make a career in reporting; all I cared about was exposing the truth as the Georgetown administration, the Lecture Fund, H*yas for Choice, and Cecile Richards

---

[54] Ford Fischer - American University •April 21, 2016. "Video: Georgetown Clamps down on pro-Life Activists at Planned Parenthood President's Speech." The College Fix, April 21, 2016. https://www.thecollegefix.com/georgetown-clamps-pro-life-activists-planned-parenthood-presidents-speech/.

tried to hide their insidious event to indoctrinate college students behind closed doors.

Four years later, shortly after the death of George Floyd, the Georgetown Lecture Fund announced via Instagram[55] that it would be embarking on an affirmative action-style diversity campaign for its speakers. The Lecture Fund said it would dedicate half of its yearly allocation of funding to "black voices," despite the fact that black people make up just over 12 percent of the population. The timing of the statement suggested a weak attempt at virtue signaling, but its contents were actually quite disturbing.

The Lecture Fund stated that it is "tasked with serious introspection" and described its new, bizarre form of reparations as a "necessary action." They go on to admonish themselves for not having more black board members, a fact they blame on recruitment methods that are not "equitable" rather than a pure lack of interest on behalf of black students. It is a sad confession of collective guilt where none should exist. It's hard to know if the students really believe that they have played a part in the oppression of their peers and thus owe them this new policy, or if they are cynically trying to get out ahead of accusations of white privilege.

Either way, the Lecture Fund somehow managed to jump the shark even further by undermining the whole point of its existence: free speech and open dialogue. The statement trashes the entire concept, arguing that certain types of speech can be "oppressive" and thus violent. It kicks off with the following quote from author Toni Morrison in 1973:

> *"Oppressive language does more than represent violence; it is violence; does more than represents*

---

[55] Georgetown Univ. "Lecture Fund on Instagram: 'Our Statement on Black Lives Matter.'" Instagram. Accessed September 6, 2022. https://www.instagram.com/p/CBdYrqAgemj/.

*the limits of knowledge; it limits knowledge....
Sexist language, racist language, theistic language—all are typical of the policing languages of
mastery, and cannot, do not, permit new knowledge or encourage the mutual exchange of ideas."*

Did you catch that piece about "theistic language"? I'll remind
you again that Georgetown is the oldest Catholic university in
the country. By Morrison's and thereby the Lecture Fund's standard, the mere existence of the university is violence. Students
who attend are risking their lives every day just by walking to
class! How amazing!

The chosen Morrison quote also reveals a common view of
speech by woke college students. They do not believe that the First
Amendment protects all speech, including objectionable speech,
and if it does, they'd like to see otherwise. A plurality of college
students polled by Brookings[56]—44 percent to 39 percent—
believe that "hate speech" is not protected by the Constitution.
Fifty-one percent, including 62 percent of Democrats, believe
students would be right to shout over a speaker who is known
for making "offensive and hurtful statements." Nearly a fifth
of college students believe using violence to shut down such a
speaker is acceptable. Why do so many college students think
violence is an acceptable response to speech? Because they think
speech *is* violence. Go back to that Morrison quote—"oppressive
language...is violence," she writes. If speech is indeed violence,
then you are merely acting in self-defense when you use violence
to stop it.

---

[56] Villasenor, John. "Views among College Students Regarding the First
Amendment: Results from a New Survey." Brookings, March 9, 2022.
https://www.brookings.edu/blog/fixgov/2017/09/18/views-among-college-
students-regarding-the-first-amendment-results-from-a-new-survey/.

My exposure of the Cecile Richards event did not come without social ramifications. Leftists on campus also found my tweets, including Brosnan, who proudly reaffirmed her stance that God is "pro-choice." (Oddly enough, while I was doing research for this book, Brosnan blocked me on Twitter and made her Instagram account private.) Others accused me of homophobia for noting that a gay man in the audience was fanning himself at the prospect of seeing Richards in person; I merely found it odd that anyone would be that excited about abortion, particularly someone who would presumably never be involved in a pregnancy. His general advocacy flew in the face of most of the commentary on campus against my male pro-life friends, who were repeatedly told that they were not allowed to have opinions about "women's bodies." This was not an acceptable explanation for my peers who were determined that it was proof of my secret hatred for gay people. I was harassed on social media for days by people who called me a "basic hoe," "problematic," and "toxic." One student, CeeJay Hayes, even went to my Twitter account, pulled some screenshots of me dissing the Black Lives Matter organization, and posted them to the official Georgetown University Facebook page. He wanted the university to punish me for tweeting things he didn't like.

The subject of my tweet about the gay man at the Richards event, Carlo Izzo, sent me a long message on Facebook insisting that people like me "scare" him and angrily informed me that I had misgendered him—"thank you for assuming my gender, I go by them/them/theirs". If you thought teens and young adults adopting invented genders was for Gen Zers on TikTok, I can assure you that young millennials were the true curators of this sad trend. Carlo went on to accuse me of supporting "toxic masculinity" and thus "helping create a culture that leads to your own oppression." Er, does that count as mansplaining? Or themsplaining?

I've always appreciated the not-so-subtle condescension from social justice warriors. They believe that their political opponents are merely not educated or intelligent enough to have reached the woke enlightenment. In my case, they could not accept that I researched and understood the concepts they preached about and still rejected them. I was accepted to the same prestigious university and studied the same disciplines and had reached my own conclusions about politics and the world. This is what is known as "critical thinking," something that used to be applauded in the university system. To the left, it was simply unacceptable.

Before I had a chance to even read Carlo's message or reply, he had reposted it as a Facebook status on his page, earning nearly 500 likes mostly from members of the Georgetown community. The hate continued to roll in from his friends and peers. Izzo said he posted the status so that others could "learn from [my] mistakes." If he meant that he wanted to scare other conservative students into shutting up, he probably succeeded. If he wanted to shut *me* up, he failed miserably.

Although I should've seen this as the obvious play for attention and praise that it was, at the time I really just wanted to put a stop to the harassment and agreed to get coffee with Carlo to discuss the situation. We each shared our thoughts on abortion and I tried to explain how attempts at public shaming will rarely make someone more amenable to your position. I also pointed out that, considering Carlo places a great emphasis on mental health, he should consider how his online dogpile could have really damaged someone with thinner skin than I have. The conversation was more productive than I expected, but that was often the case when meeting one-on-one with campus leftists.

They talked a big game online but hardly had the courage to be as venomous face-to-face.

Carlo asked me if he could post an "update" for his followers about our conversation, which I agreed to, hoping it would quell some of the vitriol that was still coming my way. He acknowledged in the post that we had a respectful conversation and that his initial reaction could have been "intimidating" and that I should not have "stereotyped" him.

"While I know we do not (and perhaps will never) agree, there is something truly respectful and empowering about being able to talk openly with another person," Carlo wrote. "In light of bringing Cecile Richards to campus, I think this type of open dialogue is the goal of a Jesuit education. We can debate our ideas but still respect the fundamental humanity of the other person."

The comments cheered Carlo on for his "mature" and "amazing" handling of the situation. In retrospect, Carlo had truly put on a masterclass in manipulation. He feigned horror over a fairly innocuous tweet that didn't even name him, earning him sympathy for his oppression. Then, he demonstrated his faux courage by sitting down with his attacker and deigning to see the humanity in them. He managed to make himself both the victim and the hero. I, naturally, was not granted similar status for having a pleasant chat with someone who sicced hundreds of angry followers on me.

Carlo was able to bask in his own glory, but within just a couple of days I was being "dragged" again, this time in the "Black GroupMe" I mentioned earlier. At the time, the group was called the "Blaxa Room of Requirement." I had a couple of moles who were kind enough to share screenshots with me at the time so I knew what was being said.

This time, my old friend Crystal incited the hate. She shared a status I had posted on my Facebook about a story in *The Hoya*.

The Hoya reported that the university was reaching out to students who may have been "affected" by some university buildings being "defaced" with pro-Trump and pro-Officer Darren Wilson "graffiti." I questioned why these messages were being described so aggressively when other chalk messages on buildings remained untouched for months. *The Hoya* suggested that these particular messages could fall under university policy that prohibits "threatening" or "grossly obscene" content on campus. I wondered, as well, if students would need a safe space to protect them from messages that could be washed off with water.

"She never stops smh..." Crystal wrote in the group chat.

The follow-ups were truly incredible. A girl name Citlalli Velasquez replied, "she's stupid," which led to a quick admonishment from Renleigh Stone.

"She's not stupid," he said. "That's dismissive and ableist. She should be dragged with specificity. She's hateful, malicious, foolish, ridiculous, useless, and acrimonious. Precision of language is key."

Another student asked why using the term "stupid" is "ableist."

"Stupid implies someone is unintelligence [sic] which is ableist. People call a bunch of different kinds of disabled folk stupid," Stone replied. "It's dismissive at the very least."

The poor grammar used in a sentence explaining why you can't call people stupid isn't lost on me. Nor is the hilarity of them being unable to even make fun of someone they hate without being politically correct!

But man, how satisfying is Crystal's exasperation? These students were legitimately bothered that all of their nasty comments and harassment campaigns couldn't stop me from saying what I think. It was like they had never encountered someone who didn't cave and grovel at the first sign of resistance.

I guess they had finally learned that mean words weren't going to get me to shut up, so they advanced to physical threats.

A couple of weeks before graduation, I was involved in more Facebook fights, one over whether or not the university needed to give low-income students tickets to the Senior Auction, and one about whether or not then-Department of Homeland Security Secretary Jeh Johnson should be allowed to speak at commencement. I didn't understand why low-income students would want to attend a charitable event where rich people bid on things we couldn't afford. I also pushed back at the ridiculous notion that Johnson should be removed as a commencement speaker because his presence would traumatize undocumented students.[57] It's not like Johnson was going to call ICE during his speech and let them come and round up the DREAMers in front of the captive audience, although that would be quite a sight. Anyway, if you don't want to live in fear of deportation, shouldn't you make sure you're in the US legally?

No, no, Amber, not more common sense! The SJWs quickly piled on. A friend of mine asked if any of them had the guts to ever say anything to me in person.

"I've encountered many of the people who write shitty things about me on Facebook," I commented. "Not one has dared say a goddamn word to me."

Shola Powell replied, "You wanna meet up?"

She posted a screenshot of her comment in the Blaxa chat, asking, "Who wants to come?" Her post got twenty-four likes on Facebook and thirty-two in the group chat. Another student replied to the Facebook comment with a meme of a woman clasping her hand over her mouth in shock.

---

[57] "Undocuhoyas Asks University to Disinvite Johnson." *Georgetown Voice*, May 10, 2016. https://georgetownvoice.com/2016/05/10/undocuhoyas-asks-university-to-disinvite-johnson/.

"Not sure if that's supposed to be a threat, but if you have something to say, you'll know where I'll be at graduation. I'll be wearing a pair of turquoise cowboy boots if you have a hard time finding me," I responded, sounding way tougher than I felt.

"It wasn't a threat…you would know if I was threatening you. Believe that," Shola responded. "I will look out for you and your turquoise cowboy boots."

Another student replied, "I applaud you for standing your ground buuuutt I'd stop now while you're not ahead because this won't end well."

After the years of harassment from these kids, I wasn't going to take her word for it that her comment wasn't a veiled threat. Maybe I was just too steeped in white working-class culture, but asking if someone wants to "meet up" during a tense argument is like asking someone to "step outside" during a bar fight. I sent an email to the Georgetown Police Department informing them of the situation and asking what I should do. This wasn't the first time I had to go to GUPD to report threats on social media, so they were familiar with what was going on.

"While these are more likely indirect threats, I do feel concerned for my safety especially considering I have had issues with online harassment in the past (these are things I have reported GUPD before)," I wrote in my email.

"Thank you for sending me this information. We will take a look at this further, but in the meantime I wanted to encourage you to reach out to Major Joseph Smith, deputy chief in GUPD, who can provide some guidance on safety planning. I have cc'ed him here. If there is any new information on this (new comments on this post, etc.), please forward those as well," the director of threat assessment replied.

I ended up meeting with Major Smith and he seemed concerned by the messages too and kindly offered to have GUPD officers present at any senior events I attended over the next week. I sent them my schedule, and I did notice what seemed to be an increased police presence at a senior party a few days later. I appreciated that they seemed to be taking the situation seriously. Still, I had no idea if the police actually ever talked to these students or tipped the administration off about their behavior.

Ultimately, isn't it just really sad that I needed police protection in order to enjoy my graduation events merely because I expressed conservative opinions on social media?

CHAPTER 8

CAMPUS REFORM

Initially I wasn't too keen on joining the media after graduation because I thought—and still think—that most reporters are scumbags. I still physically cringe, actually, when I identify myself as a journalist. However, my experience writing for my local paper and exposing the Cecile Richards event opened up some doors professionally in the industry. I chose to work for The Leadership Institute's Campus Reform as an investigative reporter because I thought they were doing really important work exposing the insanity happening on college campuses.

I figured I could always find another gig later on if it turned out I didn't like working as a reporter.

Spoiler alert: I loved it.

I was hooked after my first couple of scoops. There is something really addicting about being the first to a story. Campus Reform was the perfect fit for me because my experience at Georgetown taught me exactly how to find the craziest campus happenings. It was deeply rewarding to be able to make a difference on college campuses nationwide through my reporting, and it was a bonus that I got to be something of a support system for conservative students facing the same struggles that I had on campus.

My reporting led to numerous victories on campuses across the country. I was the first to report that American University tried to get a fraternity to cancel a badminton fundraiser for veterans over concerns that the event's title, "Bad(minton) and Boujee," could be considered "cultural appropriation." The *Washington Post* and *Barstool Sports* both covered the story, and AU ultimately promised to reach an "amicable solution" with the fraternity.

My colleague Anthony Gockowski and I reported on the trend of "Students for Hillary" groups across the country using university resources to phone bank and collect data for the former secretary of state, a potential violation of the tax-exempt status given to most nonprofit colleges. Most universities do not allow nonuniversity-funded student groups to use university resources for political activity so as to prevent these potential conflicts. Multiple Students for Hillary groups were busted for breaking their schools' policies and had to move their campaigning activities off campus.

A California State Polytechnic Institute professor faced an investigation into the use of his email account after he tried to cajole his students into voting for Hillary Clinton. The professor had used a mobile app to send a pledge to vote for Hillary Clinton to all of his students but claimed that his account on the app must've been compromised by a hacker. The mobile app company told me that there was no security breach of the professor's account. I provided this information to Cal Poly, who confirmed they'd be launching an investigation into the professor and his email communications.

Outside of reporting, the other way we showed the world how bad the colleges were getting was by going to campus with a camera and asking students some pretty basic questions. The lack of critical thinking skills was astounding. Cabot Phillips and I filmed students admitting they couldn't name any of Hillary Clinton's accomplishments as a politician, signing a petition to ban Christmas when we told them the holiday was "oppressive," and drawing blanks when we pointed out that they talked negatively about Obama's policies when they were falsely attributed to Trump. After Cuban dictator Fidel Castro died in 2016, I decided to go to American University and ask students who they thought was a better leader: Fidel Castro or Donald Trump? The majority of the students said Castro.

Our little Campus Reform team, made up of maybe half a dozen full-time employees, broke all of these stories from a small office inside the Leadership Institute building above a Trader Joe's grocery store. Each of us had our own tiny, carpeted cubicle, a desk phone, and a glitchy Microsoft Surface computer. When we scored a "victory"—usually defined as a change in campus policy or action due to our reporting—we would get a little laminated "V" to pin up on our cubicle wall. When one of our stories landed on the *Drudge Report*, we'd similarly pin up a cutout of Matt Drudge's fedora-ed head.

I ended up covering a lot of stories out of Georgetown thanks to my friends still on campus who would send me tips. My continued virtual presence on campus irked students. Georgetown's Kennedy Institute of Ethics put up a message board in June 2017 asking recent graduates to name the biggest ethical challenge they've dealt with since leaving Georgetown. One respondent wrote, "dealing with people like Amber Athey." I was still living rent free in their heads a year after I graduated!

One of my Campus Reform pieces about my alma mater completely blew up. In March 2017, I was tipped off to a Facebook post from a student named Daniel Breland. Breland had posted an email from Theresa Sanders, a theology professor at Georgetown, offering to allow him to skip a lecture on slavery and other "awful stuff." I reached out to both Sanders and Breland to ask if they'd like to comment on a student missing class over sensitive discussion topics. Neither responded.

The piece was published[58] (with Breland's name withheld), and it got picked up by a few other media outlets, but it was hardly my biggest story. Georgetown students were fired up about the article though. You'd think I was Russia and I just sent troops to invade Ukraine! Breland, who had a background in music, posted on social media that he was thinking about dropping a diss track in response. I tweeted a goading response: "Apparently the student is planning on writing a 'diss track' about me for reporting on this. Literally shaking."

Sure enough, the track dropped the next day. Breland, whose rap name was "D Breezy" at the time, titled it "Amber Alert." He accused me of being desperate to be famous, questioned why I was allowed to graduate from Georgetown, suggested I was ugly, and claimed my family was "rich off of slaves."

It is pretty ironic that Breland accused me of being "rich off of slaves" and having my "whole life handed" to me considering I grew up in rural America, was raised by blue collar laborers, and was in an organization for low income students at Georgetown. Breland grew up in a part of New Jersey with median income $30,000 above the national average and attended one of the most

---

[58] Athey, Amber. "Prof Excuses Black Student from Lecture on Slavery and Race." Campus Reform the #1 Source for College News, March 22, 2017. https://campusreform.org/article?id=8958.

expensive and elite private boarding schools in the country. But I digress.

I did my best to have a good sense of humor about the whole thing. After all, the song was well done, even if factually inaccurate, and it was undeniably funny that someone was so upset about a 250-word article that they would produce an entire song. Laughing it off was difficult, though, considering the hate that got sent my way by Breland's friends and allies via social media. I would get home from work, turn my phone off, and just flop on my twin bed for an hour or two to try to shut it all out.

The harassment only got worse when Georgetown asked Breland to perform as the opening act for the annual spring concert, which hosts 1,500 students. Apparently the university suggested he not perform "Amber Alert." It was inappropriate, I think, for the school to extend the performance invitation to someone whose biggest claim to fame in the last year was smearing an alum. Breland reached out to me over Facebook Messenger to ask if he could perform the diss track at the concert. I had no question that he would've blasted me publicly again and it would've looked weak if I said no, so I gave him permission.

The whole ordeal got funny again when I received more Facebook messages from Breland between Midnight and 2 a.m. the night of the spring concert. High off of performing, and probably a few shots of liquor deep, Breland decided to shoot his shot.

"Oh boy…you're super cute," he said.

Maybe AOC had a point when she said all of her critics secretly want to date her. I didn't reply.

I am sad to report that Breland has successfully appropriated my culture and is now a platinum-selling country artist. It wasn't enough for him to accuse me of being a fraud; he had to insert himself into my favorite Spotify country playlists. Some of his songs are really catchy, too. Damn.

Outside of my ongoing personal beefs with Hoyas, my work at Campus Reform had me really concerned for the future of our country. If our small team of two full-time reporters and part-time campus correspondents were uncovering so many examples of craziness on college campuses, how much was happening that we didn't know about?

People often ask me if colleges are really that far left. I always thought that the student body at Georgetown was generally very liberal but not in a shut-down-speakers-and-cancel-every-one-to-the-right-of-Stalin kind of way. I was friends with some members of the College Democrats and their politics were often closer to Bill Clinton than Bernie Sanders. The truth is that the crazy progressives were a smaller subset of the student body, but they were so vocal and militant that they controlled everything. Moderate Democrats were scared of upsetting them, even though they were on the same "side." Closet conservatives messaged me on social media all the time to tell me they wished they could speak up but they didn't want their lives destroyed by the left. A *Georgetown Voice* political values survey published in the fall of 2015 seemed to confirm my observations that these crybullies were a vocal minority on campus. A relatively small 35.9 percent of Georgetown students believed private organizations must pro-vide a safe space for students who listen to speakers who hold views contrary to theirs, and just 0.9 percent said organizations should not use university funds to bring speakers with views con-trary to theirs.

I think this is probably the case at most universities. My time at Campus Reform taught me that you'll usually find fewer far-left kids at state schools and more at the crunchy liberal arts col-leges. Georgetown has more than your average school because of its location in Washington, DC; it self-selects for students who are obsessed with politics. Overall, though, the campus craziness was driven by a vocal minority that were experts at getting their way.

Unfortunately, that vocal minority gets a little bit bigger every year. In 2016, 4.2 percent of college freshmen identified as "far left" in a survey by the UCLA Higher Education Research Institute. That was the first time since they started collecting data in 2000 that more than 4 percent of students identified that way. The next highest percentage of incoming freshmen who identified as "far left" was 3.9 percent in the year 2015.

This is happening for a few reasons.

First, take the concept of "silence is violence." The left claims that it is not enough to be apolitical or agnostic about their causes. Unless you are actively fighting alongside them, not only are you not an ally, but also you are complicit in the injustices they claim to be tackling. If you are already over on the left, then it won't take much bullying to convince you to go full wackjob.

Second, students are being exposed to leftist ideology at much younger ages. Kindergarten students in Washington, DC were filmed carrying "Black Lives Matter" signs and chanting in support of the group. School officials claimed the children asked to hold a march because they were "inspired" by an event called the Black Lives Matter at School Week. A public school district in Buffalo, New York, told middle schoolers through its "Emancipation Curriculum" that "all white people play a part in perpetuating systemic racism." I was the first to report in September 2021 that President Joe Biden gave the introductory remarks at a conference during which a panelist said Critical Race Theory must be taught in schools because "white kids are making assessments about their own racial superiority, or who's better than, or their own entitlement."[59] Virginia Governor Glenn Youngkin won in a shock upset over Democrat Terry McAuliffe at least in part because parents in the commonwealth were concerned about the highly racialized and sexualized content their kids were being fed in public schools. The indoctrination machine made up of teachers' unions, the Democratic Party, and the media apparently decided that college was too late to start brainwashing children.

Third, women are a huge part of the problem. In the UCLA survey, 41.1 percent of women identified as liberal or far left compared to just 28.9 percent of men. Because more women than ever are going to college, this gender divide skews the overall campus population far to the left. Young women are more likely to be enrolled in college and are more likely to have a four-year degree compared to their male counterparts, per Pew Research.[60] There are currently three women for every two men[61] attending college. Anecdotally, I found it to be the case that the left-wing women I encountered on campus did outnumber the men and were far more aggressive with their shaming and bullying tactics.

There are a lot of things we can do to combat indoctrination in our schools, but we are always going to be at least five

[59] "Biden Speaks at Conference Filled with Anti-White, Anti-Police Rhetoric." The Spectator World. Accessed September 6, 2022. https://spectatorworld. com/topic/biden-anti-white-root-institute-conference/.

[60] Parker, Kim. "What's behind the Growing Gap between Men and Women in College Completion?" Pew Research Center. Pew Research Center, November 8, 2021. https://www.pewresearch.org/fact-tank/2021/11/08/ whats-behind-the-growing-gap-between-men-and-women-in-college-completion/.

[61] Wolfers, Justin. "More Women than Men Are Going to College. That May Change the Economy." *New York Times*, November 23, 2021. https://www. nytimes.com/2021/11/23/business/dealbook/women-college-economy. html.

years behind because conservatives, frankly, underestimated the power of the SJWs.

Boomer conservatives called woke millennials the "snowflake generation." Just wait until they graduate and enter the real world, they said. Nobody is going to hire these crazies! Their employers will never allow them to have a safe space! Trigger warnings don't exist here! Suck it up, buttercup, because things are going to be really different once you get a *real* job!

"We are grooming our students to be sensitive crybabies when we need to be showing students how to deal with world situations and how to be adults—there are no 'safe spaces' in the real world," libertarian commentator Kristin Tate said in November 2016 in response to reports that college students were offered puppy cuddles and coloring books after Donald Trump's shock victory in that year's presidential election.[62]

Fox News host Pete Hegseth said in his 2019 mock commencement address to college graduates, "your debt needs to be paid off, the world doesn't care about your feelings, and your parents' basement is embarrassing."[63]

Conservative pundit Tomi Lahren practically became famous for her rants about campus snowflakes. When Notre Dame students walked out of a speech by Vice President Mike Pence in

[62] Singman, Brooke. "Coddling Campus Crybabies: Students Take up Toddler Therapy after Trump Win." Fox News. FOX News Network, November 17, 2016. https://www.foxnews.com/us/coddling-campus-crybabies-students-take-up-toddler-therapy-after-trump-win.

[63] Hegseth, Pete. "Pete Hegseth: Graduates, It's Time to Unlearn College." FOX News Network, May 19, 2019. https://www.foxnews.com/opinion/pete-hegseth-graduates-its-time-to-unlearn-college.

2017 she tweeted, "Snowflakes think this kind of crap will fly in the real world? Good luck holding a job, kids!"[64]

Actually, all of the students involved in major campus incidents seemed to have no problem getting respectable jobs after graduation. After all, they went to some of the most prestigious colleges and had resumes filled to the brim with activism, internships, and leadership positions in campus organizations. It was nice to think that this would be the end of their activism and that their employers would neuter them in the boardroom.

The optimism was very misplaced. The campus snowflakes didn't just go away or learn to deal. Instead, they took the same tactics they used to shut down debate on campuses like Georgetown to the boardroom, Hollywood, Silicon Valley, Capitol Hill, and, of course, the media. If the adults in charge of the universities couldn't figure out how to shush the snowflakes, then what made us think that the so-called "real world" would fare any better? The truth is that these entities were primed to be steamrolled by the millennial crybullies, and the media in particular was an easy mark.

---

[64] Klein, Charlotte. "'Clusterf--k': Inside the Washington Post's Social Media Meltdown." *Vanity Fair*, June 8, 2022. https://www.vanityfair.com/news/2022/06/inside-the-washington-posts-social-media-meltdown.

CHAPTER 9

DEMOCRATS WRITE THE NEWS

I left Campus Reform in March of 2017 and went to the *Daily Caller* where I started covering the media full-time. I always knew the media was biased against conservatives, but I never knew just how bad it was until I started watching cable news for eight hours a day. Watching that much CNN and MSNBC will rot anyone's brain. If I ever say something stupid, you can blame them for killing my brain cells.

The tsunami of misleading, overtly partisan, and just plain false stories that came out of the media on a regular basis was stunning. The worst part is they repeatedly lied to the American public about their political leanings. "Journalists don't root for a side," CNN's Chris Cillizza infamously said once.

During the early days of the American republic, media bias was open and accepted. Newspapers were openly affiliated with and even received funding from political parties in exchange for support in their pages. It wasn't until the mid-1800s that objective reporting as we understand it today was introduced. By the early 1900s, journalists and intellectuals of the time, such as Walter

Lippmann, believed reporters needed to rely on some version of the scientific method to accurately report facts and events to readers. Plus, newspapers could be more profitable if they avoided alienating potential readers because of their political bias.

The rise in journalistic standards meant there had to be some way of credentialing reporters to make sure they were up to snuff. While some papers settled for more extensive on-the-job training, reporters increasingly went to dedicated journalism schools or were required to obtain a college degree. Over time, journalists became more highly educated and came from wealthier backgrounds than the general population. They also become less religious,[65] due to the secular nature of modern higher education.

According to a 2014 Indiana University survey, 92 percent of journalists had a college degree compared to about 30 percent of the overall country.[66] The Journal of Expertise found that 43.9 percent of *New York Times* writers and editors and 49.8 percent of *Wall Street Journal* writers and editors attended elite universities.[67] This puts them on educational par with senators, Fortune 500 CEOs, Forbes billionaires, and federal judges.

Meanwhile, more than two-thirds of new journalists came from white collar backgrounds, whereas fewer than 10 percent came from working class backgrounds, according to a 2002 UK

---

[65] "In Theory: Do Journalists Cover Religion Well?" *Los Angeles Times*, April 20, 2012. https://www.latimes.com/socal/glendale-news-press/opinion/tn-gnp-xpm-2012-04-20-tn-pas-0421-in-theory-do-journalists-cover-religion-well-story.html.

[66] Thompson, Derek. "Report: Journalists Are Miserable, Liberal, over-Educated, under-Paid, Middle-Aged Men." *The Atlantic.* May 8, 2014. https://www.theatlantic.com/business/archive/2014/05/report-journalists-are-miserable-over-educated-under-paid-middle-aged-men-mostly/361891/.

[67] *Journal of Expertise.* https://www.journalofexpertise.org/.

survey.[68] The results are likely similar in the United States given the high cost of attending college and/or journalism school, the financial barrier to getting an internship with a national newspaper in a big city with little to no pay, and the relatively low return on investment for entry-level journalists. The average entry-level reporter in DC, for example, makes less than $50,000 a year. If you don't have wealthy parents to offset your housing costs or help you pay off your student loans, it can be really tough going until you catch a good break. Blue collar kids usually don't bust their asses working through school just to graduate and make less than they would in the trades—you have to be *really* passionate about the business.

Is it any surprise newsrooms are so liberal, then? They are staffed with the cosmopolitan, highly educated, secular elite who flock toward Chicago, New York, DC, and Los Angeles. Credentialing journalists merely reinforced the bias it sought to root out. A homogenized press meant that journalism became an echo chamber for the liberal elite. The problem only gets worse as more journalists go to university, and universities get more liberal. A *Washington Post* survey from 2020 found that of the 78 percent of journalists who identified with a particular political ideology or party—eight in ten—said they were liberal or Democrats.[69] The Media Research Center examined donations to politicians made by employees of the *New York Times*, the *Washington Post*, ABC News, CBS News, and NBC News. One

---

[68] "Focus on Journalism Training: A Job for the Wealthy and Connected." *The Guardian.* Guardian News and Media, April 7, 2008. https://www.theguardian.com/media/2008/apr/07/pressandpublishing4.

[69] Hassell, Hans, John Holbein, and Matthew Miles. "Analysis | Journalists May Be Liberal, but This Doesn't Affect Which Candidates They Choose to Cover." *Washington Post.* WP Company, April 10, 2020. https://www.washingtonpost.com/politics/2020/04/10/journalists-may-be-liberal-this-doesnt-affect-which-candidates-they-choose-cover/.

hundred and fifteen employees across the five outlets donated to Democrats compared to just seven who donated to Republicans.[70]

Watching nonstop cable news and the nightly broadcast news reports during the first two years of the Trump administration was so enlightening. Journalists everywhere finally lifted the veil of objectivity. The Media Research Center found that during a period of three months in Trump's first year in office, coverage of the president was 91 percent negative on the three broadcast news networks: ABC, CBS, and NBC. Harvard University similarly found[71] that at least 80 percent of news coverage by CNN, NBC, CBS, the *New York Times*, and the *Washington Post* was negative toward Trump.

Lucky for me, the media's Trump coverage gave me something of a masterclass in media bias. I quickly became something of an expert. I shared a tiny office, which was situated in the back of the dingy *Daily Caller* office building in downtown DC, with two to three other people at any given time. We had three TVs mounted on the walls: one for CNN, one for MSNBC, and one for Fox News. It was a big deal when I was finally offered control of the three remotes to decide which network was worth unmuting at any given time. There were a few good rules regarding the remote policy. We unmuted Republican politicians appearing on one of the liberal networks, Joy Reid, any of the giant roundtable CNN panels—particularly ones involving Ana Navarro—and

---

[70] "MRC Study: 'Objective' Papers, Networks Stuffed with Democrat-Donating Employees." Newsbusters. Accessed September 6, 2022. https://www.newsbusters.org/blogs/nb/tim-graham/2016/10/18/mrc-study-objective-papers-networks-stuffed-democrat-donating.

[71] Wemple, Erik. "Opinion | Study: 91 Percent of Recent Network Trump Coverage Has Been Negative." *Washington Post.* WP Company, December 1, 2021. https://www.washingtonpost.com/blogs/erik-wemple/wp/2017/09/12/study-91-percent-of-recent-network-trump-coverage-has-been-negative/.

any interview with Trey Gowdy, because, well, our readers loved that guy.

The crazy things pundits and reporters alike would say on the television had me more convinced than ever I was on the right side of things. My real education, though, was not memorizing the stupid sound bites from *The View* or becoming the fastest to transcribe interviews.

First, and most importantly, the media underwent a dramatic and public shift in ideology after Trump's election. During the era of objective journalism (brief as it was) reporters viewed themselves as sources of information for the public. Their mission was to present the facts as best as they could gather them. They weren't perfect at it, but most of them tried.

This disappeared and gave way to the rise of activist journalism. Journalists approached stories with a particular viewpoint and believed it was their duty to impart those ideas to consumers. They manipulated the facts to reinforce their own biases.

When Trump rose to power, journalists stopped talking about informing readers, and instead waxed poetic about holding power to account, speaking truth to power, fighting for the downtrodden, and being a voice for the voiceless. They believed that Trump was such a threat to the Republic that every institution had to join forces to fight him like a really bad sequel to a Marvel *Avengers* movie. Journalists were suddenly the only people you could trust because Trump was such a master at manipulating reality. They were the thin line stopping democracy from falling to fascism.

The truth is the media was threatened by Trump because he challenged their monopoly on information. Journalists were terrified that they would no longer get to sneakily pass their own narratives onto the public without being called out by the bad, orange man.

The new journalistic values adopted by the media were applied selectively and manipulatively to continue to boost liberal ideas. They held Republicans "accountable," but Democrats still enjoyed limp-wristed coverage. The "downtrodden" and "voiceless" only referred to Democratic interest groups, like black women and the queer community. The white men who voted for Trump because their manufacturing jobs were being shipped overseas and their sons sent to die in a forever war? Well, they just needed to check their privilege. There was no greater victim, though, than the poor, oppressed journalists. After all, Trump was *literally killing us(!)* by calling the media "fake news" and the "enemy of the people."

The *Washington Post* appropriately updated its official slogan to "Democracy Dies in Darkness"[72] but conveniently insisted it had nothing to do with Trump. Think-pieces about the unending virtues of a free press abounded.[73] MSNBC's Katy Tur declared that journalists are like firefighters. People who go clickety-clack on a keyboard all day are HEROES, dammit!

This ideological shift led to some disturbing patterns of behavior. Journalists had to literally re-write the ethics and standards of their profession in order to justify their overt bias. The journalistic process used to involve gathering and verifying facts and then presenting them to the reader. Readers could reach their own conclusions. Now, journalists approach a story having already reached a conclusion. Thanks to an overwhelmingly liberal press, the most popular conclusions are that Trump

---

[72] "Watch the Washington Post's Super Bowl Message: 'Democracy Dies in Darkness.'" *Washington Post*. WP Company, February 4, 2019. https://www.washingtonpost.com/graphics/2019/national/democracy-dies-in-darkness/.

[73] Teresa Puente, opinion contributor. "Journalists Are Defenders of Democracy." The Hill. The Hill, August 17, 2018. https://thehill.com/opinion/white-house/402349-journalists-are-defenders-of-democracy.

and Republicans are evil. They prop up these conclusions with a variety of questionable and unethical methods. When they are inevitably exposed, they do everything in their power to avoid accountability.

It's important to fully understand these methods in order to effectively combat bias and also to understand how the media made itself vulnerable to the woke kids as they left campus and entered the workforce.

The establishment media has incredible message discipline. Have you ever noticed that they all use the same language to talk about stories or describe what's happening? I started to recognize that it only took a day or two—sometimes even a few hours—into a news cycle for all of the cable news chyrons, online and print articles, and pundits to be in lockstep with their talking points. This isn't a coincidence.

In the era of online journalism, it's increasingly rare that stories get written because an editor or a reporter just comes up with a really good idea for a piece. The news moves really quickly, and websites are constantly demanding more content to sell advertisements. So, not many reporters have the luxury of taking days, months, or years to develop and source an article. Instead, journalists and media outlets are increasingly dependent on outside forces to help them craft stories and narratives. Because the media is so liberal, these outside forces tend to be, you guessed it—Democrats!

How does this work in practice? When a news story breaks, communications staffers for politicians and party activists are immediately on the phone calling their most loyal TV pundits and opinion writers and telling them exactly what to say. Republicans do this too, as I learned when I moved into commentary writing, but they're not as good at it and they simply don't have as many media stooges willing to regurgitate whatever they're fed. Sometimes these unofficial briefings happen via email, but an off-the-record phone call is better because it offers plausible deniability and no real record of what was offered.

Douglas MacKinnon, a writer in the White House for Presidents Ronald Reagan and George H.W. Bush, wrote about this phenomenon in 2020,[74] explaining how he would often show up for his television hits to find Democrats in the green room preparing by digesting liberal agitprop.

"I was always amazed to watch my Democrat counterpart either reading 'talking points' just before airtime, or literally taking instructions by phone from a Democratic White House or political organization as we waited to go live," MacKinnon said in an opinion column for *The Hill*.

These talking points aren't uttered from the lips and pens of political operatives only to disappear into the ether. Journalists are in on this game too, either appearing on the same phone calls or emails as the activists, or merely getting the memo by listening to their Democratic friends during television hits or reading their columns. Email communications between Hillary Clinton's staff and journalists released by WikiLeaks demonstrated exactly how the sausage is made.

Erskine Bowles, a major fundraiser for Hillary, emailed[75] Rebecca Quick, a CNBC anchor, in 2014 about potential criticism of Obama's Health and Human Services Secretary nominee, Sylvia Burwell. Bowles helpfully laid out a line of defense for Burwell, describing her as "informed" and "smart" and listing

---

[74] Douglas MacKinnon, opinion contributor. "Partisan-Fed Talking Points Are an Insult to Hurting Americans." The Hill. The Hill, September 5, 2020. https://thehill.com/opinion/white-house/515030-partisan-fed-talking-points-are-an-insult-to-hurting-americans.

[75] "Fw: Sylvia Matthews Burwell." WikiLeaks. Accessed September 6, 2022. https://wikileaks.org/podesta-emails/emailid/4588.

important points on her resume. Quick replied that anyone with Bowles's endorsement is "good by me" and promised to "defend" Burwell "when things get further along in the confirmation process." CNBC later offered glowing coverage of Burwell, describing her as "uniformly admired."[76]

Another email circulating within the Clinton camp included a list of names for "Columnist/Pundit Calls."[77] Curiously, a fair amount of names on the list are billed as objective reporters by their respective outlets: CNN's Wolf Blitzer, who anchors a midday news program and moderated several Republican presidential debates; Gloria Borger, CNN's chief political analyst; John Dickerson, the host of CBS's 60 Minutes; Jon Karl, the chief Washington correspondent for ABC News; Jeff Zeleny, the chief national affairs correspondent for CNN; and more.

My editors at the *Daily Caller* and I decided to start a series in the spring of 2018 tracing where political talking points originated and how they ended up dominating the narrative across the media.

We called it "Democrats Write the News."

Once we noticed a certain talking point being used ad nauseum, we would use a television database to search for its first use in the public conversation. More often than not, these phrases were originally uttered by Democrats or left-wing activists.

The first example that launched the series happened when Republican Representative Devin Nunes, then the House Intelligence chairman, released a memo in February 2018

---

[76] Morningmoneyben. "Why Sylvia Burwell? What Obama Was Thinking." CNBC, April 11, 2014. https://www.cnbc.com/2014/04/11/why-sylvia-burwell-what-obama-was-thinking.html.

[77] Greenwald, Glenn, and Lee Fang. "Exclusive: New Leak on Clinton's Cozy Press Relationship." The Intercept. The Intercept, October 9, 2016. https://theintercept.com/2016/10/09/exclusive-new-email-leak-reveals-clinton-campaigns-cozy-press-relationship/.

outlining FISA abuses by the DOJ and FBI when they obtained warrants to surveil Carter Page, a former Trump campaign official. The memo alleged that the FBI greatly mislead the FISA court, including using the unverified—and now discredited—Steele dossier as an "essential" portion of its applications for warrants.[78] Nunes also claimed that the applications did not sufficiently indicate that the Steele dossier was opposition research paid for by political opponents of Trump and Page. The Nunes memo should've been a huge blow to the legitimacy of Crossfire Hurricane, as it indicated that at least one of the Trump campaign officials accused of having improper links to Russia was illegally surveilled thanks to political kompromat. Instead, thanks to Ranking Intelligence member Adam Schiff, the Nunes memo was declared illegitimate by the press.

The same day Nunes released his memo, Schiff appeared on CNN to declare that it "cherry-picks" information from the FISA applications.

So, we have two competing narratives about the Carter Page surveillance from opposite ends of the political spectrum. Both are on the Intelligence Committee, so it seems like a classic he-said-she-said. No one in the media, at that point, had access to the original FISA documents. Can you guess who they sided with?

You got it. Adam Schiff. And not only did they accept his rebuttal as proof, but also they used that exact same term—"cherry-picked"—to describe Nunes's memo.[79] That's far too specific to be a coincidence.

---

[78] Felton, Lena. "Read the Full Text of the Nunes Memo." *The Atlantic*. Atlantic Media Company, February 2, 2018. https://www.theatlantic.com/politics/archive/2018/02/read-the-full-text-of-the-nunes-memo/552191/.

[79] Athey, Amber. "Establishment Media Parroted Dem Talking Points about the Nunes Memo." Daily Caller, February 11, 2018. https://dailycaller.com/2018/02/10/media-parroted-dem-talking-points-nunes-memo/.

CNN anchor Fredericka Whitfield stated on her program, "this memo kind of pairs it all down, and that's why critics say it's partisan because Nunes just kind of—the Chairman of the House Intelligence, Devin Nunes, just cherry-picked certain details."

CNN political commentator David Swerdlick agreed, arguing that there is a "problem" with "having memos that boil things down to a few cherry-picked facts."

The *Washington Post*'s Ruth Marcus said during an MSNBC appearance that the Republicans had "cherry-picked" from "thick documents."

MSNBC's Chris Matthews and Joe Scarborough were also fans of the term "cherry-picked," using it on their respective cable news programs.

It didn't matter that Nunes was largely vindicated by Inspector General Michael Horowitz, whose 2019 report confirmed "widespread failure"[80] in the process that led to the FISA court granting surveillance on Carter Page. The media was able to make Nunes and his memo a laughingstock when that information really mattered.

"Democrats Write the News" continued exposing the Democrat-media complex with two clear-cut examples in the aftermath of the Parkland school shooting in Florida.

Senator Richard Blumenthal used the term "weapons of war" to describe certain firearms during a CNN interview on February 21,[81] just hours before the network would host its controversial Parkland shooting town hall where Parkland activists,

---

[80] Boyd, Jordan. "Ig Finds 'Widespread' FISA Failure after FBI Director Dismissed Concerns." The Federalist, September 30, 2021. https://thefederalist.com/2021/09/30/inspector-general-finds-damning-widespread-fisa-failure-after-fbi-director-dismissed-concerns/.

[81] Datoc, Christian. "Democrats Write the News: 'Weapons of War'". The Daily Caller, March 10, 2018. https://dailycaller.com/2018/03/09/democrats-write-the-news-weapons-of-war-gun-control/.

a mostly pro-gun control crowd, and host Jake Tapper ganged up on the NRA's Dana Loesch. They won a Cronkite Award for that, by the way.

After Blumenthal used the "weapons of war" moniker, it became inescapable. Karine Jean-Pierre, who is now Biden's deputy press secretary, and Symone Sanders, who served as Vice President Kamala Harris's communications director, repeated it on CNN. MSNBC's Joy Reid, Joe Scarborough, Lawrence O'Donnell, and Ari Melber all used it in their broadcasts. They all used a politically charged, nondescriptive term to make semi-automatic weapons, particularly the AR-15—the most popular rifle in America—sound scary to average Americans. The purpose? To drum up support for banning those guns, of course.

The same phenomenon happened with the false claim that there had been "18 school shootings in the past seven and a half weeks," a statistic that was shared by Everytown for Gun Safety, a gun control advocacy group co-founded by Mayor Michael Bloomberg. That inaccurate stat was shared on the House floor by Democratic Representative Carol Shea-Porter and in a viral tweet by Senator Bernie Sanders.[82] It was such an obvious lie that it was thoroughly debunked by even the *Washington Post* and *Politifact*.

"Everytown has long inflated its total by including incidents of gunfire that are not really school shootings," the *Washington Post* wrote.

Politifact agreed that Everytown "uses a broad definition of school shooting—that is, any time a firearm discharges a live round inside a school building, or on a school campus or

---

[82]   Sanders, Bernie. "Maybe, Just Maybe, after 18 School Shootings in America in Just 43 Days of 2018 the Congress Might Want to Consider Common-Sense Gun Safety Legislation and Save Innocent Lives." Twitter, February 14, 2018. https://twitter.com/SenSanders/status/963895154607296512.

grounds. Its database includes incidents when no one was injured; attempted or completed suicide, with no intent to injure others; and cases when a gun was fired unintentionally, resulting in injury or death."

Nonetheless, this misleading statistic was repeated on television by MSNBC anchors Brian Williams and Stephanie Ruhle, CNN anchor Don Lemon, and HLN's Erica Hill.[83] According to WaPo's fact check, the number was also used in reportage by ABC News, NBC News, CBS News, *Time*, MSN, the BBC, the *New York Daily News*, and HuffPost.

Perhaps the most egregious example of the media parroting a Democratic talking point was when Hillary Clinton claimed that all seventeen intelligence agencies agreed that Russia meddled in the 2016 election. Clinton initially used this line of attack against Trump during the third presidential debate, citing an October 2016 statement from the Director of National Intelligence that said the "US intelligence community" is "confident" that Russia meddled. The fact checkers quickly backed up Clinton, asserting that because the DNI speaks on behalf of the intelligence community, this meant that all of the agencies "agreed."

Clinton repeated the claim for a second time in June 2017 during an interview, referring to a more recent DNI report released in January that reached the same conclusion about Russia and its involvement in the election.

"Read the declassified report by the intelligence community that came out in early January," said Clinton. "Seventeen agencies, all in agreement—which I know from my experience as a senator and secretary of state is hard to get—they concluded with

---

[83] DailyCallerVideo. "Democrats Write the News - 18 School Shootings." YouTube, March 16, 2018. https://www.youtube.com/watch?v=4RhAAp DIJKY.

'high confidence' that the Russians ran an extensive information war against my campaign to influence voters in the election."

The media ran with the claim. CNN,[84] the Associated Press, ABC News,[85] NBC News,[86] and NPR[87] all unquestioningly used the talking point in their reporting.

Some would use it to slam Trump, who noted that he believed only "three or four" intelligence agencies were involved in the report. Contradicting the "17 intelligence agencies" narrative, the press suggested, was only further proof that Trump was either delusional or in bed with the Russians. Add that to Mueller's list of evidence, I guess.

Maggie Haberman of the *New York Times* reported that even Trump's allies were "frustrated" by his "deflections and denials" on Russian hacking, citing the seventeen intelligence agencies point as an example: "[Trump] still refuses to acknowledge a basic fact agreed upon by 17 American intelligence agencies."[88]

[84] Murray, Sara, and Dana Bash. "Officials Struggle to Convince Trump That Russia Remains a Threat | CNN Politics." CNN. Cable News Network, June 28, 2017. https://www.cnn.com/2017/06/28/politics/officials-struggle-to-convince-trump-russia-threat/index.html.

[85] ABC News. ABC News Network. Accessed September 6, 2022. http://abcnews.go.com/Politics/week-transcript-11-17-preet-bharara-jay-sekulow/story?id=47957684.

[86] Bennett, Jonah. "Katy Tur Tweets False Claim That 17 Intel Agencies Agree on Russian Election Meddling." The Daily Caller, July 6, 2017. https://dailycaller.com/2017/07/06/katy-tur-tweets-false-claim-that-17-intel-agencies-agree-on-russian-election-meddling/.

[87] Naylor, Brian. "Intelligence Chiefs 'Stand More Resolutely' behind Finding of Russia Election Hacking." NPR. NPR, January 5, 2017. https://www.npr.org/2017/01/05/508355408/intelligence-chiefs-stand-more-resolutely-behind-finding-of-russia-election-hack.

[88] Haberman, Maggie. "Trump's Deflections and Denials on Russia Frustrate Even His Allies." *New York Times*, June 25, 2017. https://www.nytimes.com/2017/06/25/us/politics/trumps-deflections-and-denials-on-russia-frustrate-even-his-allies.html.

NBC's Chuck Todd asked on *Meet the Press*, "How stunning is that to you, that the president of the United States disputes the evidence of 17 intelligence agencies in this country?"[89]

The only problem? It wasn't true.

Trump was correct all along to say that the intelligence community report indicating Russia tried to meddle in the election was the work of just three agencies, not seventeen. I'm proud to say that the *Daily Caller*'s fact-checking team was the first to actually examine Hillary's claim with a fair eye.

"While the intelligence report she mentions does express 'high confidence' that Russia sought to undermine her campaign, it only represents the views of three agencies – the FBI, CIA and NSA," my colleague David Sivak wrote. "Former Director of National Intelligence James Clapper himself appeared in front of Congress and explicitly pushed back on the idea that '17 intelligence agencies agreed,' stating flatly that it was just three."

Clapper, when testifying to the Senate, also resisted the notion that the other seventeen agencies signed on to the report, noting that they didn't have "time" to go through that "process."

The idea that all seventeen intelligence agencies would agree on this issue made no sense to begin with. How would the Department of Energy, the Department of the Treasury, and the Drug Enforcement Agency have any expert opinion on foreign influence in an election? What about the Coast Guard? Geospatial intelligence?

The vast majority of agencies under the purview of the DNI wouldn't have been involved in the report anyway and certainly wouldn't have been able to reach any independent conclusions about it.

---

[89] "Meet the Press - June 18, 2017." NBCNews.com. NBCUniversal News Group. Accessed September 6, 2022. https://www.nbcnews.com/meet-the-press/meet-press-june-18-2017-n773816.

As *Daily Caller* reporter Rachel Stoltzfoos pointed out, the only agencies that would feasibly be involved were the State Department intelligence, Department of Homeland Security, the FBI, the CIA, and the NSA.

"Five tops, narrowed down at the speed of common sense and Google," Stoltzfoos snarked at the time.[90]

Why does the distinction matter if, ultimately, the agencies that count did conclude that Russia was behind email hacks and election meddling? First of all, it's an obvious exaggeration for political purposes. Hillary wanted to embarrass Trump and really drive the point home that 1. He doesn't know what he's talking about, and 2. His election was illegitimate.

What's more concerning about the difference is what it reveals about the press. The mistake happened, in part, because journalists do not approach claims made by Democrats with any skepticism.

Washington Post media critic Erik Wemple hinted at this in his own column about the media's "17 intelligence agencies" disaster.

"Whatever your take on the fact-checks, the media laundered and recycled a Clinton talking point without too much exploration of the intricacies through which the intelligence community reaches its conclusions," Wemple wrote.[91]

Wemple is right, and the media's relationship with the left goes well beyond just the repetition of talking points. The media

---

[90]   Stoltzfoos, Rachel. "The Media Perpetuated a Clinton Lie for 9 Months. What It Means for the Russia Narrative." The Daily Caller, July 10, 2017. https://dailycaller.com/2017/07/09/the-media-perpetuated-a-clinton-lie-for-9-months-what-it-means-for-the-russia-narrative/.

[91]   Sivak, David. "Fact Check: Did 17 Intel Agencies 'All Agree' Russia Influenced the Presidential Election?" The Daily Caller, August 7, 2017. https://dailycaller.com/2017/06/01/fact-check-did-17-intel-agencies-all-agree-russia-hacked-the-dnc-podesta.

uses Democrats as anonymous sources for articles without questioning their motives, uses the left's hand-picked "experts" to prop up spurious "facts" that support a certain narrative, accepts opposition research performed by left-wing activist groups without verifying the information themselves, and diminishes Democratic scandals by framing them around Republicans "seizing" or "pouncing" on the issue. The reality is that the vast majority of news we consume originates in this information pipeline between Democrats and the media.

Naturally, when the Democratic party shifts further to the left, so does media coverage.

CHAPTER 10

REVOLVING DOOR

The media's reliance on the Democrats for information and narrative-building produces a lot of mistakes. The media tends to skip the all-important verification process when publishing stories that are favorable to Democrats or negative toward Republicans. This violates the first principle in the Society of Professional Journalists' Code of Ethics: Seek Truth and Report It. The media doesn't want to admit that they've failed to adhere to this principle, because when mistakes only happen in one direction, it would suggest the media allowed politics to overshadow professional responsibilities. So, the media violates another SPJ principle: Be Accountable and Transparent. Hiding mistakes and pretending they didn't happen is a hallmark of a biased media that is loyal not to seeking truth but to advancing leftist narratives.

The "17 intelligence agencies" lie was a stunning example of media bias, but not just because it showed how the media will recycle a Democratic claim without a hint of skepticism or additional research. It also showed how the media covers its ass when it gets something wrong.

The media is really good at avoiding accountability for its lies. Most outlets would just ignore my media reporting, even if it clearly and decisively proved them wrong. It usually took really concerted and widespread campaigns from conservatives to get them to admit errors. Even when they did, they downplayed their errors or blamed them on others.

One of the media's favorite tactics to minimize their errors is by refusing to use the word "correction." Instead, they prefer to use "update," "note," or "clarification." The term "update" implies that the outlet simply didn't have enough information available to them at the time of an article's publication to do accurate reporting. A "note" suggests they are providing the reader with more context or information. And a "clarification" insultingly insinuates that readers misinterpreted the original report, thus requiring the reporter to set the record straight. "Correction" is only used in really dire cases; otherwise, it is avoided at all costs so as to avoid admitting that the media did anything wrong.

For example, the *New York Times* was one of the only outlets to use the term "correction" when it fixed its article claiming the seventeen intelligence agencies agreed on Russian meddling.

"The assessment was made by four intelligence agencies— the Office of the Director of National Intelligence, the Central Intelligence Agency, the Federal Bureau of Investigation, and the National Security Agency. The assessment was not approved by all 17 organizations in the American intelligence community," the correction read.

However, in a longer article in July 2017 explaining why the correction needed to be made, the *New York Times* shifted blame to Trump for the error.

"Trump Misleads on Russian Meddling: Why 17 Intelligence Agencies Don't Need to Agree," the headline read.[92]

"President Trump said on Thursday that only 'three or four' of the United States' 17 intelligence agencies had concluded that Russia interfered in the presidential election—a statement that while technically accurate, is misleading and suggests widespread dissent among American intelligence agencies when none has emerged," the *Times* argued.

So even while admitting they screwed up, the *Times* tried to pass the buck onto someone else.

The Associated Press used the more deceptive "clarification"[93] designation to update four stories about the DNI report on Russian meddling, acknowledging that not all seventeen intelligence agencies were involved in the report.

NPR, which operates on taxpayer dollars, was arguably the most deceptive. It took them a full year after every other media outlet to start issuing corrections and "clarifications" on the multitude of stories they ran featuring "17 intelligence agencies." Articles they ran in May[94] and February[95] of 2017 received cor-

---

92 Rosenberg, Matthew. "Trump Misleads on Russian Meddling: Why 17 Intelligence Agencies Don't Need to Agree." *New York Times*, July 6, 2017. https://www.nytimes.com/2017/07/06/us/politics/trump-russia-intelligence-agencies-cia-fbi-nsa.html.

93 Rutz, David. "New York Times, Associated Press Correct Claims That All 17 Intelligence Agencies Agreed on Russian Interference." *Washington Free Beacon*, July 6, 2017. https://freebeacon.com/national-security/new-york-times-associated-press-correct-claims-that-all-17-intelligence-agencies-agreed-on-russian-interference/.

94 Montanaro, Domenico. "Why the Russia Investigation Matters and Why You Should Care." NPR, May 24, 2017. https://www.npr.org/2017/05/24/529781094/why-the-russia-investigation-matters-and-why-you-should-care.

95 Kelly, Mary Louise. "Where's the Director of National Intelligence?" NPR, February 16, 2017. https://www.npr.org/sections/parallels/2017/02/16/515590646/wheres-the-director-of-national-intelligence.

rections on July 18, 2018. The handful of edits were all made just two days after a July 16, 2018, piece made the same error.[96] That more recent article received a "clarification" and prompted a public memo from NPR's standards editor warning reporters to "be careful."

"While the DNI does speak on behalf of 17 intelligence agencies, the work that led to the assessment about Russian interference came from three of the 17—the CIA, FBI and NSA," Memmott said in his guidance. "Don't specifically attribute the conclusion to all 17 intelligence agencies."[97]

Despite these sweeping edits, NPR managed to miss at least one article that still spouted the seventeen intelligence agencies lie. An article published in January 2017 did not receive an update until over two and a half years later![98] NPR popped an editor's note into it in September 2019, reiterating Memmott's preferred language: "While the DNI does speak on behalf of 17 intelligence agencies, the work that led to the assessment about Russian interference came from three of the 17—the CIA, FBI and NSA."

Online journalism is a gift to outlets that like to avoid accountability.

Issuing timely corrections is a key part of journalistic integrity. However, the massive number of stories being published and pushed online on a daily basis means that mistakes get

---

[96] Kelly, Mary Louise, and Mara Liasson. "Trump Refuses to Back Intelligence Agencies' Election Interference Findings." NPR, July 16, 2018. https://www.npr.org/2018/07/16/629588424/trump-refused-to-say-he-believes-intelligence-agencies-election-interference-fin.

[97] Memmott, Mark. "Guidance on '17 Intelligence Agencies.'" NPR, July 18, 2018. https://www.npr.org/sections/memmos/2018/07/18/630057400/guidance-on-17-intelligence-agencies.

[98] Naylor, Brian. "Intelligence Chiefs 'Stand More Resolutely' behind Finding of Russia Election Hacking." NPR, January 5, 2017. https://www.npr.org/2017/01/05/508355408/intelligence-chiefs-stand-more-resolutely-behind-finding-of-russia-election-hack.

memory-holed really quickly. Hardly anyone is going back to articles that are a couple days old—let alone a couple of years old!—to make sure the information within is still accurate. NPR gets to publish an incontrovertible falsehood that advances a certain narrative and, by the time they get around to issuing a correction, their readers have already moved on.

Take the Hunter Biden laptop story. Nearly every major media outlet ignored the *New York Post*'s stellar reporting in 2020 on Hunter's hard drive, which had been picked up from a laptop repair shop in Delaware. The abandoned hard drive not only contained lewd and graphic photos and videos of the drug and sex-addicted president's son but also carried several suspicious emails about Hunter's business dealings abroad. It raised major questions about then-candidate Joe Biden's connections to these foreign deals...meanwhile, the press was wholly uncurious. They, along with social media companies, issued a fatwa against anything having to do with the laptop—that is, unless they were calling it fake or Russian disinformation. It wasn't until a year and a half later that media outlets, like the *New York Times*[99] and the *Washington Post*,[100] started quietly admitting that the laptop existed and appeared to have belonged to Hunter Biden. By that point, it was too late to make much of a difference. The election was long over. Sixteen percent of Biden voters said they would

---

[99] Board, Post Editorial. "Washington Post, New York Times Finally Admit Hunter's Laptop Is Real - but Only to Protect Joe Biden Some More." *New York Post*, April 2, 2022. https://nypost.com/2022/04/01/new-york-times-finally-admit-hunters-laptop-is-real-but-only-to-protect-joe-biden/.

[100] Golding, Bruce. "Washington Post Joins New York Times in Finally Admitting Emails from Hunter Biden Laptop Are Real." *New York Post*, March 30, 2022. https://nypost.com/2022/03/30/washington-post-admits-hunter-biden-laptop-is-real/.

have voted differently if they had known about Hunter's laptop.[101] In other words, the media that ignored the story and the social media companies that actively suppressed it, engaged in a form of electoral fraud, for which no one was held accountable. More on this later.

The same phenomenon, where media outlets correct themselves long after the damage is done, is common on social media. News outlets fire off a tweet featuring breaking news, a salacious scoop, or a nasty quote from a politician. When the information in those tweets is proven false, most news outlets won't even bother to delete the original. Instead, they send out a quote tweet with the "corrected" information. The quote tweet gets a fraction of the amount of engagement as the original, and the original is free to continue to be shared by people who have no idea it's not accurate.

Take Brian Ries, a senior editor at CNN, who, in 2018, tweeted a *Baltimore Sun* story that suggested a Trump supporter heiled Hitler during a musical.[102]

"A man stood up and shouted, 'Heil Hitler! Heil Trump!' during a Baltimore performance of 'Fiddler on the Roof' last night. Audience members started running. 'I'll be honest, I was waiting to hear a gunshot. I thought, "Here we go,"' one said," Ries wrote.

The tweet received nearly eleven thousand likes and eight thousand retweets.

---

[101] Anthony, James. "Flashback: 16% of Biden Voters Would Have Voted Differently If Hunter Biden Laptop Story Was Not Suppressed by Media, Big Tech." The Post Millennial, March 17, 2022. https://thepostmillennial.com/flashback-16-of-biden-voters.

[102] "Journalist Thinks Tsunami Warning Triggered by the Alaska … - Twitchy." Accessed September 7, 2022. https://twitchy.com/gregp-3534/2018/11/30/journalist-thinks-tsunami-warning-triggered-by-the-alaska-earthquake-is-proof-climate-change-is-real/.

The next day, Ries responded to himself with new information from a *New York Times* report. It turns out that the man at the musical was yelling in *protest* of Trump, not in support of him.

"Police report: Man who shouted at Baltimore theater had been 'drinking heavily,' told cops he yelled because the program scene 'reminded him of his hatred for President Trump.' Huh," Reis followed up.

The clarification, as the media likes to call it, received fewer than sixty likes and fifty retweets.

The other sneaky way that the press avoids accountability is through what's referred to as "stealth edits." A stealth edit is when an online publication changes the language in a story without informing the reader. This would be near impossible during the print days of journalism, because there was always a physical record of the first edition of the story. However, catching a stealth edit made by a digital publication requires an archive or screenshot of the original.

The purpose of the stealth edit is obvious: The media doesn't want its readers to know that they ever got anything wrong.

I busted out the *Washington Post* on an egregious stealth edit in June 2018.

One of the most covered stories at the time was about family separations on the southern border. The media alleged that President Donald Trump implemented a policy that called for the systematic separation of migrant children from their parents. The hand-wringing articles over the so-called "family separation policy" were filled with misinformation.

The Flores agreement, settled in 1997, laid out certain requirements for the detention of illegal migrant children that made it nearly impossible to house them with their parents.

First, there are only about four thousand beds available in detention centers built specifically for families. Once the family centers are full, children will be separated from their parents because they have to be placed in detention centers that still meet the requirements under Flores. The adults will go to a separate, less nice facility. During the height of the border crisis under Trump, more than one hundred thousand people were crossing the border illegally every month, so this happened a lot.

Second, Flores also establishes a maximum time limit that children are allowed to be held in detention. If a family immigration case takes longer than that established time limit, then the child would be released but the adult would remain in detainment until the case is concluded. If you are catching and releasing a lot of illegal migrants, like President Barack Obama, then you won't come up against the Flores time limit as often. Trump, however, required that nearly every illegal migrant be held in detention while their cases were adjudicated, which meant more frequent family separations. This was meant to combat the high percentage of illegal migrants fearing possible deportation who would not return for their court dates after being released.

There was also an important safety aspect to the Flores agreement—placing children in separate detention centers potentially could prevent sexual and physical abuse by unrelated adults. We also learned under the Trump administration, thanks to mandatory DNA tests, that a significant portion of adults and children claiming to be family members were actually not related. Why were they doing this? Well, again, it goes back to the Flores agreement. Because prior administrations would often release so-called "family units" to avoid dealing with the Flores requirements, illegal migrants started crossing the border with children, using them as their free meal ticket into the US.

In short, "Trump is separating families!" was hardly as clear cut as the media made it seem.

The media could not defend itself when presented with these pesky facts about family separations at the border, so they went for fully emotion-driven reporting instead. The line was that separating any family at the border, regardless of the reason, was cruel and inhumane. The defining image of this narrative was a photo snapped at the border that showed a child crying with arms outstretched as her mother was patted down by Border Patrol agents. That photo was used on an infamous *Time* magazine cover that photoshopped the crying girl to make it appear she was pleading with a cold, uncaring President Trump.

The photo was not an image of family separation, as the media claimed. It more accurately depicted the situation at the border as described by President Trump. The young girl was only briefly set on the ground while the mother was patted down; they were never actually separated. We also learned that the mother was not fleeing violence and seeking asylum but looking for a job in the US, had taken her daughter without her husband's permission, and left her three other children behind––and had been previously deported.[103]

Washington Post writer Aaron Blake criticized *Time* for helping spread inaccuracies about the photo. He admitted that the media's goal in reporting on family separations was not to inform, but to "forc[e] action on this policy." He warned his colleagues that skeptics could be turned off by policy changes if they believe the media is "overselling the problem by using misleading information and images."

---

[103] Athey, Amber. "Everything the Media Got Wrong about the Crying Girl on the Time Cover." The Daily Caller, June 22, 2018. https://dailycaller.com/2018/06/22/media-wrong-about-time-cover/.

"The use of this photo damaged that entire effort—no matter how pristine the motives were," Blake confirmed.

Other reporters at the *Washington Post* apparently didn't get the memo that their abandonment of journalism standards in favor of blatant activism was actually hurting their cause. An article by Eli Rosenberg marveled at the *Time* cover as a "powerful...statement on family separation."

The *Washington Post* quietly edited the story when media critics pointed out the mistake. They changed the headline to "Time and New Yorker covers make powerful statement about the border crisis" and no longer described the mother-daughter pair as being "separated" at all. This is a major distinction, but the *Post* opted not to inform readers that anything had changed.

That is, until I reached out to the *Washington Post* press office pointing out that their own editorial policy requires corrections to be noted at the top of a story. They finally added a "clarification" hours later.

"Clarification: The initial version of this story said the child depicted on Time's cover had been separated from her mother, based on the magazine's account. As the *Washington Post* and others have since reported, the child was not separate from her mother during their encounter with a border patrol agent. The story has been updated," a new note at the top of the article said.

The *Post* did not explain to me why that "clarification" wasn't included in the first place. It's doubtful that they ever would have alerted readers to their error if I hadn't caught their stealth edit. Can you imagine how often this happens when we aren't paying attention?

Outside of their ideological coziness, there is another important reason why the media is willing to destroy its credibility to advance the goals of the Democratic Party and its left-wing allies. Reporters who toe the line are handsomely rewarded by the left in the form of exclusive stories, swanky cocktail parties, and job offers.

The idea of the "Georgetown cocktail party" is mocked by the left as an imaginary right-wing trope.[104] These soirees may not always take place in Georgetown, nor do they always occur during happy hour, but it is true that politicians and their PR firms court reporters with meet-and-greets at hotel rooftop bars, holiday parties at downtown multimillion-dollar row houses with passed hor d'oeuvres, and dinners at high-end steakhouses.

Leaked emails from 2015 showed the Clinton campaign schmoozing reporters with home-cooked dinners and cocktails.[105] Before Clinton announced, John Podesta whipped up a meal for more than two dozen reporters at his home in Washington, DC. Reporters were later treated to Friday night cocktails at the home of Joel Benenson, Clinton's chief strategist, in New York. The goals for the meetings were described as "setting expectations," "framing the race," and just enjoying one another's company.

These types of meetings aren't exclusive to the left, and all parties involved will tell you they are innocuous. I've admittedly been to quite a few of them myself. They are important tools of source development for journalists. There are few better bonding experiences in DC than getting drunk together, and doing so with people in power can lead to exclusive stories and interviews down the line. However, it's important not to get swept up in the glamour and free stuff and allow it to soften your coverage.

---

[104] "The Right's Mythologized Georgetown Cocktail Party Circuit Cabal." Daily Kos. Accessed September 7, 2022. https://www.dailykos.com/stories/2014/5/12/1298779/-The-Right-s-Mythologized-Georgetown-Cocktail-Party-Circuit-Cabal.

[105] Greenwald, Glenn, and Lee Fang. "Exclusive: New Leak on Clinton's Cozy Press Relationship." The Intercept, October 9, 2016. https://theintercept.com/2016/10/09/exclusive-new-email-leak-reveals-clinton-campaigns-cozy-press-relationship/.

This was always easier for me because my default position is that most politicians are morally degenerate lying scumbags, even the ones who are "on my side." I've earned myself social media blocks, lost job opportunities and speaker invitations, and been blacklisted by people and organizations within the conservative movement because of my unwillingness to run with certain stories or ideas. I'm not some paragon of moral virtue, but I think it's fair to say that most journalists are probably a bit more worried about losing access over negative coverage. This is especially true among the left because Democratic politicians and activist groups are way more willing to freeze out reporters who don't play ball. Plus, there's the added component of left-wing journalists who already agree with and idolize Democratic politicians.

If a dirty martini isn't enough to temper an aggressive journalist, a job opportunity might be. The government-to-media pipeline is a well-documented phenomenon. Reporters and pundits who provide friendly coverage to incoming administrations are offered well-paid and forward-facing roles in communications. When a new administration takes over, those staffers are redirected back to the media, where they are billed as "experts," "analysts," and most disturbingly, paraded as straight news reporters.

I don't have any particular problem with government officials offering commentary on news networks so long as they are properly identified and not treated as objective sources of information. This is often not the case. There are also a whole host of other conflicts of interest that can arise in these situations.

Axios reported on April 1, 2022, that Biden press secretary Jen Psaki was planning on leaving the White House to take a job with NBC, serving as a commentator on MSNBC and a news program host on Peacock, the company's streaming service. Press secretaries joining the media are nothing new—see Nicolle Wallace, Dana Perino, and Kayleigh McEnany—but Psaki's situation was unique. She was still taking questions from the podium while actively negotiating a deal with a media company that has White House reporters in the briefing room.

Psaki was asked about this conflict by none other than Kristen Welker, a White House correspondent for NBC News. It was almost as if NBC and Psaki were prepared for ethical questions about her move to the private sector. NBC helpfully demonstrated that they will still ask "tough questions" of Psaki despite actively courting her for work, and Psaki was able to talk about her own attempts to abide by ethical guidelines.

"I have taken the ethics, legal requirements...very seriously in any discussions and any considerations about any future employment just as any White House official would and I have taken steps beyond that to ensure there's no conflicts," Psaki said.

She also claimed that the same ethical considerations apply to government officials seeking work in "any industry." She is being deliberately obtuse if she thinks her situation isn't especially prickly given the potential for softer coverage from NBC-affiliated networks. Or that she might, even subconsciously, call on NBC-affiliated networks more frequently.

"I hope that all of you...would judge me for my record and how I treat you and I try to answer questions from everybody across the board," Psaki asserted.

Sorry, but that's not good enough when we're talking about a public employee in a country that's supposed to have an independent press.

The perception of conflict was so obvious that NBC News president Noah Oppenheim held an emergency meeting for his journalists, who worried that Psaki's hiring could tarnish the brand.[106] Aside from the hilarity of NBC reporters suddenly worrying about ethics, Oppenheim nonetheless assured them that MSNBC's programming decisions had nothing to do with NBC News. NBC News, he claimed, was still dedicated to news reporting, while MSNBC was a separate opinion arm. This seems a pretty irrelevant distinction given that Psaki's show will be streamed on Peacock, which is owned by NBC News's parent company, NBCUniversal. Plus, there's already a lot of overlap between the opinion programming on MSNBC and the news reporting at NBC News. Chuck Todd, Andrea Mitchell, and Hallie Jackson, despite technically working under the NBC News umbrella, also host shows on MSNBC.

Even Judd Legum, the founder of left-wing blog *ThinkProgress*, tweeted his concerns about Psaki's imminent move to cable.

"I don't think Psaki should be negotiating for a job with a media company while she still serves as press secretary," Legum said. "She currently plays a powerful role in determining what outlets get access. It creates, at a minimum, the appearance of a conflict."

While journalists anxiously tried to conceal their ties to the Biden administration, the Democratic Party fabulously blew their cover. In a fundraising email, the Democratic Congressional Campaign Committee claimed Psaki's goal as press secretary was not to speak on behalf of the Biden administration, but to "restore trust" in the media. She would finally be joining "intrepid

---

[106] Darcy, Oliver. "NBC News Journalists Vexed by MSNBC's Move to Hire White House Press Secretary Jen Psaki | CNN Business." Cable News Network, April 7, 2022. https://www.cnn.com/2022/04/06/media/jen-psaki-nbc/index.html.

journalists" at MSNBC, whose job is to "hold dangerous, far-right Republicans accountable."[107]

At least Democrats can be honest about their relationship with journalists and how they operate. They don't need a veneer of ethics.

There are many other examples of this "revolving door" between government and the media that have led to ethical conflicts.

Let's take Jim Sciutto. Sciutto started his career as the moderator and producer of a PBS news show aimed at college students, moved to Asia Business News to cover Hong Kong, and then served as the senior foreign correspondent for ABC News until late 2011. Four years later, in 2015, Sciutto was hired by CNN to serve as the network's chief national security correspondent and would go on to anchor the daily news program "CNN Newsroom" alongside Poppy Harlow.

That gap in his resume between leaving ABC News and joining CNN? Oh yeah, Sciutto joined the Obama administration. He served as the chief of staff and senior adviser to U.S. ambassador to China Gary Locke.[108]

Viewers would be forgiven for thinking that Sciutto is merely a career journalist. CNN has done a really good job at covering up the fact that he was a political appointee for a Democratic presidential administration. Sciutto provides reports on daily news stories, conducts interviews, and breaks stories. Somehow, he's been allowed to cover the tail end of the Obama administration, the Iran Deal, the United States' deal to lift sanctions on a

---

[107] "House Democratic Campaign Arm Fundraises off Psaki's Plans to Join MSNBC." Yahoo! Accessed, September 7, 2022. https://www.yahoo.com/lifestyle/house-democratic-campaign-arm-fundraises-165646318.html. l

[108] ABC News. ABC News Network. Accessed September 7, 2022. https://abc-news.go.com/blogs/headlines/2011/12/jim-sciutto-leaving-abc-news-to-become-chief-of-staff-to-the-u-s-ambassador-to-china.

Chinese telecommunications firm, and other major international stories without ever disclosing his political history. If you check out Sciutto's bio on CNN's website, they mention that he served as a chief of staff to Locke but conveniently leave out which administration he served under.

How can we trust seemingly objective journalists' reporting when they aren't even honest with viewers about their career moves? In Sciutto's case, it turns out we can't. Sciutto has been responsible for sharing a lot of misinformation and clear bias during his tenure at CNN.

In 2017, he claimed that the Obama administration cared more about civilian casualties than the Trump administration. In February 2018, he falsely claimed that the Steele dossier was first funded by Republicans (as a refresher, a Republican firm paid for standard opposition research against Trump, but that research was not included in the Steele dossier, which was funded exclusively by Democrats.) Sciutto tweeted incorrectly in September 2018 that Christine Blasey Ford, Supreme Court Justice nominee Brett Kavanaugh's accuser, was not offered the chance to testify about her alleged sexual assault in private. According to Senate Judiciary Chairman Chuck Grassley, Blasey Ford was offered public or private testimony on multiple dates. Sciutto's original tweet got nearly twenty thousand likes—his correction, just a few hundred.[109] A few months later, Sciutto accused the Trump administration of lying about catching terrorists crossing the

---

[109] Athey, Amber. "CNN's Jim Sciutto Spreads Fake News about Offer to Kavanaugh's Accuser." The Daily Caller, September 20, 2018. https://daily-caller.com/2018/09/20/cnn-sciutto-fake-news-kavanaugh/?dg.

southern border illegally; the Department of Homeland Security backed up Trump's version of events.[110]

CNN had a long habit of either employing or producing Obama affiliates and failing to identify them as such. John Kirby, a State Department spokesperson for Obama, was given free rein to bash President Donald Trump's foreign policy without revealing his former employer. Laura Jarrett, a "justice reporter" for the network, was tasked with covering Trump's Justice Department despite apparently having no reporting experience. Prior to joining CNN, Jarrett worked as a lawyer for a private practice. Most importantly, she is Valerie Jarrett's daughter. Valerie Jarrett served as a special advisor to President Obama. CNN conducted at least seven interviews with Valerie Jarrett while never disclosing that her daughter worked for the network.

At least two CNN employees left their journalism careers to work for the Obama administration as well. Sasha Johnson, a political producer, left CNN in 2009 to serve as press secretary for Obama's Department of Transportation. CNN war correspondent Aneesh Raman quit his job in 2008 to intern for the Obama campaign and eventually became a domestic policy speechwriter for the administration.

When it's not a government position, you can bet it's a job with a left-wing activist group. Kate Smith, a CBS News reporter who covered abortion—and was often criticized by the right for her obvious bias toward pro-abortion advocates—joined Planned Parenthood in April 2022 to help the organization's news content.

How can we trust network coverage if reporters are secretly angling for government jobs and vice versa? The revolving door between the media and politics has become so commonplace that

---

[110] Athey, Amber. "DHS Shuts down Fake News from CNN's Jim Sciutto." The Daily Caller, December 13, 2018. https://dailycaller.com/2018/12/13/dhs-cnn-jim-sciutto-fake-news-terrorists/.

Democrats oftentimes can't seem to tell the difference between the two industries. Speaker Nancy Pelosi chastised the media as if they were her own staffers in the fall of 2021, demanding they "do a better job" of "selling" Biden's $3.5 trillion "Build Back Better" spending bill.[111]

[111] Joe Concha, Opinion Contributor. "Pelosi Hilariously Scolds Media for Not 'Selling' $3.5t Spending Bill: 'Do a Better Job." The Hill, October 15, 2021. https://thehill.com/opinion/finance/576903-pelosi-hilariously-scolds-media-for-not-selling-35t-spending-bill-do-a-better/.

CHAPTER 11

INSIDE THE WHITE HOUSE

After just a few years working in conservative media, I viewed the White House press corps with great disdain. Watching press briefings was an exercise in anger management, as reporters either asked Trump and his administration officials the same questions over and over again or teed up "gotcha" questions to try to get a good sound bite for the evening news broadcast.

Nonetheless, in January 2019, the *Daily Caller* promoted me to White House Correspondent. It felt odd to be joining the ranks of the White House Correspondents Association (WHCA) after I spent the past two years reporting on them critically and mocking them on social media. I certainly wouldn't be welcome with open arms, nor would I necessarily want to be. My goal was to approach the job with a different perspective from the other WHCA members and hopefully ask the questions that Americans really cared about. If NBC, CNN, and PBS were asking about Russiagate, I wanted to be asking about immigration. If they were asking about palace intrigue stories, I wanted to ask about the economy or foreign policy.

The White House is a very bizarre place to work, mostly because there is a constant mismatch between expectations and reality. The first time I made it through the security hut, the grandeur of the North Portico and the meticulously manicured grounds of the North Lawn took my breath away. Once you're on the grounds, you take a paved pathway toward the West Wing, passing green media tents lined up like little pine trees on your right. This is where reporters do their live television shots with the White House in the background. In the colder months, you'll see correspondents wrapped up in scarves and huddled under blankets between hits to stay warm. It's surreal.

But then you enter the James S. Brady briefing room, and it is like a slap in the face. The briefing room is an overcrowded dump. Reporters working for outlets unlucky enough to be without an assigned workspace, like myself, had to post up in the little fold-down chairs in the briefing room. When gathering for a press briefing, we're kicked out of our seats for the more important outlets and shoved into the aisles like canned sardines. Past the back of the briefing room where the cameras are lined up, there are small desks with deteriorating chairs on stained carpet, tiny offices the size of telephone booths for the more established outlets, a grimy kitchenette, and the infamous vending machine where I spent way too much money on diet coke. I tried to avoid going into the basement, which was somehow even more grim. No matter where you were in the briefing room and accompanying workspace, it would be difficult to have two people standing shoulder to shoulder at any given time.

Pretty on the outside, ugly on the inside. I'm often reminded of what David Martosko, the former political editor of the *Daily Mail* and an all-around standup guy, once told me while puffing a cigar at approximately nine o'clock in the morning:

"Welcome to hell!"

Working at the White House was sometimes hell but also a hell of an experience. I got to attend so many once-in-a-lifetime events: the late Japanese Prime Minister Shinzo Abe arriving at the White House for a State Dinner, Israeli Prime Minister Benjamin Netanyahu and Trump delivering remarks from the Diplomatic Room, the Washington Capitals visiting the Oval Office after winning the Stanley Cup, golfer Tiger Woods receiving the Presidential Medal of Freedom in the Rose Garden, riding with the presidential motorcade, and watching Air Force One take off from Joint Base Andrews, to name a few. I have so many incredible memories from my time as a White House correspondent.

Outside of these moments, though, reporting from the White House briefing room was not exactly glamorous. The drab workspace led to a general culture of disrespect among the press corps, who weren't exactly winners themselves. In fact, most of them were complete slobs. They constantly left empty food wrappers and water bottles on their desks and dropped crumbs all over the floor. If a White House reporter isn't on camera for a living, chances are they are overweight and unattractive. I made an effort to look my best when I was on the White House grounds, but despite making way more money than me, these reporters strolled around in ill-fitting suits from the 1980s, stained khakis, pencil skirts bursting at the seams, and cardigans about to unravel.

The outer appearance seemed to be a reflection of their internal misery. I'm not a psychologist, but I can tell you that any job entailing working long hours, cutting back on family time, spending way too much time in DC, missing holidays, and eating garbage food on a daily basis is not good for the soul. I got burned out on full-time White House coverage within a year. Anyone who stays longer than a few years is either a glutton for punishment or hoping they'll get that big break. The latter group is filled with the horrible narcissists who appear on camera every day or dream of doing so. Their job is to poke and prod the press secretary with ridiculous questions until they finally snap, putting themselves at the center of the story, and delivering a delicious made-for-TV moment. This is why the Trump administration often discussed the idea of moving the press briefings to audio only. The hunger to become famous drives a lot of White House reporters to deliver pretty bad coverage. So many reporters practically abused Trump's press secretaries during briefings. Kayleigh McEnany was constantly accused of being a liar, and Sarah Sanders had the displeasure of having her family weaponized against her by the ever-distasteful Brian Karem. Karem, who nobody in the press corps actually liked, as far as I could tell, leveraged briefing room meltdowns[112] into a CNN contributor gig.[113] April Ryan charted the same course, getting hired at CNN after Sean Spicer asked her to stop shaking her head in response to an answer to one of her questions.[114] And we all know the story of Jim Acosta, who generally acted like an ass at nearly every press briefing and used it to get a book deal.[115]

---

[112] Athey, Amber. "CNN Analyst Brian Karem Defends Press Briefing Meltdown." The Daily Caller, June 17, 2018. https://dailycaller.com/2018/06/17/cnn-brian-karem-defends-meltdown/.

[113] Athey, Amber. "CNN Hired the Playboy Reporter Who Had a Meltdown at a WH Press Briefing." The Daily Caller, September 8, 2017. https://dailycaller.com/2017/09/08/cnn-hires-playboy-reporter-who-had-outburst-at-press-briefing/.

[114] Press, the Associated. "CNN Hires April Ryan as Political Contributor." The Hollywood Reporter, April 3, 2017. https://www.hollywoodreporter.com/tv/tv-news/cnn-hires-april-ryan-as-political-contributor-990912/.

[115] Flood, Brian. "Jim Acosta's CNN Role Further Muddled by Upcoming Book: 'You Can't Tell the Difference between Him and a Paid Pundit.'" FOX News Network, May 23, 2019. https://www.foxnews.com/entertainment/cnn-jim-acosta-book-reporter-paid-pundit.

Unfortunately for these folks, they are really only useful to the media when they can act as foils to Republican administrations. They were discarded as soon as they could no longer antagonize the Trump administration because, beyond that, they weren't actually very good reporters. Karem was denied membership to the WHCA in 2021[116] and his appearances on CNN seem to have all but disappeared. He left his job at the Montgomery County *Sentinel*, and his LinkedIn profile says he is covering the White House as a freelancer. *Playboy* magazine, where he also used to work, shut down operations in 2020. April Ryan moved to a new website, *The Grio*, and, according to a search of TV clipping service Grabien, is appearing on CNN very infrequently. She hasn't had a viral briefing room moment in quite a while. Acosta was moved off the White House beat when Biden was elected and given his own show at CNN. You'd think that would be considered a reward, but millions used to watch his temper tantrums in the briefing room, even if only to make fun of him. Now, a measly half a million viewers tune in for his program compared to the two to three million who usually watch his competitors at Fox News.[117] CNN, it seems, is where careers go to die. Just ask Chris Wallace.

Some of the reporters at the White House were pleasant, particularly if they also worked for conservative or independent media outlets. A lot of them were entitled jerks.

---

[116] Talcott, Shelby. "Playboy's Brian Karem Says His White House Correspondents' Association Membership Has Been Declined." The Daily Caller, January 29, 2021. https://dailycaller.com/2021/01/29/playboy-brian-karem-white-house-correspondents-association-membership-declined/.

[117] Ellefson, Lindsey. "CNN Ratings Sink with Brianna Keilar, Jim Acosta in Chris Cuomo Time Slot." TheWrap, January 26, 2022. https://www.thewrap.com/cnn-9-ratings-cuomo-keilar-acosta/.

I was sitting down in the briefing room one day working on an article when a reporter for an outlet I had never even heard of proudly declared to me that he didn't know how I could possibly work for the *Daily Caller*.

"I wouldn't be able to work for an outlet that's so blatantly partisan!" he asserted.

I nearly laughed in his face, both at the idea that the *Daily Caller* was any more "partisan" than any other outlet represented at the White House and that this untalented loser would ever be in the position to turn down a job offer.

One sunny day, I was lined up to attend an event in the Rose Garden when I saw a certain on-camera CNN reporter getting into it with a Trump communications staffer. Most official events open to the press were limited to one reporter from each outlet, and this was no different. There was already one CNN reporter in the Rose Garden, and this on-camera talent demanded she be let in as well because she had to get her stand-up shot. Eventually, she stormed into the Rose Garden and threw her own colleague out of the event.

White House reporters are really good at weaseling their way into places they don't belong. I was lined up in the upper press area one day with about six other reporters from conservative outlets. We were all invited to attend a background briefing with a senior administration official. It was incredibly rare that right-wing reporters got any special privileges at the White House, even during the Trump administration. We were often frozen out of other background briefings and left begging for interviews and exclusives. Still, mainstream media reporters tried to elbow their way into our briefing that day. Goons from CBS, CNN, and other outlets joined us in line and played dumb when administration officials asked them if they were invited. Luckily, they were sent empty-handed back to the briefing room. I would say they left with their tails between their legs, but I don't think these people are capable of feeling shame.

Mainstream reporters were usually only kind to us outsiders when they could get something useful in return. The *Daily Caller* is a member of the White House print pool, so once a month I was on pool duty. This basically means that you follow around the president for the day and report on his movements to the rest of the press corps. It was a relatively easy job. White House officials told you where to go and when to be there. The rest of it was just following basic instructions, writing down things as they happened, and making sure the right people were cc'ed on emails. Several correspondents still seemed floored that I picked it up pretty quickly and heaped praise on me after my first day of pool reporting. This reinforced my prior impression from media reporting that most reporters are pretty dumb. Mostly, though, correspondents have to be nice to whomever is on pool duty that day because the pool reporter gets more access to the president. The pool reporter can thus ask questions on behalf of, share audio and photos with, or gather more event information or color for other reporters and outlets.

The only other time reporters from mainstream outlets started buzzing around me was when WHCA board elections were around the corner. People I had talked to once or twice would catch me outside of the White House and assure me that they understood the needs of smaller media outlets. Sometimes they'd remind me of how much they "helped" me in the past year from their board seat, and I had literally zero idea what they were talking about. The worst was when Anita Kumar, a *Politico* reporter and former WHCA board member, blatantly ignored my emails, including one asking to join the supplemental print pool when I moved over to *The Spectator* in 2020. A few months later, she had the gall to call my cell phone out of the blue and ask me to give her my vote for the WHCA president and the at-large seat (a candidate for WHCA president must also win a board seat to fill the president role). I voted for her opponent, Kelly O'Donnell, just to spite her.

Kumar and O'Donnell tied for the at-large seat, 197–197, but O'Donnell won the race for president by thirteen votes. The board gave the election to O'Donnell. Every vote counts!

Kumar now works as a standards editor for *Politico*. We'll get into that later.

The most important thing to understand about White House reporting is that the entire system is set up to benefit establishment and corporate media outlets. Contrary to popular belief, whichever administration is in the White House plays a relatively small role in determining press access. They determine who gets a press pass, but most other decisions relating to coverage are outsourced to the White House Correspondents Association.

The WHCA creates the seating chart in the briefing room, determining who is most likely to be called on by a press secretary. They place correspondents from the large broadcast and cable networks in the front rows. Only a couple of conservative outlets are given seats at all, and they are plopped in the back. Everyone else has to stand in the aisles, throw some elbows to retain some personal space, and pray they get called on. The *Daily Caller* just recently gained a seat in the briefing room—we did not have one when I covered the White House. The *Spectator* does not have one either. To get a good space in an aisle during the Trump administration, you had to arrive about an hour before the briefing to save your spot, while the reporters with seats can stroll in after the two-minute warning. The conservative and independent outlets forced into the aisles are placed at a huge disadvantage because they are out of the press secretary's line of sight. If you've ever watched a press briefing and felt like everyone was asking the same questions, it's because the corporate media drones are usually the only ones getting any. The WHCA revamped its seating chart in February 2022, the first time they had done this in about five years. The first three rows are occupied by the following outlets: NBC News, Fox News, CBS News, the Associated Press, Reuters, CNN, the *Wall Street Journal*, CBS News Radio, *Bloomberg*, NPR, the *Washington Post*, the *New York Times*, *USA Today*, *Politico*, AP Radio and PBS Radio, McClatchy, the foreign pool, AFP, the *Los Angeles Times*, and ABC News Radio. Of the forty-nine seats in the briefing room, just nine are occupied by right-leaning news outlets. If you exclude Fox News, WSJ, and Fox Radio, then you're down to six. Of those six, five are seated in the back rows.

The WHCA's protection of certain outlets extends to its public statements and, unofficially, the way members selectively come to each other's defense. The WHCA filed an amicus brief when the Trump administration revoked Jim Acosta's (of CNN) hard pass, released a statement defending CNN's Kaitlan Collins when she was barred from an event, and filed another amicus brief to challenge the revocation of Brian Karem's hard pass. However, the WHCA voted to remove conservative One America News Network (OANN) from the briefing room rotation for not abiding by their contrived social distancing guidelines, even though OANN's correspondent had been personally invited to be in the briefing room by the Trump administration. All of the WHCA reporters would jump on their social media accounts to defend one another when Trump was even slightly sarcastic in response to one of their questions. When a reporter from a conservative outlet even got a question, the rest of the press corps would complain. Much like the woke college kids who believed conservatives shouldn't be allowed to speak on campus, the WHCA didn't believe that conservatives should get to ask questions in the briefing room. Jim Acosta accused my colleague at the time, Saagar Enjeti, of asking softball questions during a joint presser between Trump and Brazilian president Jair Bolsonaro.[118]

Saagar asked Bolsonaro, "A number of Democrats who are running to replace the president have embraced socialist ideas… If a candidate who embraced socialism were to replace the president, how would it affect your relations with the United States?"

It was a perfectly newsy question considering Bernie Sanders, a self-proclaimed Democratic socialist, was polling quite well at the time, and that socialism is accused of destroying Brazil's economy. Acosta disagreed, and in his criticism of Saagar, even incorrectly claimed that the questions was directed to Trump, not Bolsonaro.

Acosta claimed the question "was asked in a way that really teed it up like a game of tee ball here in the Rose Garden. The president was just sort of served up a softball there when he was asked whether or not the Democrats are advancing a lot of socialist ideas."

Acosta had previously whined that Trump might call on conservative outlets who ask "softballs." His consternation over conservative colleagues was especially disgusting because none other than Fox News came to his defense when Trump tried to pull his hard pass.

Back in 2017, reporters fretted after press secretary Sean Spicer called on the *New York Post*, *LifeZette*, and *Breitbart* during

---

[118] Hall, Colby, and By. "Jim Acosta Incorrectly Mocks 'Socialist' Question Asked by Daily Caller's Saagar Enjeti: 'Served up a Softball.'" Mediaite, March 19, 2019. https://www.mediaite.com/trump/jim-acosta-incorrectly-mocks-socialist-question-asked-by-daily-caller-reporter-he-served-up-a-softball/.

briefings.[119] They were livid when the *Daily Caller*'s Kaitlan Collins, who they would later champion as their hero when she moved to CNN, got a question at a Trump press conference.[120]

Back to April Ryan for a second. In addition to taking care of its preferred outlets, the WHCA also does favors for its personal friends. Ryan was given a permanent seat in the briefing room when she covered the White House for the American Urban Radio Networks, where she worked for more than two decades. In 2020, Ryan moved to *TheGrio*, a website that covers African American issues and is owned by Allen Media Group. Even though it usually takes media outlets years to get an assigned briefing room seat, the WHCA quickly made sure that Ryan's seat with the American Urban Radio Networks was reassigned to *TheGrio*. It's also worth pointing out that, until 2016, *TheGrio* was launched and owned by NBC.

Television correspondents and wire services—Reuters, the Associated Press, and the like—are also given priority when it comes to other White House events. Whenever we are set to cover a president's arrival or departure, or an event in the Rose Garden or East Room, we have to line up in a predetermined order. Let's use an example. Imagine that Trump was leaving the White House to fly to a rally in Iowa. Typically, before he boarded Marine One, he would stop and answer questions from the press gaggle. That gaggle is not assembled randomly. Photographers, cameras, and sound are sent out first to set up their equipment. Then, members of the rotating press pool head out. Next up,

---

[119] Pfeiffer, Alex. "Spicer Calls on a Conservative Outlet First and Pisses off Reporters Yet Again." The Daily Caller, January 24, 2017. https://dailycaller.com/2017/01/24/spicer-calls-on-a-conservative-outlet-first-and-pisses-off-reporters-yet-again/.

[120] Landler, Mark. "A Trump News Conference Filters out the Tough Questions." *New York Times*, February 14, 2017. https://www.nytimes.com/2017/02/13/us/politics/donald-trump-reporter-questions.html?_r=0.

WHCA members, who are allowed to line up thirty minutes prior to the departure. Correspondents for larger outlets game the system by sending out their producers or junior reporters to hold their spots in line, an advantage those of us operating solo don't have. Television correspondents also have the benefit of having their cameramen, who are already set up, holding a place for them at the front of the rope. By the time the rest of us reporters could get out to the gathering location, we were two to three rows back in the crowd and effectively frozen out of getting any questions. I had to fight a little dirty to make sure I could get a decent spot in the gaggle. I always wore flats or sneakers on arrival or departure days so I could run ahead of other reporters once our line was let through. If a photographer was set up on a ladder, I'd sneak behind them and stand on the first rung so I could be taller than the people in front of me. Sometimes, being small was an advantage because I could maneuver my way closer to the front of the gaggle with some strategically placed elbows. The system is similar for events in the Rose Garden. A certain number of establishment outlets get assigned seats in the back two rows, while the television correspondents get the prime standing space. Everyone else has to crowd around the back and sides of the garden. There were many times I nearly ended up face down in the thorny rose bushes after being pushed out of the way by a photographer or ruined a good pair of heels by sinking into the grass on a dewy day.

The WHCA's rules are self-reinforcing, so the system is never challenged. It doesn't make sense for reporters from smaller outlets to be at the White House every day because they don't have a set working space or an assigned seat in the briefing room, and they can't count on getting decent positioning at other events. Their time is usually better spent working from an office. However, in order to get more access, the WHCA requires you to have a physical presence at the White House as often as possible. It's like an abusive relationship. You have to accept being treated like dirt for years and allow your work product to suffer with the vague hope that, one day, the WHCA will let you into their club.

Access to the White House was even more limited under the Biden administration. The journalists who loved to complain about Trump's alleged "attacks on the free press" were slowly forced to admit that the Biden administration was way more restrictive. Even though White House Press Secretary Jen Psaki returned the tradition of the daily press briefing, access to the president himself all but disappeared. Trump used to almost always stop and talk to reporters while leaving or arriving at the White House. He took impromptu shouted questions during pool sprays in the Oval Office and gave tons of interviews. Biden gave just one press conference and just twenty-two media interviews during his first year in office.[121] Biden often tells the press at the end of events that he is not supposed—sometimes it's not "allowed"—to be taking questions.

"We need more access to Biden himself," Jonathan Karl, ABC News White House Correspondent and former WHCA president told the Committee to Protect Journalists.[122] "Press access to him is so far very limited. Press conferences are few and far between. His people seem to wall him off from the press."

WHCA members claim that Biden's rhetoric toward the press is at least less hostile than Trump's, but that's hardly true. Biden bizarrely flipped out on CBS's Ed O'Keefe on the campaign trail when he was asked a question about Senator Bernie Sanders. He called Fox News's Peter Doocy a "stupid son of a bitch." When

---

[121] "'Night and Day': The Biden Administration and the Press." Committee to Protect Journalists, January 13, 2022. https://cpj.org/reports/2022/01/night-and-day-the-biden-administration-and-the-press/.

[122] Ibid.

the *Daily Caller*'s Shelby Talcott asked if there are Democrats who want to defund the police, Biden bafflingly asked her if there are Republicans who think "we're sucking the blood out of kids." He accused another Fox News reporter of asking a "stupid question" about Ukraine. Biden lashed out at CNN's Kaitlan Collins after she asked if he is confident Vladimir Putin will "change his behavior," stammering, "What the hell...what do you do all day?" and telling her she might be "in the wrong business."[123]

A few months after Biden called Doocy a "stupid son of a bitch," Psaki was asked about the situation during a taping of *Pod Save America*. Biden called Doocy to apologize for the comment, but instead of following her boss's lead, Psaki doubled down.

"He works for a network that provides people with questions that, nothing personal to any individual, including Peter Doocy, but might make anyone sound like a stupid son of a bitch," Psaki laughed.[124]

So much for Biden's promise to fire any staffer who disrespects others. Psaki's comments were especially gross because she was confirmed to be leaving the White House for MSNBC at this point. She was being paid by taxpayers to bash the competitor of her future employer. Swampy!

It's also worth pointing out that Fox does not feed questions to Doocy. I can't say the same for NBC's Peter Alexander, who I saw taking a list of questions from a producer ahead of a Trump press gaggle one fine afternoon.

---

[123] "6.19.21." You're in the wrong business. https://mailchi.mp/thefirsttv/fourth-watch-jun-19-21.

[124] Getahun, Hannah. "Jen Psaki Says Fox News Provides Questions That Make Peter Doocy Sound like 'Stupid Son of a Bitch.'" Business Insider. https://www.businessinsider.com/psaki-says-fox-news-questions-may-make-doocy-sound-stupid-2022-4.

The Biden administration loved using the COVID-19 pandemic as an excuse to freeze out the press corps. The WHCA complied with the White House's requests to cut back on press briefing attendance so that reporters could "socially distance," and again weaponized the seating chart to reward legacy media outlets. Toward the start of the pandemic, briefing room attendance was limited to just twelve seats out of the normal forty-nine. The large corporate outlets and wire services kept their seats, but every other WHCA member had to rotate through just one seat. It would take several months for these outlets to get a chance to be in the briefing room. The pandemic seating chart was later expanded to twenty-four seats, but most of us still were rotating through just a couple of seats. I got to be in the briefing room just once during this time period, on June 2, 2021. It was just one day after the *Washington Post*[125] and *BuzzFeed News*[126] published redacted emails from Dr. Anthony Fauci, the White House's top COVID-19 advisor. The most shocking in the bunch showed that Dr. Fauci was warned the novel coronavirus could've been "engineered," even while publicly dismissing the so-called "lab leak theory" as a conspiracy not based in fact. Republicans in Congress called for Fauci to be fired. It seemed obvious to me that any reporter worth his salt should ask White House Press Secretary Jen Psaki if the Biden administration was concerned by the contradictions between Fauci's private and public statements about the virus and if it still had confidence in him. No one in the room asked about them, and Psaki ended the briefing

---

[125] Damian Paletta, Yasmeen Abutaleb. "Anthony Fauci's Pandemic Emails: 'All Is Well despite Some Crazy People in This World.'" *Washington Post*, June 1, 2021. https://www.washingtonpost.com/politics/interactive/2021/tony-fauci-emails/.

[126] Bettendorf, Natalie. "Anthony Fauci's Emails Reveal the Pressure That Fell on One Man." BuzzFeed News, June 2, 2021. https://www.buzzfeednews.com/article/nataliebettendorf/fauci-emails-covid-response.

before I could be called on for a question. The *Washington Post* presumably had a reporter in the room that day and didn't think their own story was worth bringing up to Psaki.[127] Psaki wasn't asked about the emails until the next day by Fox News. When press access is restricted to outlets with the orthodoxical political perspective, the American public loses.

Sadly, things got worse in January 2022. The WHCA held an emergency meeting and voted unanimously to "temporarily" reduce the briefing room to fourteen seats, citing the rise of the Omicron variant. At the time, the press corps was 99 percent vaccinated and we knew that Omicron was a mild strain of COVID-19. This time, the WHCA didn't throw a single bone to smaller outlets. The rotating seat available to all WHCA members? Gone. Only outlets that already had a permanently assigned seat in the briefing room would be allowed entry. This new rotation made certain that you'd be lucky to have one right-leaning outlet in the briefing room on any given day.

Navigating this stacked deck as a conservative reporter was certainly difficult at times. I tried to follow the rules as much as possible because I knew they'd be looking for any excuse to throw me out of the White House. I was polite and cordial to these gremlins in person, even though I had spent two years as a media reporter blasting them in articles and on Twitter. When on pool duty, I kept my head down and did my job well. I even occasionally attended board meetings!

Even though the WHCA was effectively a left-wing cabal, it could not escape the leery eye of the woke. During Q&A at a WHCA event in downtown DC, the board was caught flat-footed

---

[127] Boyd, Jordan. "White House Press Corps Doesn't Ask Psaki Any Questions about Fauci's Emails." The Federalist, June 2, 2021. https://thefederalist.com/2021/06/02/white-house-press-corps-doesnt-ask-psaki-any-questions-about-faucis-emails/.

when one member accused them of systemic racism. Brittany Shepherd, a White House correspondent for *Yahoo! News* at the time, demanded to know why there weren't more people of color on the WHCA board.

It was oddly satisfying to watch the board members sputter through excuses for their lack of diversity. One board member pointed out that there are simply not many people of color in journalism overall, let alone covering the White House. He started to convey that maybe people of color just don't want to be journalists, but quickly decided against it, instead promising that the WHCA was looking into ways to recruit more diverse reporters. The question eventually was kicked over to one of the Latino members of the board, who presumably could answer safely.

The fear I saw in the eyes of the WHCA board over one measly question confirmed to me that even the most seasoned, prominent reporters were terrified of being smeared by the progressive left. If the White House Correspondents Association, with its liberal bias and tight grip controlling coverage of some of the most powerful people in the world, was not immune to the perils of wokeness, then what did that mean for the rest of the media?

CHAPTER 12

THE WOKE TAKEOVER

The story of how the media went woke is really a story of self-immolation.

The media spent years cozying up to the Democrats, left-wing activist groups, and liberal academics for story ideas, scoops, and on-the-record quotes. News reporting at major outlets, which were filled with liberal, cosmopolitan elites, became indistinguishable from the Democratic Party platform. This reliance on the left for content, however, made the media vulnerable to the same pressures being exerted on Democratic leadership. In recent years, young radicals like The Squad have pushed the Democrats further to the left than ever before, crowding out moderate voices. New litmus tests for Democratic members emerged: You must support abortion until birth, amnesty for illegals, a green energy overhaul of the economy, special protections for LGBTQ+ Americans, and believe that America is a fundamentally evil place. The blue dogs like Conor Lamb, Tim Ryan, and Joe Manchin are a dying breed who no longer have a place in their own party. As the messaging from Democrats lurches leftward, naturally so does the content published by mainstream media outlets.

Still, there's a far more insidious thing happening to the media. News organizations are routinely responding to a mixture of internal and external pressures from the most maniacal left-wing activists.

Corporate media outlets were acutely aware of allegations that they were too exclusive in their hiring practices. Many news outlets decided to hire less experienced reporters, who instead padded their resumes with campus activism and internships with left-wing organizations. The exact type of woke students I encountered at Georgetown started filling up newsrooms. These young people made no efforts to hide their progressive sympathies and refused to let go of their hostility to classically liberal principles like free speech and diversity of thought. They believed that media outlets should be used as just another megaphone for radical ideas. And why shouldn't they? Newsrooms made clear they were willing to abandon objectivity in favor of taking down Trump and saving democracy. Their abandonment of journalistic standards made it even easier for activist-minded reporters to make the case that the media should be a tool for political progress rather than information.

Editors couldn't put the genie back in the bottle. Wesley Lowery, a thirty-something Pulitzer Prize–winning journalist, argued that objective truth is worthless if it is "decided almost exclusively by white reporters and their mostly white bosses." Even facts couldn't escape the clutches of left-wing identity politics.[128]

---

[128]   Lowery, Wesley. "A Reckoning over Objectivity, Led by Black Journalists." *New York Times*, June 23, 2020. https://www.nytimes.com/2020/06/23/opinion/objectivity-black-journalists-coronavirus.html.

The mostly left-leaning corporate press were flummoxed by the takeover. They had spent the last decade denying that there was even an illiberal shift taking place on college campuses, let alone that it might pose a problem for institutions that hire from universities. The woke millennials pressured their editors to update style guides to reflect progressive values, lobbied for unions and diversity officers, and bullied and publicly shamed anyone who didn't go along with their demands. Newsroom leaders complied, hoping the kids would stop. Instead, just like the campus administrators that gave in to the campus mobs, they were eaten alive.

Each year, thanks to constant internal revolts and the complete absence of real leadership from editors and publishers, the woke millennials take another bite out of objective news coverage and reshape media outlets into their personal platforms for crazier and crazier ideas.

As the inmates take over the asylum, their views are reinforced by relentless Twitter mobs who gang up on media outlets that step out of line. These keyboard warriors signal boost unacceptable tweets to their online circles, leading to aggressive pile-ons, ratios, nasty direct messages, angry emails, canceled subscriptions, and boycotts. Twitter may not be real life, but online harassment campaigns can often feel just as oppressive as face-to-face bullying, particularly to people who aren't prepared to deal with them. News outlets usually end up apologizing and changing their behavior so as not to face the wrath of the social media activists.

Pew Research found that Twitter users are younger, more likely to identify as Democrats, more highly educated, and wealthier than the general population. That same study found that most tweets come from just 10 percent of Twitter users, and that individuals in that group are more likely to be politically active, female, and Democrats.[129] This puts corporate media outlets in an even tighter spot—the Twitter mobs are actually their most loyal consumers. Outlets like the *New York Times*, the *Washington Post*, the *LA Times*, CNN, and MSNBC spent years cultivating audiences among the wealthy, politically active coastal elites by feeding them liberal propaganda.

Newsroom leaders are simultaneously terrified of the damage dealt by the Twitter mob but reliant on them for engagement and clicks to sell advertisements and subscriptions. The media could shift back to the center to win over average Americans. But even the nonwoke reporters are still mostly liberal, so they internalize bad faith social media criticism from their "side." This further undermines the case for impartiality and reinforces a harmful feedback loop that pushes the media further and further left.

The media only has itself to blame for its rapid destruction. They opened the gates and wheeled in the Trojan Horse. Now let's explore exactly how it happened.

---

[129] Wojcik, Stefan, and Adam Hughes. "Sizing up Twitter Users." Pew Research Center: Internet, Science & Tech, January 7, 2021. https://www.pewresearch.org/internet/2019/04/24/sizing-up-twitter-users/.

CHAPTER 13

MEDIA MATTERS

Media Matters, founded by David Brock and funded by George Soros, bills itself as a media watchdog. In practice, it is dedicated to canceling right-wing journalists and media personalities. Media Matters "reports" on commentary that it deems objectionable, then encourages its followers to participate in advertiser boycotts and harassment campaigns. For example, if a Fox News personality says something that a Media Matters researcher finds offensive, Media Matters lists the companies who advertise on that person's show. Left-wing activists and liberal wine moms call the companies en masse and demand they stop running advertisements on Fox News. The goal is to make the most effective conservative communicators unprofitable and thus dispensable.

Being a Media Matters researcher is the perfect job for a former college activist like Madeline Peltz. Remember, Peltz was one of the Oberlin College students who affirmed by signing the *Oberlin Review* letter against Dr. Christina Hoff Sommers's appearance on campus that she believes in deplatforming and silencing people with whom she disagrees. Peltz carried these same values into her current job, where she mostly binges Fox News' *Tucker Carlson Tonight* and finds reasons to target Tucker's advertisers and call for the network to fire him.

Peltz's big break came in 2019 when she stumbled across old audio recordings of Tucker on shock jock Bubba the Love Sponge's radio show.[130] Tucker was heard making some uncouth, edgy jokes—par for the course for the Howard Stern-esque radio programs of the 2000s but wholly unacceptable for the pearl-clutching left.

Other researchers contributed to the exposé of the Tucker tapes, including Courtney Hagle, a former Northeastern University student who used her 2017 internship at the Department of Justice to record a private event with then-Attorney General Jeff Sessions. Hagle demanded to know where the DOJ stood "on issues of LGBT rights" and inaccurately referred to a "ban" on transgender individuals serving in the military during the Trump administration.[131] Only a woke college student would think it is appropriate or ethical to secretly record her boss during an off-the-record meeting, and it explains perfectly why Hagle landed at Media Matters.

Peltz's article was seized upon by the mainstream media. It was the perfect opportunity to take a shot at arguably the most

---

[130] Peltz, Written by Madeline. "In Unearthed Audio, Tucker Carlson Makes Numerous Misogynistic and Perverted Comments." Media Matters for America. https://www.mediamatters.org/tucker-carlson/unearthed-audio-tucker-carlson-makes-numerous-misogynistic-and-perverted-comments.

[131] ABC News. ABC News Network. https://abcnews.go.com/Politics/guarded-sessions-spars-interns-internal-doj-video/story?id=51623744.

powerful man in cable news. The *Washington Post*,[132] CNN,[133] *USA Today*,[134] CBS News,[135] *Business Insider*,[136] and numerous other outlets pounced.

Tucker refused to budge an inch to the cancel mob coming after him. He would not apologize for any "naughty" comments made on the radio program "over a decade ago," instead inviting detractors to watch his show every night to learn what he thinks. And sure enough, he told them. Media Matters, he said, is a "bully" designed to spin up "the great American outrage machine" and silence dissenters.

Media Matters and Peltz took the first shot but were suddenly framed as the victims once Tucker responded to the hit. The *Washington Post's* Eli Rosenberg—the same reporter who falsely claimed that the little migrant girl on the *Time* cover was separated from her mother—ran a glowing profile of Peltz, who

[132] Chiu, Allyson. "Tucker Carlson Unapologetic over 'Misogynistic' Comments on Statutory Rape, Insults against Women." *Washington Post*, March 14, 2019. https://www.washingtonpost.com/nation/2019/03/11/tucker-carlson-calls-women-extremely-primitive-newly-surfaced-audio/.

[133] Stelter, Brian. "Tucker Carlson Defiant against Outrage over Audio Clips: 'We Will Never Bow to the Mob' | CNN Business." Cable News Network, March 12, 2019. https://www.cnn.com/2019/03/11/media/tucker-carlson-bubba-the-love-sponge-audio-clips/index.html.

[134] Cummings, William. "Tucker Carlson Refuses to Apologize amid Uproar over Past Comments on 'Extremely Primitive' Women." USA Today. Gannett Satellite Information Network, March 12, 2019. https://www.usa-today.com/story/news/politics/2019/03/11/fox-tucker-carlson-bubba-love-sponge-comments-spark-uproar/3127666002/.

[135] Picchi, Aimee. "Here's What Tucker Carlson Said That's Sparking Calls for an Ad Boycott." CBS Interactive, March 12, 2019. https://www.cbsnews.com/news/tucker-carlson-bubba-the-love-sponge-women-called-dogs-and-primitive-calls-for-boycott-media-matters-2019-03-11/.

[136] Goggin, Benjamin. "Tucker Carlson Refuses to Apologize after Tapes Surface of Him Calling Women 'Primitive' and Comparing Them to Dogs." Business Insider. https://www.businessinsider.com/tucker-carlson-wont-apologize-for-bubba-the-love-sponge-tapes-2019-3.

was twenty-four at the time.[137] He dishonestly painted Carlson's comments about bullies and outrage machines as a direct reference to Peltz rather than to the incredibly powerful left-wing activist organization of which she is a part.

"In reality, credit for the tapes' publication is due to Peltz: a twenty-something in her first adult job who lives in the basement of a DC house she rents with five other people, a few cats, and a dog named Noodles," Rosenberg wrote without a hint of embarrassment.

The message? Nothing to see here, folks. Just a little ol' twenty-something girl going after the biggest name in the media. This was the same reaction from campus leftists whenever you criticized them. No matter how many times they struck at their opponents, you were not allowed to defend yourself without being accused of oppressing them.

The truth is that Media Matters has an outsized influence on the political landscape because of its acceptance as a reliable source by the mainstream media. Seemingly objective reporters use Media Matters research in their articles, quote their employees as experts, and defend them whenever possible. Why? So reporters can spread left-wing messages without implicating themselves as biased. Wacky, radical ideas presented as fact are conveniently sourced to an outside organization in case of backlash.

Tucker and my former colleague Vince Coglianese reported on the Media Matters and mainstream media feedback loop

---

[137] Rosenberg, Eli. "Tucker Carlson Says He's the Victim of a Powerful Bully. Meet the 24-Year-Old Who Found the Tapes." *Washington Post*, March 14, 2019. https://www.washingtonpost.com/arts-entertainment/2019/03/14/tucker-carlson-says-hes-victim-powerful-bully-meet-year-old-who-found-tapes/.

in 2012.[138] After speaking to current and former staffers, they learned that Media Matters was in direct contact with officials at the Obama White House and executives at MSNBC. They also had a rotating list of reporters with which to dump their opposition research: Greg Sargent at the *Washington Post*, Ben Smith, who was at *BuzzFeed*, and Brian Stelter, who was at the *New York Times*, to name a few. Over at the White House, none other than Jen Psaki, then a deputy communications director for Obama, was a receptive contact for Media Matters.

Media Matters has caused several high-profile firings, including Lou Dobbs, Jeffrey Lord, and Rick Santorum. They've pushed numerous Fox News guests onto the company's PR blacklist. They've launched campaigns for cable and satellite television services to drop Newsmax and One America News, and were successful on the latter.[139] Beyond driving the cancel culture, Media Matters bears a lot of responsibility for the way activist groups impact the media's framing of issues and their use of language. Earlier, I explained how the media takes many of its cues from Democratic politicians and left-wing organizations. Well, as activist groups have gotten more woke, so has media coverage.

In January 2022, Florida Republicans started working to pass the "Parental Rights in Education" bill, a fairly standard anti-indoctrination effort that banned the teaching of developmentally

---

138 Coglianese, Tucker Carlson and Vince. "Inside Media Matters: Sources, Memos Reveal Erratic Behavior, Close Coordination with White House and News Organizations." The Daily Caller, September 7, 2015. https://dailycaller.com/2012/02/12/inside-media-matters-sources-memos-reveal-erratic-behavior-close-coordination-with-white-house-and-news-organizations/.

139 "After Months of Outrage from Free Press and Allies, DIRECTV Drops One America News Network." Free Press, January 15, 2022. https://www.freepress.net/news/press-releases/after-months-outrage-free-press-and-allies-directv-drops-one-america-news.

inappropriate lessons on sex and gender to children in kindergarten through third grade. The bill also required schools to notify parents about major changes to their child's physical and mental state while carving out reasonable exemptions for cases of suspected parental abuse.

I searched far and wide for the first known use of the bill's de facto nickname: "Don't Say Gay." A group called "Equality Florida" first tweeted out that moniker on January 19, 2022.[140] Equality Florida falsely claimed that the Parental Rights in Education bill would "block teachers from talking about LGBTQ people or issues" and urged its supporters to contact state legislators and tell them to oppose the legislation. By the next day, several Democratic lawmakers in Florida were promising to fight the legislation, and *Newsweek* ran an article repeating Equality Florida's allegation that the bill could "block kids with LGBTQ parents from discussing family in class."[141] Chasten Buttigieg, the husband of Transportation Secretary Pete Buttigieg, insisted on Twitter that the legislation would "kill kids."

The Hill appears to be the first mainstream media outlet that actually used the false "Don't Say Gay" nickname in an article

---

[140] Florida, Equality. "Alert FL Lawmakers Are Voting Tomorrow on the Dangerous 'Don't Say Gay' Bill That Would Block Teachers from Talking about LGBTQ People or Issues. Rush a Message to Committee Members Telling Them to Vote No on HB 1557: Https://T.co/tn4e5oeyej Pic.twitter.com/f8dsmmws0x." Twitter, January 19, 2022. https://twitter.com/equalityfl/status/1483912126867681280?lang=en.

[141] Thomas, Jake. "Florida Bill Could Block Kids with LGBTQ Parents from Discussing Family in Class, Critics Say." Newsweek, January 21, 2022. https://www.newsweek.com/florida-bill-could-block-kids-lgbtq-parents-discussing-family-class-some-say-1671450.

headline on January 21, 2022.[142] The article was published under the outlet's "Changing America" project, which we'll get into later.

By the next week, the *Guardian*,[143] CNN,[144] *Vanity Fair*,[145] and the *Washington Post*[146] were unflinchingly using "Don't Say Gay," only sometimes stopping to attribute the misleading moniker to "critics." Other mainstream outlets soon took the hint, and Media Matters had spent the early part of the year sending out warning signs to others who didn't comply with their preferred narratives on transgender issues.

Well before joining the fight on "Don't Say Gay," Media Matters was framing the acceptable parameters for reporting on legislation that would ban biological men from competing in women's sports. Their big rub was that news outlets would report on these "anti-trans" laws without interviewing transgender people.

"Florida print media rarely spoke to transgender people in reporting on a bill banning trans athletes from competing," Media

[142] Migdon, Brooke. "House Committee in Florida Passes 'Don't Say Gay' Bill." The Hill, January 21, 2022. https://thehill.com/changing-america/respect/equality/590838-house-committee-in-florida-passes-dont-say-gay-bill/.

[143] "Florida: Republican Panel Advances Bill to Ban LGBTQ+ Discussion in Schools." The Guardian News and Media, January 24, 2022. https://www.theguardian.com/us-news/2022/jan/24/florida-republican-committee-dont-say-gay-bill.

[144] "Florida Lawmaker Says 'Don't Say Gay' Bill Is a 'Step Backward' - Cnn Video." Cable News Network, January 24, 2022. https://www.cnn.com/videos/politics/2022/01/24/florida-dont-say-gay-bill-reax-nr-vpx.cnn.

[145] Levin, Bess. "Surprise: Florida Republicans Want to Ban Talk of Sexual Orientation and Gender Identity in Schools." *Vanity Fair*, January 26, 2022. https://www.vanityfair.com/news/2022/01/florida-dont-say-gay-bill.

[146] Wojcik, Stefan, and Adam Hughes. "Sizing up Twitter Users." Pew Research Center: Internet, Science & Tech, January 7, 2021. https://www.pewresearch.org/internet/2019/04/24/sizing-up-twitter-users/.

Matters wrote in the spring of 2021.[147] The article also accused news outlets of "misgendering" trans women by referring to them as "biological males." It also wasn't appropriate, Media Matters claimed, for news outlets to give equal weight to voices in favor of and against sports bans, because it wrongly suggested that "trans rights" are up for debate. A majority of Americans believe transgender people should play on sports teams that correspond with their sex, but Media Matters was strong-arming news outlets into pretending that the issue was settled.

Media outlets couldn't get away with backing off coverage of transgender issues either. Media Matters criticized major TV outlets for their scarce coverage of transgender sports bans.[148] Liberal outlets had an obligation to weigh in, Media Matters said, otherwise they were complicit in allowing Fox News to air its "anti-trans" news packages without pushback. Media Matter shamed its liberal allies in the media into taking the radical, left-wing side on an issue likely to alienate the average American viewer. Just a few years ago, it would have been unthinkable to defend an adult male like UPenn swimmer Lia Thomas jumping into the pool with women and parading around the women's locker room with male genitalia flapping in the breeze. Now, media outlets had to comply or face the wrath of Media Matters and the rest of the pro-trans lobby.

---

[147] Wexler, Written by Casey, and Zachary Pleat Research contributions from Alex Walker. "Florida Print Media Rarely Spoke to Transgender People in Reporting on a Bill Banning Trans Athletes from Competing." Media Matters for America. https://www.mediamatters.org/local-news/florida-print-media-rarely-spoke-transgender-people-reporting-bill-banning-trans.

[148] Wexler, Written by Casey, and Zachary Pleat Research contributions from Alex Walker. "Florida Print Media Rarely Spoke to Transgender People in Reporting on a Bill Banning Trans Athletes from Competing." Media Matters for America. https://www.mediamatters.org/local-news/florida-print-media-rarely-spoke-transgender-people-reporting-bill-banning-trans.

Ari Drennen, the LGBTQ program director at Media Matters, was responsible for much of the organization's ensuing coverage on the Parental Rights in Education—er, "Don't Say Gay"—bill. Drennen authored a piece complaining about the influence of the "Libs of TikTok" Twitter account, which reposts videos of wacky teachers indoctrinating their students with radical race and gender ideology. Drennen would end up being quoted and Drennen's piece cited in the *Washington Post* when the outlet doxxed the owner of "Libs of TikTok." We'll dig into the full story there later.

Drennen's foray into left-wing politics started, like most of today's young activists and reporters, on campus. Drennen attended Middlebury College in Vermont under the name "Zach" and was identified as a male under his college sailing records. Drennen authored a regular political column for the campus newspaper called "Apply Liberally"[149] and served on a student panel protesting against Middlebury's "hypocritical" investment in fossil fuels.[150] Post-graduation, Zach Drennen worked on the press team for the Hillary campaign in 2016 and as a communications manager with Climate Advisers, a policy group seeking to lower carbon emissions. Drennen continued to cover climate issues at the Center for American Progress, a left-wing think tank, and, at some point, changed his name to Ari and started presenting as a woman. Not long after Drennen transitioned, he moved to Media Matters and started shaping wider media coverage of transgender issues.

---

149 "About." Apply Liberally, May 2, 2013. https://zachdrennen.wordpress.com/about/.

150 Daniel Ross is a Los Angeles-based journalist with bylines in Truthout, and Daniel Ross is a Los Angeles-based journalist with bylines in Truthout. "Opinion: Can We Reach 100 Percent Renewable Energy in Time to Avert Climate Catastrophe?" Common Dreams, August 28, 2019. https://www.commondreams.org/views/2019/08/28/can-we-reach-100-percent-renewable-energy-time-avert-climate-catastrophe.

The *Post*, a mainstream corporate news outlet, treated Drennen as an expert on the Parental Rights in Education bill. Readers were not informed of Drennen's long history as a left-wing political activist nor his personal interest in the issue. His comments were used as justification for a Bezos-backed cancelation campaign that outed a private citizen for holding the wrong political opinions.

Media Matters will do anything to silence debate on left-wing causes. Just a few years into my career, I became a target of one of their cancel campaigns by speaking negatively about the Democratic "Squad" in Congress.

I don't really like talking or even writing about this because it's embarrassing and painful to be constantly reminded of one of your biggest mistakes. I've only written about it once before and that was for the "Canceled" edition of the *Spectator*'s monthly US magazine. However, if there's any place to retell my side of the story, then it's my own book, dammit.

In February 2019, I was on NRA TV to talk about recent anti-Semitic comments from Reps. Ilhan Omar and Rashida Tlaib. This was something of a running trend for the pair, who often couched their anti-Semitism under the guise of being pro-Palestine or in support of the BDS movement, which calls for boycotts, divestments, and sanctions on Israeli industries.

Timothy Johnson, a Media Matters researcher who has been working with the left-wing activist group since before I graduated high school, decided that this could not stand. He posted a screenshot of my interview on NRA TV alongside additional screenshots of Holocaust jokes I made in high school.

The jokes were admittedly very offensive and I am not proud of them. However, they were not evidence of some secret anti-Semitism that I'd been harboring for years. The truth is that I am a practicing Catholic, and in the spring of 2012, I started dating a Jewish guy from a nearby high school. Our religious differences were never an issue, but our friend group liked to crack jokes to one another about how we must secretly hate each other. We further poked fun at the dynamic by googling and sending each other the most offensive jokes we could find about Jews and Catholics. In my case, these were Holocaust jokes. In his case, jokes about Catholic priests being pedophiles. No harm, no foul.

Years later, I started working in conservative media and saw conservatives across the industry getting smeared by the left for jokes, statements taken out of context, old tweets, and the like and decided it would be a good idea to clear my tweet history. I believe it was in 2017 that I deleted anything I had tweeted more than a year prior.

This didn't stop Timothy Johnson, who apparently couldn't get a job anywhere else with his art history degree from George Washington University. He had either saved screenshots of the tweets for years or got them from someone else who did. What kind of sicko holds onto screenshots of high school tweets for years, waiting for the most opportune moment to strike? Very disturbing and evil, if you ask me.

Anyway, Johnson posted the tweets in 2019 and all hell broke loose. I was receiving countless messages telling me I was a horrible person and that I better kill myself. The *Daily Caller* got emails and phone calls demanding I be fired. The left even managed to track down my sister-in-law's Instagram and sent her the screenshots, asking if she knew that I was a bigot. My old progressive buddies from Georgetown celebrated my apparent demise on their social media accounts, declaring that it "couldn't have happened to a nicer person."

I drafted an apology. I didn't explain the circumstances involving my Jewish boyfriend because I didn't want to be seen as making excuses for the tweets. I agreed that they were bad. I felt sorry for sending them and I didn't mean to hurt anyone.

Here was my apology:

> *"I sincerely apologize for past tweets of mine from when I was in high school. At the time they were written, they were intended as jokes among high school friends. I understand now that they were not funny and are in fact extremely harmful. This past behavior does not reflect who I am today and will be one of the regrets I carry with me for the rest of my life. Hope that in due time, I hope that I shall earn forgiveness or my grave error in judgment and demonstrate that I am no longer the stupid person who made those awful statements."*

I regret apologizing. Not because I wasn't sorry, but because the people coming after me didn't deserve one. They were not interested in forgiveness, only destruction. They threw the apology back in my face:

> *Too little, too late, Amber!*
> *You should've known better.*
> *You don't deserve forgiveness.*
> *You work for the Daily Caller, so clearly you haven't learned anything.*
> *How can we believe you're no longer a bigot when you're still openly a conservative?*
> *Your parents clearly raised you to be a racist.*
> *A tiger can't change its stripes.*

The responses to my apology made clear to me that there was a deep cynicism behind modern attempts at "canceling" political enemies. Much like the left-wing students at Georgetown threw around accusations of racism and homophobia to keep me from campus activism, Media Matters and its allies were using whatever tools available to them to keep me out of the media. They knew that I was good at my job. They knew that my message was getting out to millions of people each month. So, they had to shut me up by whatever means possible. They could not accept an apology because that would defeat the purpose of smearing me in the first place.

I managed to keep my job—barely—but the tweets still follow me, three years after they were made public by Timothy Johnson and ten years after I first sent them as a teenager. Every time I say something that the left doesn't like, whether it's speaking out against biological men competing against women in sports or defending a Republican politician from a dishonest media hit job, there are always people in my mentions using my high school tweets to discredit me.

Media Matters' cynical use of racism, transphobia, homophobia, or any other accusation of bigotry is especially craven because they ignore these things when they happen in-house. Angelo Carusone, the president and CEO of Media Matters, has his own history of anti-Semitic and transphobic content on his personal blog.

Carusone complained that "trannies" are considered "attractive," warned people to stay away from "tranny bars," and downplayed the sexual abuse of young girls in Japan, writing, "lighten up, Japs." In other posts, Carusone referred to "Jewish gold" and said that his boyfriend is adorable "despite his Jewry."

When confronted with these posts, Carusone, without a shred of self-awareness, said they were being used in "bad faith." He later alleged to the *Washington Post*—clearly a reliable friend of Media Matters—that the blogs were meant as a "right-wing parody," a dubious claim considering the rest of the blog championed left-wing causes and Democratic political candidates.[151] There were no calls for Carusone to resign from his post, nor internal backlash from staff.

It would be easy to laugh off Media Matters as a goofy left-wing blog if the mainstream media hadn't granted them legitimacy. Unfortunately, they've been given a huge platform to smear and destroy conservatives, spread wild lies with impunity, and frame public debate around radical, left-wing standards.

Oh, and they do it all tax-free, thanks to their status as a nonprofit organization.

---

[151] Hasson, Peter. "Media Matters President Misleads about Offensive Blog Posts––with Brian Stelter's Help." The Daily Caller, March 14, 2019. https://dailycaller.com/2019/03/14/media-matters-carusone-stelter/.

CHAPTER 14

POLITIC—OH NO!

C asual news consumers outside of the DC beltway may not be familiar with *Politico* but for denizens of the swamp, it is pretty much required reading. *Politico* grew its readership on the wildly successful "Playbook," a daily round up of the biggest political stories and DC gossip in one easily digestible morning newsletter.

Politico used to be considered one of the less biased corporate outlets in political journalism. Reporters at left-wing outlets would often complain that *Politico* was being too nice or too fair to Republicans. Other times, they'd take issue with the outlet's play-calling approach to politics, crying that this style did not treat life-or-death policy decisions with the seriousness they deserved. Oddly enough, the supposedly corporation-hating left never seemed to have much problem with the fact that *Politico*'s national security newsletter was sponsored by defense contractor Lockheed Martin or that its COVID-19 newsletter was sponsored by pharmaceutical lobbyist PhRMA. Hmm.

As *Politico*'s readership and influence grew, so did its newsroom. A former *Politico* reporter told me that the outlet began hiring less experienced reporters who made no effort to conceal their progressive sympathies and were keen on newsroom efforts to promote so-called diversity and inclusion, enact arbitrary new reporting standards, and develop style guides that contained partisan language on everything from abortion to LGBTQ issues. Another current reporter says newsroom activism escalated after the death of George Floyd in the summer of 2020, after which *Politico* sent out a new style guide to reporters updating some of its standards on race. In June 2020, the company elevated Robin Turner, a copy editor and manager of diversity initiatives, to a full-time director of editorial diversity initiatives.

These simmering issues fully burst into the open in January 2021. *Politico*'s longtime Playbook writers, Anna Palmer and Jake Sherman, announced in the fall that they were leaving the company to start their own media venture. Instead of immediately choosing a replacement, *Politico* said they would have a rotating cast of guest writers for the daily newsletter. Seeking a bit of ideological diversity, *Politico* gave guest writing spots to PBS's Yamiche Alcindor, MSNBC's Chris Hayes, the *Free Beacon*'s Eliana Johnson, and former *New York Times* opinion editor James Bennet.

When *Politico* leadership let *Daily Wire* founder and conservative radio host Ben Shapiro take the reins, the newsroom revolted.

Shapiro's Playbook was standard, run-of-the-mill conservative thought. He mostly wrote about why Republicans didn't want to vote to impeach Trump over the Capitol riot, explaining that the party felt the Democrats' goal was not just to punish Trump for his rhetoric but also to make all conservatives complicit in the events of January 6.[152]

---

[152] Shapiro, Ben. "Politico Playbook: The Real Reason Most Republicans Opposed Impeachment." POLITICO, January 14, 2021. https://www.politico.com/newsletters/playbook/2021/01/14/the-real-reason-most-republicans-opposed-impeachment-491399.

The young progressive staffers decided that their bosses had gone a bridge too far. The problem wasn't that Shapiro was a conservative, they claimed, but that he was a bigot who did not deserve to use Playbook as a platform for his incendiary views. Internal message boards lit up with complaints from staff who demanded leadership apologize for publishing Shapiro.

Matt Kaminski offered the staffers a dialogue. As one former *Politico* reporter put it, Kaminski asked the mob to put down their pitchforks and torches and invited them into the castle. More than 240 staffers showed up on a Zoom call to share their "disappointment" with leadership over the Shapiro Playbook, according to the *Washington Post*.[153] One former employee who was on the call said a young staffer expressed that having Shapiro write for them was like giving a platform to David Duke, the former leader of the Ku Klux Klan.

Shapiro, it's worth reminding, is an Orthodox Jew.

Kaminski, to his credit, refused to apologize for allowing Shapiro a guest spot on Playbook, telling staffers that it was important for their audience to hear from conservative voices.

"What sets Politico apart in this intense political and media moment is that we rise above partisanship and ideological warfare—even as many seek to drag us into it," *Politico* said in a statement. "It's a core value of the publication that is unchangeable, and that above all protects our ability to do independent journalism. It's a part of our mission."

---

[153] Zadi, Elahe. "Politico Brought Ben Shapiro on as a 'Playbook' Guest Author to Bring Balance. It Brought a Backlash Instead." *Washington Post*, January 15, 2021. https://www.washingtonpost.com/media/2021/01/14/playbook-ben-shapiro/.

More than one hundred *Politico* staffers elevated the Playbook issue to publisher Robert Allbritton.[154] They signed a letter demanding *Politico* update editorial standards, increase newsroom diversity, and issue an apology to staff for publishing Shapiro. Although it does not seem *Politico* ever apologized, it was still too late. The staff Zoom meeting allowed the internal groupthink that had developed inside the newsroom, particularly among younger reporters and staffers on the business side, to be brought into the light. Woke employees realized they had many like-minded allies, and they were determined to band together and flex their muscles.

One month later, the left-wing Twitter mob was equally as desperate for a scalp over the Shapiro incident and a public spat between reporter Tara Palmeri and White House press secretary TJ Ducklo. (Ducklo threatened to "destroy" Palmeri, who was reporting on an inappropriate relationship between Ducklo and *Axios* reporter Alexi McCammond.) *Politico* top brass forced reporter Marc Caputo to publicly apologize for retweeting a meme about Kamala Harris that her rabid fan club, the KHive, deemed "sexist."[155] *Politico* editors often told employees to ignore Twitter because it wasn't "real life" but were also allowing social media backlash to dictate personnel decisions.

By March 2021, *Politico* was again plagued by internal troubles. Newsroom activists seized on an article titled "GOP seizes on women's sports as unlikely wedge issue." The article, authored by political reporter Gabby Orr, explored how Republicans

---

[154] Sarnoff, Marisa. "More Than 100 Politico Staffers Reportedly Send Letter to Publisher Over Ben Shapiro's Edition of Playbook," Mediaite, January 25, 2021, https://www.mediaite.com/news/more-than-100-politico-staffers-re-portedly-send-letter-to-publisher-over-ben-shapiros-edition-of-playbook/

[155] Goldblatt, Daniel. "Politico Reporter Apologizes for Sharing Sexist Meme of Kamala Harris." TheWrap, February 27, 2021. https://www.thewrap.com/marc-caputo-politico-apologizes-kamala-harris-meme/.

sought to position themselves as defenders of women's sports against transgender athletes.

A source briefed on the situation said Orr was informed by *Politico*'s Director of Editorial Diversity Initiatives Robin Turner that two colleagues had voiced concerns about her story. Turner wanted to arrange a meeting to discuss them. During the course of that meeting, Orr was probed about her employment history at the *Washington Examiner*, a center-right outlet, and asked why the story omitted any transgender voices—though the piece had quoted Kate Oakley, senior counsel at the Human Rights Campaign, an activist organization dedicated to LGBTQ+ issues, extensively.

Orr's colleagues also complained that she quoted conservatives, such as American Principles Project director Terry Schilling and former White House policy adviser Stephen Miller, without "contextualizing" their comments. Miller was quoted as saying that he believed that the issue of transgender athletes in women's sports would help Republicans win the midterm elections because the left's position would alienate "non-ideological voters." Schilling pessimistically praised left-wing activists for their ability to convince the American public that transgender people were facing a wave of violence even though when "you look at the numbers…it's, like, 40 people." Orr, her colleagues argued, should have explicitly told readers that those remarks were offensive and transphobic.

One meeting attendee took issue with the phrase "biological women," which appeared three times in the piece, but only by individuals Orr quoted. Her colleagues again described the phrase as offensive to transgender readers.

Turner suggested at the meeting's conclusion that Orr's colleagues serve as "sensitivity readers"—i.e., individuals who could make sure Orr wasn't causing offense—prior to publication of future stories about transgender issues.

Orr had written a 5,000-word *Politico* magazine cover story on the same subject only six months earlier that extensively quoted transgender individuals and had not drawn internal complaints. Multiple sources point back to that Shapiro Zoom meeting as the moment that emboldened *Politico* staff to start pushing back on colleagues who did not write about issues in the overtly partisan way they desired. They also all confirmed that multiple other *Politico* reporters were given warnings about their coverage of transgender issues.

On July 2, 2021, the company held a seminar with three transgender individuals charged with helping the newsroom learn to report on transgender issues in a "more comprehensive and inclusive way." Tre'vell Anderson, editor at large at *Xtra*, Bethany Grace Howe, CEO of the TransHealth Data Collective, and Kate Sosin, LGBTQ+ reporter at *The 19th*, lectured reporters on a Zoom call about the inherent transphobia in their reporting.

I obtained a copy of an email from *Politico* editors summarizing "highlights" from the seminar. The panelists informed reporters that what they consider the "neutral" position on transgender issues was probably created by "white, cisgender men" and thus cannot be trusted to be accurate. Gendered words, they said, can be rooted in "exclusion" and can actually cause "trauma" for transgender and gender-neutral individuals. One former *Politico* reporter who attended the seminar said the panelists complained that the word "mother" could potentially be offensive when used by reporters and mocked reporters who had a hard time grappling with the grammatical implications of referring to singular individuals as "they/them."

"So many non-trans journalists get caught up in the 'meaning' of certain words that they don't realize the many ways that a certain word can mean different things to different people, and the ways in which various languages carry trauma and carry triggering motivations for folks and how our feelings about the meaning of certain words are rooted in exclusion," Anderson said.

The panelists warned journalists that they cannot simply cover "both sides" of the transgender issue, because they could be elevating transphobic voices.

"The job of journalists historically always has been to speak truth to power and it's a violation of journalistic ethics to entertain any conversation that paints transphobia as legitimate," Sosin said.

"Giving these people the balance of both sides does disrespect to the idea that there are facts and that not all 'facts' are created equal," Howe echoed.

What do these folks consider to be antitrans or transphobic? Sosin has said that the phrase "biological male" is an "antitrans slur" and that women not wanting to share a bathroom with a man is transphobic. Howe complained on Twitter that they were called "sir" on the phone by a FedEx employee. Anderson has described bills banning biological males from women's sports as "antitrans" legislation. Factual language, honest mistakes, and reasonable concerns about deep-rooted biological differences will not be tolerated by the trans lobby.

These radical views on gender permeated the newsroom, according to a source who overheard an editor arguing with colleagues about using "birthing people" over "birthing moms" because the latter could be seen as offensive and exclusive.

One former *Politico* staffer said the constant newsroom tensions over questions of diversity and inclusion spiraled into attempts by younger staffers to unionize. The newsroom union, this staffer explained, was merely an extension of the woke crowd showing their true colors after the Shapiro firestorm. According to reporting by the *Daily Beast*, unionization advocates were forced to address questions on whether or not they were the "woke police" after some White House reporters expressed concerns about the effort. During early discussions, the union considered asking *Politico* to allow reporters to attend political activism events in their free time, but that idea was scrapped. *Politico* officially recognized the union, which was formed under NewsGuild, in November 2021.

A few weeks after the transgender seminar, *Politico* appointed a new "standards editor" to oversee the tone of editorial content. Anita Kumar, my old friend from the White House Correspondents Association, was given the newly minted title of "Senior Editor, Standards & Ethics." Laughably, her biography says the standards editor's focus will be "accuracy, fairness, clarity and nonpartisanship."

A style guide sent to staff in January 2022 reads more like a game of Media Matters mad libs than a document for journalists. Here are some examples of noninclusive words that *Politico* reporters should avoid using in their articles:

- Mankind
- Man-made
- Manhunt
- Crack the whip—unacceptable because of origins in slavery
- Waiter or waitress—"server" should be used instead
- Biological gender, biological sex, biological woman, biological female, biological man, or biological male
- Illegal immigrant or illegal alien
- Cake walk—"originated during slavery" and thus perpetuates "racist motifs"

- In reference to illegal migration: onslaught, tidal wave, flood, inundation, surge, invasion, army, march, sneak and stealth
- Anchor baby
- Chain migration—this is a term used by "immigration hard-liners"
- Peanut gallery—"The cheapest seats often occupied by Black people and people with low incomes"
- Third-world countries—too "derogatory"

Reporter should also not:

- Say that a transgender person "identifies as" a certain gender—this questions their existence
- Describe the current situation at the border as a "crisis"— According to the style guide, "While the sharp increase in the arrival of unaccompanied minors is a problem for border officials, a political challenge for the Biden administration and a dire situation for many migrants who make the journey, it does not fit the dictionary definition of a crisis."
- Portray migrants as a "negative, harmful influence"

The style guide also has a special section for "Standards on Culture & Inclusivity". Some quoted highlights (emphasis *Politico*'s):

– Do not use "pro-choice" or "pro-life" outside of quoted material. **Use abortion rights, abortion rights supporter or anti-abortion**—When describing abortion issues, consider using gender-neutral language like "people who seek abortions" or "patients who seek abortions" rather

than "women who seek abortions," as there are nonfe-
male-identifying people who are able to become pregnant.
- **Late-term abortion**—Do not use; opt instead for "abortion later in pregnancy"
- Generally, avoid references to a transgender person
being born a boy or girl, and opt for phrasing such as
"identified at birth as boy/girl." A person's biology does
not take precedence over their gender identity, and such
oversimplifications can invalidate the person's current,
authentic gender.
- Consider using gender-neutral language like "pregnant
people" or "people using birth control," rather than
"pregnant women," as there are nonfemale identifying
people who are able to become pregnant, require reproductive healthcare, etc.
- Unlike Black, white should not be capitalized in any
instances, even when referring to race
- **Crippling**—When possible, substitute a different word
to avoid the negative association with the word "cripple,"
which is offensive and should not be used.... The same
substitution rule goes for words like "paralyzing."

Kumar sent out another email to staff in March 2022 promising that she and other senior editors "have been engaged in
conversations" on the topic of transgender coverage "with many
journalists in the newsroom for several weeks."

"We've been working on identifying ways to strengthen our
content, including updating our stylebook, holding small group
discussions and organizing additional training," Kumar wrote.

Thanks to the constant complaints by woke staffers, transgender coverage at *Politico* now reads like pure propaganda over
well-informed and reasoned reportage. A piece in Playbook

Nightly authored by Renuka Rayasam and published in late March "explained" the issue of medical transitions for children to readers.[156] The article referred to puberty blockers, hormone therapies, and surgeries for children as "gender-affirming medical care" and quoted three "transgender health experts," all of whom downplayed potentially life-altering and damaging side effects of such treatments. Effects of hormone therapy on future fertility and bone density, one of the doctors claimed, for example, could be "reversed."

Politico continues to make poor choices that will accelerate its descent into madness. The same month Kumar sent her email assuring staff that more would be done for the trans lobby, *Politico* hired Dafna Linzer over from NBC News. Linzer now serves as the publication's executive editor. In March 2019, Linzer allegedly tried to bully HuffPost reporter Yashar Ali out of reporting on a scoop about the dates of that year's Democratic National Committee primary debates. After Ali reached out to the DNC for confirmation, he received a call from Linzer, who demanded he wait an hour to publish the story so the DNC could have time to call its delegates first. Ali said Linzer got "exasperated" when he wouldn't agree. NBC News and Linzer declined to comment on the story.

Given all of the power seized by left-wing activists in the newsroom over the past few years, the last thing *Politico* needs is an editor that's willing to shill for the DNC. It seems unlikely that Linzer will try to halt the woke left who have seized editorial control.

---

[156] Rayasam, Renuka. "The Transgender Care That States Are Banning, Explained." POLITICO, March 25, 2022. https://www.politico.com/newsletters/politico-nightly/2022/03/25/the-transgender-care-that-states-are-banning-explained-00020580.

CHAPTER 15

THE HILL TO DIE ON

A similar internal staff revolt unfolded at *The Hill*, another DC-based political news organization, over the past few years.

Just as when *Politico* staffers lambasted their editors for publishing Ben Shapiro and demanded an apology, low-level reporters and editors at *The Hill* sought to usurp editorial control through a series of formal complaints that were selectively leaked to outside media outlets.

In the last six months of 2017, reporter John Solomon was a star in right-wing media. Solomon published a number of major stories that were damaging to Democrats, including one that found prominent lawyer Lisa Bloom had sought payments for women who might accuse President Donald Trump of sexual misconduct. Solomon was also focused on reporting on corruption between US government officials and Ukraine and Russia, the Clinton Foundation, and Russiagate.

Young staffers at *The Hill* were not pleased that their outlet was being used to undermine the left. They were also quite unhappy that Solomon had become a frequent guest on Fox News host Sean Hannity's primetime opinion program.

In January 2018, they demanded that management launch an internal review of all of Solomon's reporting, which they alleged fell short of appropriate journalistic standards. Regarding the story about Lisa Bloom paying sexual misconduct accusers, staff wanted to know if *The Hill* assigned a female editor to read the article before publication for sensitivity purposes.[157]

These staffers were communicating about their grievances with Solomon's reporting over their work email accounts, boldly using company resources to organize official complaints against their bosses. These official complaints went over the heads of their direct supervisors and were instead presented to the company's owner and executive editor, according to a source familiar with the situation. Then, the staffers leaked everything to the media to publicly shame *The Hill* into acting.[158]

"They basically made it out like they ran the show," the source said.

By May 2018, Solomon was reassigned to the opinion side of the operation, while staffers internally pushed for more action against the conservative reporter bringing disrepute to the mostly liberal newsroom. Over the next year, Solomon continued to rile up his left-wing colleagues by reporting on alleged corruption between the Biden family and Ukraine, with a tight focus on Hunter Biden's seat on the board of Ukrainian energy company

---

[157] Wemple, Erik. "Opinion | Staffers at the Hill Press Management about the Work of John Solomon." *Washington Post,* December 1, 2021. https://www.washingtonpost.com/blogs/erik-wemple/wp/2018/01/17/staffers-at-the-hill-press-management-about-the-work-of-john-solomon/.

[158] Wemple, Erik. "Opinion | Staffers at the Hill Press Management about the Work of John Solomon." *Washington Post,* December 1, 2021. https://www.washingtonpost.com/blogs/erik-wemple/wp/2018/01/17/staffers-at-the-hill-press-management-about-the-work-of-john-solomon/.

Burisma. Solomon left *The Hill* in the fall of 2019 to launch his own news outlet, and *The Hill* quickly announced in a staffwide memo that it would be conducting an independent, internal review of all of his work. The memo was, naturally, immediately leaked to *Politico*.

"Because of our dedication to accurate, non-partisan reporting and standards, we are reviewing, updating, annotating, and when appropriate, correcting any opinion pieces referenced during the ongoing congressional inquiry," editor-in-chief Bob Cusack wrote.

A few months later, *The Hill* announced the results of the investigation and gave the young staffers what they wanted. The news outlet said that Solomon had "failed to identify" key information about his sources, some of whom were known to be unreliable, under criminal investigation, or that some were his own lawyers.[159] *The Hill* also took some responsibility by claiming that they should've made a clearer distinction between Solomon's opinion columns and his work as a news reporter.

Although there seemed to be some issues with Solomon's reporting, the situation was inappropriately handled. Low-level staffers should not have been weighing in on the practices of senior editors or newsroom leadership, nor should they have been leaking internal documents and communications to outside news publications. These were the oft-used tactics of the campus mob, which used relentless protest and public-shaming devices to get people in power to comply with their demands. Leadership at *The Hill* was supposedly warned about the consequences of incentivizing the mob within its newsroom but ignored those concerns, putting more blood in the water.

---

[159] "The Hill Finds John Solomon 'Failed' to Identify Key Details of Sources." POLITICO. https://www.politico.com/news/2020/02/19/hill-john-solomon-failed-disclose-details-115976.

The staffers were emboldened by the success they had in delegitimizing Solomon and decided to shift their concerns to questions of race and diversity in the newsroom. This manifested itself in the summer of 2020 during the Black Lives Matter protests against George Floyd's death.

"The staff was trying to set the editorial direction around the types of phrases that are being used around anti-racism," a former *Hill* staffer told me, "and trying to censor anybody who would try and speak out against the narrative."

None of *The Hill's* articles about the police shooting of Jacob Blake in Kenosha, Wisconsin, for example, mentioned that Blake had confirmed having a knife that day and picking it up off the ground during his interaction with police. *The Hill* hardly covered violence stemming from the Floyd protests outside of the opinion section, except when Portland police officially declared riots outside of a law enforcement building in the downtown area.

A couple of months later, *The Hill* hosted a "Diversity & Inclusion Summit,"[160] alleging that "significant barriers to justice, equal opportunity and inclusion still exist for many Black, Hispanic, LGBTQ+ and minority Americans."

"What will it take for diversity, inclusion, and equity to become more than just buzzwords?" *The Hill* asked in its description of the event, which featured Democratic lawmakers and numerous left-wing activists. Just one Republican, a congresswoman from Puerto Rico, spoke during the summit.

The Hill's genuflection to the left seemed to only embolden its young, woke staffers. A *Hill* editorial project called "Changing

---

[160] Sponsors: International Franchise Association, National Association of Realtors. "Diversity & Inclusion Summit." The Hill, April 6, 2022. https://thehill.com/event/524205-diversity-inclusion-summit/.

America" that was launched in the fall of 2019[161] to take a "centrist" approach to citizenship has become indistinguishable from the now-defunct *ThinkProgress* blog. The website was the first to use the "Don't Say Gay" moniker in a headline to describe Florida's Parental Rights in Education, even though the nickname was created by a left-wing LGBTQ+ group and doesn't accurately reflect the contents of the bill.

Other articles on the Changing America website offered to "[debunk] myths about trans women in sports," and fretted that the United States was falling behind on climate goals, which would certainly mean "record droughts and tropical storms." They described medical transitions for transgender individuals as "gender-affirming care" and claimed that new passports with an option to put "X" for gender over "male" or "female" can be "critical to the health and safety of nonbinary" individuals.

Why would *The Hill* invest money in a project that is so out-of-touch with the concerns of average Americans other than to virtue signal about how woke they are? Perhaps the "Changing America" site is a cynical ploy to prevent future hand-wringing from competitors about how they dared to publish investigative pieces that were damaging to the Democrats.

---

[161] Wemple, Erik. "Opinion | 'Changing America': The Hill Is Launching a 'Centrist' Site on Citizenship." *Washington Post*, November 5, 2019. https://www.washingtonpost.com/opinions/2019/11/05/changing-america-hill-is-launching-centrist-site-citizenship/.

CHAPTER 16

DEMOCRACY DIES IN WOKENESS

The *Washington Post* started grappling with wokeness a few years ago when Editor Marty Baron cracked down on reporters sharing left-wing hot takes on social media, worried that the paper would lose its remaining thin veneer of objectivity.

Wesley Lowery, who I previously quoted as believing that objectivity is a tool of the white man, was the first to face Baron's wrath in 2019. Lowery posted several tweets criticizing the *New York Times* for publishing an article about the Tea Party that didn't note that the movement was "essentially a hysterical grassroots tantrum about the fact that a black guy was president."[162] The *Times*, fresh off its publication of the "1619 Project," dutifully added more "context" about race to the article. The *Post*,

---

[162] Tani, Maxwell. "Washington Post Threatened Reporter Wesley Lowery over Tweets." The Daily Beast, February 3, 2020. https://www.thedailybeast.com/washington-post-threatened-another-star-reporter-wesley-lowery-over-his-tweets.

however, was not happy with Lowery. Baron suggested that if Lowery was going to share opinions on his Twitter account, then he would need to be reassigned to the opinion pages of the *Post* or go work for an advocacy organization. If it happened again, Baron warned, Lowery would be fired.

The following year, the *Post* took issue with another ill-advised tweet from reporter Felicia Sonmez. Shortly after basketball superstar Kobe Bryant and his young daughter were announced dead in a helicopter crash, Sonmez linked to an article accusing Bryant of sexual assault. Sonmez got thrashed on social media for essentially spitting on a dead man's grave, and the *Washington Post* placed her on paid leave.

This time, though, the *Post* had announced its decision publicly. Colleagues and reporters at other news outlets started piling on the *Washington Post* for punishing Sonmez. She was quickly reinstated.[163] It was the beginning of the end for the *Post*'s ability to keep the mob at bay.

Sonmez would later reveal that the *Washington Post* banned her from reporting on sexual assault cases because she had publicly identified herself as a victim. The paper was allegedly worried that allowing her to cover that beat could give the appearance of nonobjectivity. It was an admittedly touchy subject. Many women are victims of sexual assault, and it does not necessarily make them incapable of covering the issue fairly. However, Sonmez also had a history of approaching the issue a bit like an activist. The ill-timed Bryant tweet was one example. In one article, she suggested that Trump should've offered "words of comfort" to women like

---

163   Darcy, Oliver. "Washington Post Reinstates Reporter Who It Suspended over Kobe Bryant Tweets, Saying She Didn't Violate Policy." Cable News Network, January 29, 2020. https://www.cnn.com/2020/01/28/media/washington-post-felicia-sonmez-kobe-bryant/index.html.

Christine Blasey-Ford, whose sexual assault accusation against Brett Kavanaugh had more holes than swiss cheese.[164]

The public backlash was too much to bear, and the *Washington Post* reversed its decision barring Sonmez from sexual assault coverage.[165] She eventually sued her employer, but a judge dismissed the case in March 2022, stating that she had not proven that the *Post* had discriminated against her because she was a victim of an assault.[166]

"News media companies have the right to adopt policies that protect not only the fact but also the appearance of impartiality," the judge ruled.

While the *Washington Post* eventually would win the legal battle, other changes were brewing in the newsroom.

The newspaper lent a hand to cancel culture in 2020 when it wrote about a Halloween party two years earlier that took place at a *Post* cartoonist's home. The article explained that a woman showed up to the party in a "Megyn Kelly Blackface" costume that was supposed to be a joke about Kelly's comments about insensitive Halloween costumes, not an attempt at racism. Several party-goers yelled at the woman and told her she was ugly. The

---

[164] Dawsey, Josh, and Felicia Sonmez. "Trump Mocks Kavanaugh Accuser Christine Blasey Ford." *Washington Post*, October 3, 2018. https://www.washingtonpost.com/politics/trump-mocks-kavanaugh-accuser-christine-blasey-ford/2018/10/02/25f6f8aa-c662-11e8-9b1c-a90f1daae309_story.html.

[165] Farhi, Paul. "Washington Post Reverses Prohibition on Reporter from Writing about Sexual Assault." *Washington Post*, March 30, 2021. https://www.washingtonpost.com/lifestyle/media/washington-post-reverses-prohibition-on-reporter-from-writing-about-sexual-assault/2021/03/29/c0ee-3be0-90c5-11eb-9668-89be11273c09_story.html.

[166] Farhi, Paul. "Washington Post Reverses Prohibition on Reporter from Writing about Sexual Assault." *Washington Post*, March 30, 2021. https://www.washingtonpost.com/lifestyle/media/washington-post-reverses-prohibition-on-reporter-from-writing-about-sexual-assault/2021/03/29/c0ee-3be0-90c5-11eb-9668-89be11273c09_story.html.

woman left the party in tears and later called the *Post* employee who hosted to apologize for causing offense.

Two female millennials who were at the party were apparently not satisfied with this conclusion. They decided to contact the host and demand the name of the woman who showed up in blackface. It's unclear why, exactly, the *Post* decided to write this up as a news article. My best guess is that they were trying to get ahead of the incident, worried that the two young women would blast the *Post* publicly for being complicit in the woman's racism. The *Post* included the name of the woman, who is a private citizen, in the article, and got her fired from her job.[167] Bravo to everyone involved!

The *Post*'s foray into wokeness didn't stop at assisting private citizens in policing each other's Halloween costumes. Not only did the *Post* start hiring more millennial staff from Ivy League schools, but also in the spring of 2021 it brought on Sally Buzbee as executive editor, replacing the more hard-nosed Marty Baron.

Buzbee is a wealthy, white, liberal, middle-aged woman. I usually refer to these types as the "liberal wine moms," but I don't know if Buzbee drinks. Nonetheless, she made clear when she was brought on to the *Post* that she would play ball with the woke left. In an interview with *Politico*,[168] she said that newspapers need to be "inclusive in our culture and also in our coverage."

"One of the most substantial things that has changed is that newsrooms are now focused on diversity and having the

---

[167] Soave, Robby. "The Washington Post's Halloween Costume Hit Job Is a New Low for Cancel Culture." Reason.com, June 18, 2020. https://reason.com/2020/06/18/washington-post-blackface-halloween-costume-cancel-culture/.

[168] Fossett, Katelyn. "Six Questions with Sally Buzbee, the Washington Post's New Executive Editor." POLITICO, May 14, 2021. https://www.politico.com/newsletters/women-rule/2021/05/14/six-questions-with-sally-buzbee-the-washington-posts-new-executive-editor-492859.

important but sometimes difficult conversations that are necessary for progress," she added.

In practice, these "difficult conversations" usually lead to the demand that white people feel guilty for existing, racism be redefined as "prejudice plus power," marginalized groups be allowed to say whatever they want with no consequences, and truth and facts that are inconvenient to certain narratives about race and gender be buried.

Sure enough, not long after Buzbee was appointed, the newspaper officially updated its style guide to appease the militant trans lobby. Travis Lyles, the *Post*'s Instagram editor (gag), shared the happy news on Twitter:

"@washingtonpost officially updated its stylebook guidance on how we reference pregnancy and pregnant individuals in our writing to be more inclusive," Lyles cheered.

The *Post* didn't go quite as far as some other outlets, acknowledging that using "pregnant people" can be seen as exclusionary to women, but still urged reporters to keep transgender and nonbinary individuals in mind when reporting on pregnancy.

"While biology dictates who can be pregnant, it does not always reflect gender identity," the *Post* warned.

I referred to this as "antitruth nonsense" on Twitter and was promptly blocked by Lyles. The irony of a man blocking a woman for objecting to how women get spoken about by his newspaper is not lost on me.

Outside of its editorial standards, the *Post* started allowing younger reporters to write straight-up hit jobs on conservatives who were saying things they didn't like. The newspaper drew major backlash when reporter Taylor Lorenz doxxed a private citizen for reposting embarrassing and disturbing left-wing TikToks, but we'll get into that later.

On March 28, 2022, Alex Epstein, a philosopher and author of two books on the benefits of fossil fuels, received an email from a *Washington Post* reporter by the name of Maxine Joselow. Joselow, who covers climate change, warned Epstein that she was going to write a piece accusing him of racism and wanted to offer him the chance to comment.

According to her email, a copy of which I've obtained, she had been sent materials from a "watchdog group" called *Documented*. According to the *Documented* website, they are dedicated to "pulling back the curtain on those in power to expose corruption."

"We publish and report on documents, audio, video and other materials that lay bare corporate interests and their network of operatives' best laid plans to rig the system," they assert.

I find it laughable that a watchdog worried about "corporate interests" would share information with a billionaire-owned corporate media outlet, but the "investigations" published on their website make quite clear that they are interested in holding Republicans and conservative groups "accountable"—no one else.

Joselow, who has her pronouns listed in her LinkedIn bio like a true ally, lapped up the tip she received from *Documented*.

"I'm reaching out again because I obtained materials from the watchdog group *Documented* that show Alex Epstein wrote pieces in college that attacked the Reverend Martin Luther King, Jr., and demeaned non-White, non-Western civilizations. I am planning to publish a story about those materials on the morning of Wednesday, March 30th," Joselow wrote.

The allegations, which she listed in full, reveal that Epstein wrote a couple of slightly edgy political essays while at Duke University—twenty-three years ago! One article praised MLK's civil rights activism but also noted his personal failings, such as cheating on his wife and plagiarizing an article. As far as I know, it's not racist to use publicly available history to contextualize the life of MLK. Joselow also panned Epstein for praising western civilization. Joselow admitted that Epstein never mentioned race or ethnicity in his own arguments in favor of western civilization, but somehow she had determined that he was, once again, being racist.

It's shocking that Joselow was so quick to smear someone as a bigot considering when she was the editor-in-chief at her campus newspaper at Brown University, she had to apologize for allowing two "racist" opinion pieces to be published.[169] How quickly people forget!

In the spirit of full disclosure, I had recently moderated a debate on climate change between Epstein and General Wesley Clark, but that was my first and only time meeting Epstein in person. I didn't get the sense that he was a secret racist, but I suppose people can sometimes be sneaky about these things.

Epstein decided to get out ahead of the hit piece, publishing a full response on his Twitter account. He told Joselow in an email response, "I consider your intended piece to be so beyond the pale in terms of false content, terrible methodology, and bad motives that commenting on it to you (with you choosing whether and how to use it) would only help you perpetrate an injustice against me."

He added, "I await your apology, resignation, or firing. And I hope you never again try to destroy an innocent person's life and work to advance your political agenda."

Epstein's full Twitter thread unapologetically and conclusively defended against the planned hit piece, allegation by allegation.

---

[169] Writer, Staff. "Brown Newspaper Issues Apology after 'Racist' Columns." *The Providence Journal*, October 7, 2015. https://www.providencejournal. com/story/news/education/2015/10/07/brown-newspaper-issues-apology-after/33319879007/.

With a complete lack of self-awareness, Joselow's editor accused Epstein of "vitriol and baseless attacks" and suggested he was trying to intimidate her. Other *Washington Post* reporters jumped in to defend their colleague, even though she was the one trying to falsely malign someone else's character. This is the M.O. of the cancel mob, particularly when run by journalists. They believe they can use their platforms to smear with impunity, and if you fight back, all of a sudden you are considered the aggressor.

Epstein refused to back down, and the article Joselow published a week later was stripped of all accusations of racism.[170]

The *Post* didn't learn its lesson, instead attempting another dirty smear on my friend and former colleague Saagar Enjeti. Elizabeth Dwoskin, a Columbia Journalism School graduate, emailed Enjeti's podcast producer to ask for comment on a tweet he sent about top Twitter lawyer Vijaya Gadde.

Enjeti noted that Gadde, who reportedly cried in a staff meeting after Elon Musk purchased Twitter, was responsible for censoring the Hunter Biden laptop story on the platform and "gaslit the world" about it on Joe Rogan's podcast. Musk replied to the tweet, writing "Suspending the Twitter account of a major news organization for publishing a truthful story was obviously incredibly inappropriate."

Dwoskin suggested in her email to Enjeti's producer, sent at 2:00 AM, that Enjeti was responsible for racist attacks being lobbed at Gadde. Enjeti and Gadde are both Indian, but only the left-wing brown person can be a victim in woke world.

---

[170] Epstein, Alex. "Victorya Week Ago, @Washingtonpost Planned to Run a Hit-Piece Designed to Cancel Me and My Book Fossil Future as 'Racist.' Thanks to My *Preemptive Public Refutation*, the Post Delayed the Piece a Week and Removed 90% of Its Unjust Attacks--Including All References to Racism. Pic.twitter.com/oepkvk3d4K." Twitter, April 6, 2022. https://twitter.com/AlexEpstein/status/1511771747804069888.

Dwoskin published her article at 3:00 AM, just one hour after she emailed Enjeti's producer in the middle of the night. The article initially claimed that Enjeti didn't "immediately respond for comment." Dwoskin also did not cite any examples of verified Twitter users attacking Gadde for her race, instead only quoting an unnamed user who said she would "go down in history as an appalling person." Pretty tame, as far as Twitter attacks go.

Enjeti responded on Twitter that Gadde is a public figure—in fact, a public-facing corporate executive who makes $17 million a year—and that he should be allowed to mildly criticize her policies without being held responsible for random accounts going after her. Others noted the hypocrisy in Dwoskin's logic—she may be sparking racism against Enjeti by writing an article attacking him!

If the *Post* is going to play the woke cancel culture game, they clearly have to get a lot better at it.

CHAPTER 17

THE FAILING *NEW YORK TIMES*

The *New York Times*, once considered a newspaper of record, has fallen head first down the woke rabbit hole.

The truth is that the *Times* has always been a useful propaganda tool for the establishment, from its award-winning coverage denying Stalin's famine in Ukraine to its reporting that the WMDs were totally real. But the *Times* really opened itself up to trouble with its breathless reporting of Russiagate, shorthand for the conspiracy theory that President Donald Trump colluded with the Russian government to win the 2016 presidential election. The *Times* was acutely aware of journalism's massive shift from print to digital and desperate for subscribers. The paper's mostly liberal, cosmopolitan readers who were horrified by Trump's shakeup of the establishment inhaled the suggestion that he would soon be in prison. Wine moms scoured the pages of the *Times* for evidence of Trump's crimes, whether from super hero special counsel Robert Mueller or Trump's overhyped tax returns. The *Times* leaned in and gave these readers exactly what they wanted, even if it was all based on unfounded rumors and poorly sourced innuendo.

The *New York Times* won a Pulitzer Prize for its coverage of Trump and Russia, even though Mueller's report found no convincing evidence of a conspiracy.[171] The *Times* and its biased reporters slandered a duly elected president and were rewarded for it by what used to be one of the most prestigious award organizations in the world.

The *Times* probably could have continued to beat Russiagate into the ground, except it became clear that there were no indictments of Trump affiliates coming down the line. The *Times* had already lost any remaining grip it had on normal people, who were now quite certain that it was fake news. Its most loyal liberal readers, who had been told for years that Trump would be finished any day now, might start getting suspicious too.

Unfortunately for the *Times*, its new army of young, woke reporters plucked from the Ivy League would never allow the paper to return to pre-Trump times. They believed that a journalist's real job wasn't to factually present a story, but to shove their personal enlightenment down the throats of their readers.

The writing was on the wall when these staffers angrily tweeted that their paper had hired a climate denier, Bret Stephens, who they deemed unfit for publication.[172] How could the *Times*

---

[171] Adams, Becket. "Maybe It's Time the *Washington* Post and the *New York Times* Return Those Russian Collusion Pulitzers." *Washington Examiner*, November 5, 2021. https://www.washingtonexaminer.com/opinion/maybe-its-time-the-washington-post-and-the-new-york-times-return-those-russian-collusion-pulitzers.

[172] Mullin, Benjamin. "New York Times Journalists Immediately Begin Subtweeting Bret Stephens' Defense of Climate Change Skepticism." Poynter, April 30, 2017. https://www.poynter.org/reporting-editing/2017/new-york-times-journalists-immediately-begin-subtweeting-bret-stephens-defense-of-climate-skepticism/.

ever accurately present both sides of the political debate if the squishiest of all centrists was too extreme for the newsroom? The staffers didn't want that, anyway. Fairness was a concept from a bygone era, one that existed long before their lives and democracy were *literally at risk* thanks to Trump.

By the summer of 2019, *New York Times Magazine* editor Jake Silverstein was planning to publish the "1619 Project," a rewriting of American history focused almost entirely on race. Editor Dean Baquet was also dutifully shifting the paper's focus to appease his younger, more ideological staffers, who believed that the *Times* had a moral obligation to paint Trump as an evil racist.

It didn't matter how much Silverstein and Baquet sought to placate the warped minds of the millennials. They had already raised their pitchforks.

Times staff and readers were livid that an early August 2019 headline claimed—accurately!—that Trump had spoken against racism. Following two mass shootings in El Paso, Texas, and Dayton, Ohio, the president gave a speech at the White House denouncing "racist hate" and "white supremacy."

"In one voice our nation must condemn racism, bigotry and white supremacy," Trump said. "These sinister ideologies must be defeated."

The front-page *Times* article[173] used the headline "Trump Urges Unity vs. Racism."

Democratic politicians, including Rep. Alexandria Ocasio Cortez, *Times* readers, and staff were outraged. The *Times* headline had not included the proper *context* to remind people that even though Trump said a good thing, he is still most certainly

---

[173] Crowley, Michael, and Maggie Haberman. "Trump Condemns White Supremacy but Stops Short of Major Gun Controls." *New York Times*, August 5, 2019. https://www.nytimes.com/2019/08/05/us/politics/trump-speech-mass-shootings-dayton-el-paso.html.

still a bad man. There is no room for nuance of character among the rabid millennials who have toxified our political debate by turning it into a Harry Potter-esque tale of good versus evil.

The headline was promptly changed to "Assailing Hate but Not Guns." Ahhh, much better!

Matt Purdy, a deputy managing editor for the *Times*, issued a statement claiming that editors were trying to be "nuanced" but did "not hit it right." The editors "should have done better," he said, kneeling to the mob.[174]

A week later, the mob had already found another target. Jonathan Weisman, the deputy Washington editor for the *Times*, was under fire for "racist" tweets. Weisman somewhat clumsily attempted to make the point that progressive politicians like Ilhan Omar, Rashida Tlaib, and John Lewis are probably not representative of the larger geographical regions they are from. The left interpreted this to mean that Weisman, who is Jewish, doesn't believe that people of color can be fully American. Weisman sealed his fate when he sent another tweet misidentifying the race of a black congressional candidate. The *Times* demoted Weisman from his leadership position and prohibited him from using social media over his "serious lapses in judgment."[175]

Trying to stave off a major internal staff revolt, Dean Baquet held an employee town hall on August 12.

[174] *New York Times*. "A Times Headline about Trump Stoked Anger. A Top Editor Explains." *New York Times*, August 6, 2019. https://www.nytimes.com/2019/08/06/reader-center/trump-mass-shootings-headline.html.

[175] Tracy, Marc. "A Times Editor Is Demoted as the Paper Discusses Its Coverage of Race." *New York Times*, August 13, 2019. https://www.nytimes.com/2019/08/13/business/media/times-editor-weisman-demoted.html.

The contentious meeting went for about seventy-five minutes.[176] Baquet opened by admitting that he had built the newsroom around the now-debunked Russia story. He asked staffers to help him tell the "new story"—a story about Trump's "character" with a "deep investigation" into the country's racism.

Baquet had let the genie out of the bottle, then desperately tried to squeeze it back in. Baquet cautioned staff that the *Times* is still considered an "independent" newspaper. Twitter, he said, cannot determine its editorial direction.

"Our role is not to be the leader of the resistance," Baquet told his staff.

All hell broke loose.

Throughout the rest of the meeting, staffers demanded to know why the word "racist" wasn't used more often to describe Trump's actions, chastised Baquet for only holding a meeting after the paper was criticized publicly, suggested setting up an external critic for the paper, and asserted that all *Times* coverage should start from the fact that "racism is in everything."

Older staffers tried to shake the kids awake, declaring, "We have to remember we are not advocates for the left…We are not f—ing part of the resistance!" The kids ran to competitors to complain.[177]

"When the stakes are so high and so many people feel personally threatened and there's real danger in the air, the show don't tell approach feels inadequate," one staffer said.

---

[176] Feinberg, Ashley. "Here's the Transcript of the New York Times Town-Hall Meeting." Slate, August 15, 2019. https://slate.com/news-and-politics/2019/08/new-york-times-meeting-transcript.html.

[177] Darcy, Oliver. "Inside the New York Times as It Debates Its Coverage of Trump and Racism | CNN Business." Cable News Network, August 14, 2019. https://www.cnn.com/2019/08/14/media/new-york-times-criticism/index.html.

The message was clear. The *Times* could stand up for its editorial independence, but its own staffers would deem it complicit in the racism and bigotry perpetuated by Trump.

Two days after that tense town hall, The *New York Times Magazine* published the "1619 Project" online. The project alleged that the "true founding" of the United States was not established by the 1776 Declaration of Independence from Great Britain but the arrival of the first slaves in 1619.[178] Nikole Hannah-Jones, who developed the project, claimed that the primary motivation for the American Revolution was not to seek liberty but to protect the institution of slavery in the colonies. The booklet-length article's intention was to reinforce the woke left's narrative about systemic racism: America was irrevocably tied to its "original sin" of slavery, and the legacy of slavery will forever reverberate throughout society.

Historians panned the "1619 Project" as ahistorical hogwash,[179] but the *Times* didn't care. They couldn't diminish the great Nikole Hannah-Jones, the shiny trophy editors held up to their woke staffers to say, "See, we're not racist!" Instead, they offered measly "clarifications" of the project's biggest misrepresentations and stealth edited the rest to avoid accountability. Oh, and they got another Pulitzer for their efforts.

Hannah-Jones took her special status and ran straight to the bank. She hardly writes for the *Times* anymore but rakes in cash through speeches and diversity trainings. She bullied the University of North Carolina into granting her tenure only to reject their offer, earned a journalism professorship at Howard

---

[178] "The 1619 Project." *New York Times,* August 14, 2019. https://www.nytimes.com/interactive/2019/08/14/magazine/1619-america-slavery.html.

[179] Silverstein, Jake. "An Update to the 1619 Project." *New York Times,* March 11, 2020. https://www.nytimes.com/2020/03/11/magazine/an-update-to-the-1619-project.html.

University, and has developed the "1619 Project" into educational curricula for public schools. Yeah, you can thank the spineless *New York Times* for most of the rise of critical race theory in K-12 education, ensuring that the next generation of students turns out even more messed up than the millennials.

Just a year later, the *Times* would be embroiled in another newsroom scandal.

Following the death of George Floyd at the hands of Minneapolis police officer Derek Chauvin, race relations in the US were more fraught than ever. Left-wing activist groups, with the help of the media, established a narrative that black people were being systematically hunted down by police. It didn't matter that police killings of unarmed black men were actually falling each year. Black Lives Matter and Antifa activists flooded streets across the country, demanding police reform and the defunding of police departments. Many of the protests turned violent, with agitators burning and looting storefronts, assaulting police and citizens, and in Seattle, establishing a lawless autonomous zone known as the Capitol Hill Occupied Protest and later the Capitol Hill Autonomous Zone…or "CHAZ/CHOP" for short.

Corporate media outlets excused the violence, worried about upsetting their woke staffers and the consumers who agreed with the protesters and their goals. MSNBC's Ali Velshi unironically described a riot in Minneapolis as "not generally speaking unruly" while standing in front of a burning building.[180] CNN

---

[180] "MSNBC's Ali Velshi Downplays Riot in Front of Burning Building: 'Mostly …'" https://www.realclearpolitics.com/video/2020/05/28/msnbcs_ali_velshi_downplays_riot_in_front_of_burning_building_mostly_a_protest_not_generally_speaking_unruly.html#!

ran a chyron that said the riots were "fiery but mostly peaceful."[181] A number of other outlets wrote sneering articles minimizing property damage by assuring small business owners that they would be covered by insurance.

The *New York Times*'s op-ed section somehow managed to retain some semblance of journalistic integrity during the woke takeover of the newsroom. Opinion editor James Bennet was brought on in 2016 to bring more ideological diversity to the opinion section and was responsible for hiring the aforementioned Bret Stephens and Bari Weiss. It's not like Bennet was bringing in any firebrand conservatives—let's be honest, "ideological diversity" to the *Times* means progressive or liberal—but under his tenure, the opinion pages sought a more balanced approach to political debate. This mindset was applied to the post-Floyd so-called "summer of love", a label that Seattle Mayor Jenny Durkan unironically gave the riots during a CNN interview.

Most Americans sympathized with the protests but opposed unrest and violence. As riots got out of control, what should be the federal government's response?

The *Times* published an opinion piece, titled "Send In the Troops," from Republican Senator Tom Cotton, who recommended using harsh measures to quell the riots.[182] Cotton argued that Trump should send the military to embattled areas across the country. He painted a picture of the violence taking place in American cities and cited historical precedent for using federal troops to keep peace domestically.

---

[181] Concha, Joe. "CNN Ridiculed for 'Fiery but Mostly Peaceful' Caption with Video of Burning Building in Kenosha." The Hill, August 27, 2020. https://thehill.com/homenews/media/513902-cnn-ridiculed-for-fiery-but-mostly-peaceful-caption-with-video-of-burning/.

[182] Cotton, Tom. "Tom Cotton: Send in the Troops." *New York Times*, June 3, 2020. https://www.nytimes.com/2020/06/03/opinion/tom-cotton-protests-military.html.

The backlash was swift and immediate. *Times* staffers didn't just argue that Cotton's opinion was wrong—they were incensed that the piece was ever published. Staffers started a social media campaign accusing the opinion editors of putting their black colleagues in harm's way. Taylor Lorenz, Lydia Polgreen, James Poniewozik, Jazmine Hughes, Taffy Brodesser-Akner, John Williams, Jennifer Szalai, Tracie Lee, Melissa Guerrero, Chase Turner, Tiffany May, Alexandra Alter, Jessica Silver-Greenberg, Gregory Schmidt, and countless others all shared the same message:

"Running this puts black people, including black @nytimes staff, in danger."

The staffers who took issue with the op-ed didn't dare grapple with its substance, which was wholly reasonable. Instead, they misrepresented Cotton's argument entirely. They claimed that Cotton called for sending in troops to handle mere protesters, not rioters—people who were mauling and looting businesses and attacking police. They made the case that Cotton's view on this issue was totally outside the bounds of acceptable commentary, even though the majority of Americans, including a plurality of Democrats, supported using the military to put down riots. They continued to couch their revulsion of dissenting opinions in the false claim that the Cotton op-ed shouldn't have been published because it was riddled with inaccuracies. They took great issue with Cotton saying that Antifa was involved in the riots—"hey, we've debunked that already!" they cried. My friend and *Townhall* reporter Julio Rosas, who was on the ground at many of these riots, witnessed the Antifa infiltration of peaceful protests. Attorney General Bill Barr confirmed that the violence appeared to be driven by "anarchic and left-extremist groups."

The more you dig into the *Times* staffers' arguments against the Cotton op-ed, the less it seems they are actually fearful for their lives, and the more it seems a cynical ploy to cover for their own weak, if not favorable, coverage of the violence against communities and the police. Former *New York Times* reporter Nellie Bowles all but confirmed this after her ceremonious exit from the Gray Lady. Bowles said she was informed by editors that a story she wrote about the Kenosha riots and their effects on local businesses wouldn't run until after the 2020 election.[183]

Opinion Editor James Bennet tried to defend publishing the Cotton op-ed,[184] arguing that the paper "owes it to our readers to show them counter-arguments." Publisher A.G. Sulzberger sent an internal memo to staff echoing Bennet's comments but assured staff that he understood their concerns.

"One of my most important responsibilities as we do so is to protect your safety so that you can do your vital work," Sulzberger wrote.

Times staff were naturally dissatisfied with the Sulzberger memo. Editors were at a loss for how to fix this public relations and morale nightmare, so they abandoned all defense of the op-ed and fully genuflected to the mob. A *Times* spokeswoman conceded that the Cotton op-ed was the result of a "rushed" process and that it did not "meet our standards," even though the Cotton team assured that the op-ed went back and forth several times for edits.[185] Sulzberger said the op-ed should have never

[183] Shaw, Jazz. "Reporter Claims NY Times Sat on Her Kenosha Riots Story until after Election." HotAir, November 20, 2021. https://hotair.com/jazz-shaw/2021/11/20/reporter-claims-ny-times-sat-on-her-kenosha-riots-story-until-after-election-n430527.

[184] Tracy, Marc. "Senator's 'Send in the Troops' Op-Ed in the Times Draws Online Ire." *New York Times*, June 4, 2020. https://www.nytimes.com/2020/06/03/business/tom-cotton-op-ed.html.

[185] Lowry, Rich. "The inside Story of the Tom Cotton Op-Ed That Rocked the New York Times." National Review, June 5, 2020. https://www.nationalreview.com/2020/06/tom-cotton-new-york-times-op-ed-inside-story/.

been published. Bennet resigned from the paper. Jim Dao, a deputy opinion editor, was reassigned. The *Times* published an article placing the ultimate blame for editing of the op-ed on Adam Rubenstein, a young staffer in the editorial section.[186] He left the paper six months later.

The employees that the *Times* chooses to protect and the ones they throw under the bus tells you everything you need to know about who is really running the newsroom. Bari Weiss, who left the paper in July 2020 with a scathing resignation letter, exposed this toxic dynamic.

"What rules that remain at The Times are applied with extreme selectivity. If a person's ideology is in keeping with the new orthodoxy, they and their work remain unscrutinized. Everyone else lives in fear of the digital thunderdome. Online venom is excused so long as it is directed at the proper targets," Weiss said.

Bennet faced no disciplinary action when he inserted language into an editorial accusing Sarah Palin of inciting violence against Gabby Giffords. That error led to a lawsuit against the *Times*.[187] However, he was forced out when he published a Republican member of the Senate Armed Services Committee, who held an opinion shared by the majority of the country.

Bari Weiss and Nellie Bowles received no public support from the *Times* as young staffers bullied them on Slack channels,

---

[186] Tracy, Marc, Rachel Abrams, and Edmund Lee. "New York Times Says Senator's Op-Ed Did Not Meet Standards." *New York Times,* June 4, 2020. https://www.nytimes.com/2020/06/04/business/new-york-times-op-ed-cotton.html.

[187] Erik Wemple. "Williamson, However, Didn't Write the Incorrect Stuff in the Editorial about How a Map Circulated by Palin's PAC Allegedly Served as 'Political Incitement' for a 2011 Mass Shooting in Arizona. That Stuff Was Inserted by Her Editor, James Bennet. 2/." Twitter, February 4, 2022. https://twitter.com/ErikWemple/status/1489629412135948290.

publicly whined about their articles, and leaked complaints to other news outlets.[188] At best, *Times* leadership would privately applaud Weiss for her personal courage.

Adam Rubenstein, who was simply doing his job, was offered up as a sacrificial lamb to the mob who demanded justice for publishing anything to the right of Stalin.

Donald McNeil, who had been with the *Times* for forty-five years, was forced out in 2021 after he repeated the n-word when recounting an incident where a student was suspended for using it.[189] Baquet initially offered minor punishment for McNeil, but the mob wanted more. Certainly having learned from the Cotton op-ed situation that they can get whatever they want if they cry loud enough, these staffers eventually convinced Baquet to jostle McNeil into resigning.

Meanwhile, others who toed the correct editorial line earned public statements on the *Times* social media accounts praising them for their invaluable contributions to the paper.

Taylor Lorenz was a favorite sacred cow of the paper. We'll get into more of her unethical and politicized reporting later. In 2021, Lorenz decided to make International Women's Day, which is typically reserved for celebrating historic female achievements or speaking about the ongoing persecution of women in some foreign countries, all about her.

"For international women's day please consider supporting women enduring online harassment. It's not an exaggeration to say that the harassment and smear campaign I've had to endure

---

[188] "Resignation Letter." Bari Weiss. https://www.bariweiss.com/resignation-letter.

[189] Ellison, Sarah, and Jeremy Barr. "A Star Reporter's Resignation, a Racial Slur and a Newsroom Divided: Inside the Fallout at the New York Times." *Washington Post*, February 12, 2021. https://www.washingtonpost.com/lifestyle/2021/02/12/donald-mcneil-new-york-times-fallout/.

over the past year has destroyed my life. No one should have to go through this," Lorenz whined on Twitter.

Lorenz's stunningly tone-deaf tweet was roundly mocked on social media and covered by Fox News host Tucker Carlson, who rightfully called Lorenz "privileged." She lost it. Lorenz insisted that Tucker repeatedly said her name during the segment to "drill into" his followers' heads who they were supposed to go after. How else was he supposed to refer to her? "Unnamed *New York Times* reporter?"

The *New York Times* released an official statement defending Lorenz.[190]

"In a now familiar move, Tucker Carlson opened his show last night by attacking a journalist. It was a calculated and cruel tactic, which he regularly deploys to unleash a wave of harassment and vitriol at his intended target," the *Times* alleged. "Journalists should be able to do their jobs without facing harassment."

Times leadership seemed incapable of reeling in Lorenz's Twitter habit, which frequently earned them negative PR and was arguably in violation of the company's social media policy. Instead, they asked Lorenz to meet with Maggie Haberman to discuss appropriate social media use. Lorenz responded by eviscerating Haberman on Slack channels, referring to her as a "bitch."[191] The pair got into it again after Lorenz left the paper for the *Washington Post*—even though her former employer constantly defended her despite her many public missteps, Lorenz bashed the *Times* for allegedly not giving her enough room to

---

[190] Communications, NYTimes. "Our Response to Tuesday Night's 'Tucker Carlson Tonight' Broadcast. Pic.twitter.com/lkvaljcrl5." Twitter, March 10, 2021. https://twitter.com/NYTimesPR/status/1369747504565256193.

[191] Lachlan Cartwright, Maxwell Tani. "Inside the Drama Shaking up the NYT Styles Section." The Daily Beast Company, May 20, 2021. https://www.thedailybeast.com/inside-the-drama-shaking-up-the-new-york-times-styles-section.

grow her personal brand. Haberman took umbrage to the idea that reporters should even have a brand, and the two spat back and forth on Twitter. Haberman declined to comment on the situation for this book, telling me that Lorenz is a "good reporter."

The *Times* backed up another toxic left-wing employee, Mara Gay, a member of the editorial board who said it was "disturbing" to see scores of American flags during a trip to Long Island.

"I saw, you know, dozens and dozens of pickup trucks with explicatives [sic] against Joe Biden on the back of them, Trump flags, and in some cases just dozens of American flags, which is also just disturbing…Essentially the message was clear. 'This is my country. This is not your country. I own this," Gay said during an MSNBC appearance.[192]

The *Times* quickly leaped to her defense.

"New York Times editorial board member Mara Gay's comments on MSNBC have been irresponsibly taken out of context," the paper said. "Her argument was that Trump and many of his supporters have politicized the American flag. The attacks on her today are ill-informed and grounded in bad-faith."

The paper has made it quite clear that you only earn its protection when you push the correct narratives. Otherwise, they will toss you straight into the lion's den made up of angry Twitter leftists and the young staffers who bullied their way into power.

Weiss, in a Twitter thread about the Tom Cotton op-ed, reaffirmed the idea that campus mob politics had won the newsroom.

"I've been mocked by many people over the past few years for writing about the campus culture wars. They told me it was a sideshow. But this was always why it mattered: The people who

---

[192] Wulfsohn, Joseph A. "NYT Panned for Mara Gay Defense Following Her 'Disturbing' American Flags Remark: 'Every Word Here Is a Lie.'" FOX News Network, June 9, 2021. https://www.foxnews.com/media/new-york-times-defends-mara-gay-american-flag-disturbing.

graduated from those campuses would rise to power inside key institutions and transform them," Weiss said.

The *Times*'s fear of its own staff has caused it to feed absolute garbage to the American public.

In July 2021, the paper ran an article insisting that the American flag can be considered "divisive."[193]

In January 2022, the *Times* used the word "menstruators" to describe young women who got their period. In an attempt to be "inclusive" to the less than 0.5 percent of individuals who were born female but believe themselves to be male, the *Times* threw away the concept of womanhood and dehumanized the 160 million women in the United States.[194] Even though the trans lobby (as demonstrated at *Politico*) has the power to change the language of the biggest news outlets in the world, broken woke brains still somehow consider them the marginalized class.

The following month, the *Times* ran a subway ad in New York City featuring a person named Lianna who says she is "breaking the binary," "queer love in color," and "reimagining Harry Potter without its creator"—because J.K. Rowling, who very reasonably believes that biological men should not be allowed in women's spaces, is a horrible bigot.[195] Hilariously, the ad finishes by insisting that this is proof that the *New York Times* is "independent."

National security reporter Matthew Rosenberg was recently secretly recorded by Project Veritas complaining about the woke takeover at the *Times*. He said that young Ivy League graduates

---

[193] Nir, Sarah Maslin. "A Fourth of July Symbol of Unity That May No Longer Unite." *New York Times*, July 3, 2021. https://www.nytimes.com/2021/07/03/nyregion/american-flag-politics-polarization.html.

[194] Makhijani, Pooja. "Menstruation Gets a Gen Z Makeover." *New York Times*, January 20, 2022. https://www.nytimes.com/2022/01/20/well/sustainable-period-products.html.

[195] "*The New York Times* Erases JK Rowling." UnHerd, February 18, 2022. https://unherd.com/thepost/the-new-york-times-erases-jk-rowling/.

get hired after being "indoctrinated" and believe they can impart their new, progressive values on the newsroom.

"They're not the majority, but they're a very vocal loud minority that dominates social media," Rosenberg said, adding that they'd be considered "toxic" and "shunned" from newsrooms if not for their large followings on Twitter.

Rosenberg confirmed that Times leadership has "taken the path of least resistance," which has only made things worse.

The *Times* has, in the past year, attempted to pull reporters back from limitless social media use —even encouraging some reporters to leave Twitter and the dramatics on Slack entirely. The retirement of Dean Baquet and the hiring of his replacement, Joe Kahn, still confirms that they still don't quite get the real existential threat to the newsroom.

Baquet, on his way out the door, said that the Times' mission is to deliver the "best version of the truth,"[196] a nice form of doublespeak that allows reporters the right to decide what is true, not, you know, what is objective reality. Khan, meanwhile, stunningly claimed that one of the driving forces behind recent strife at the *Times* is a lack of diversity. He committed to hiring a "newer, more diverse generation of journalists all across the organization"[197]—exactly the "solution" that got them into this mess.

Times reporters who still believe in journalistic principles ought to run for their lives. The young staffers who have abandoned journalistic principles in favor of woke activism are

[196] Yorker, The New. "'The Job of the New York Times Should in the End Be to Come out with the Best Version of the Truth.' A New Interview with @Deanbaquet, Ahead of His Expected Retirement. Https://T.co/Uw2Fqg43pY." Twitter, February 22, 2022. https://twitter.com/newyorker/status/1496138268043362312?s=21.

[197] McCreesh, Shawn. "The inside Man." Intelligencer, April 19, 2022. https://nymag.com/intelligencer/article/joe-kahn-new-york-times-profile.html.

chomping through the old guard. They harass and bully dissenters out of the newsroom and publicly smear their employer until leadership complies with their demands. Instead of cleaning house, Khan is inviting the sickness inside.

CHAPTER 18

TAYLOR MADE

Few media activists are quite as detestable as Taylor Lorenz, a one-woman wrecking ball with a bad case of Peter Pan syndrome.

The strangest thing about Lorenz is that no one quite knows her real age. The Wikipedia citation regarding this conundrum is one of my favorite entries on the entire website, so I will quote it in full here:

"According to Politico, Lorenz's birthday is October 21. In February 2016, CBS News stated that she was 30, and in September 2020, Fortune listed her age as 35. Additionally, the New York Times—prior to her employment with the newspaper—stated that her age was 31 in August 2018. However, in a Tweet in March 2022, Lorenz said that she was 43 years old."

Truly one of the great mysteries of our time.

Even if she might miss the official age cut off by a few years, Lorenz is the archetypal woke millennial as they've been discussed in this book. She grew up in Old Greenwich, Connecticut, one of the wealthiest areas in the country, and was sent to a Swiss boarding and a private liberal arts college. She worked in the fashion industry before getting really into Tumblr, which led to a career in social media and, eventually, journalism.

Lorenz covers the internet beat—influencers, social media, TikTok, and the like. Most of her stories seem more fit for the pages of an issue of *Tiger Beat* than a real journalistic outfit. Headlines from her time at the *Daily Beast* include "Memers Take Over Brooklyn for 'IRL Party'" and "Instagram's Slime Stars Pivot to Soap."

But, between the stories about teen YouTubers and the latest TikTok trends, are shockingly unethical pieces of reporting that range from self-interested articles on internet regulation to hit jobs attempting to cancel influencers whose politics she doesn't like. Lorenz, like so many modern journalists, is merely an arm of the left-wing cancel mob, and is deeply committed to using her large platform to punish people for thought crimes.

One of Lorenz's first major stories was at the *Daily Beast* in 2018 when she inexplicably exposed a group of Instagrammers for the sin of…having a conservative mother.

Claudia, Jackie, Olivia, and Margo Oshry collectively ran a series of uber popular Instagram accounts, the most popular of which was "Girl with No Job," with about three million followers. The accounts mostly posted memes, funny tweets, food pictures, and otherwise humorous content. The sisters were mostly apolitical outside of normal expressions of patriotism and praise of First Lady Melania Trump's outfits. Some of them had older tweets criticizing President Barack Obama.

It's unclear what exactly prompted Lorenz to find out more about the Oshry sisters' family, but she discovered that their mom is Pamela Geller, an activist against Islamic extremism in the

United States.[198] Geller protested against the building of a mosque at Ground Zero in New York City, held a free speech-oriented contest for people to draw the prophet Mohammed, which was threatened by two gunmen, and has had assassination attempts made against her by members of ISIS.

The Oshry sisters attempted to hide the identity of their mother, never posting photos of her or referencing her on their social media pages. Nonetheless, Lorenz exposed their dirty little secret. In her reporting, she described Geller as "anti-Muslim," an "extremist," and a conspiracy theorist. Lorenz rhetorically wondered why the sisters tried so hard to avoid publicly affiliating with their mother, as if being attached to the label "islamophobia" wouldn't be a death knell for mostly apolitical content creators. It almost seemed like she was making fun of the fact that she had just blown up these sisters' lives.

Lorenz certainly knew that revealing Pamela Geller as the mother of the Oshry sisters would nuke their social media careers. She did it anyway and offered no explanation as to why the information about their mother was newsworthy, especially considering the sisters did not run expressly political accounts. To any rational outsider, it looked like Lorenz was merely trying to punish the sisters for the sins of their mother. It was a cancellation campaign, plain and simple.

After Lorenz published her article, Claudia Oshry submitted the following statement:

> *"We want to be clear to our audience and fans that our political and cultural beliefs are not*

---

[198] Lorenz, Taylor. "The Instagram Stars Hiding Their Famous, Muslim-Hating Mom, Pamela Geller." The Daily Beast, March 1, 2018. https://www.the-dailybeast.com/the-instagram-stars-hiding-their-famous-muslim-hating-mom-pamela-geller.

> *anti-Muslim or anti-anyone. Our views are sep-*
> *arate from our mother's. Being raised by a single*
> *parent, we were taught to make our own choices*
> *based on our personal beliefs. We are inspired to*
> *think for ourselves and we do. We do not condone*
> *discrimination or racist beliefs of any kind."*

It was too little too late for the brands who wanted nothing to do with this reputational disaster and for the one-time fans who were horrified that their favorite meme accounts could be the product of women unlucky enough to be birthed by an "anti-Muslim." One day after Lorenz's article dropped, Oath, a tech platform, canceled a show featuring the Oshry sisters and promised an "investigation" into its programming.[199] Claudia's agent and manager dropped her, as did several partners. The cancel campaign continued from internet warriors who pounced on Lorenz's report. They dug up tweets from Claudia Oshry when she was sixteen years old and declared her a racist, prompting a tearful apology from the Instagrammer. Former coworkers of some of the sisters at *Huffington Post* and Yahoo! got in on the action too, declaring them unprofessional and stating that they were horrified to find out that their mother is Pamela Geller. The entire saga was a horrible game of guilt by association.

The Oshry sisters may have been Lorenz's first target, but they wouldn't be her last. Lorenz clearly learned from her days on Tumblr that there is great Internet clout in destroying people you don't like. My friend Saagar Enjeti, host of the show *Breaking*

---

[199] Maxwell Tani, Taylor Lorenz. "Oath Cancels Show Starring Muslim-Hater Pamela Geller's Instagram-Star Daughters." The Daily Beast, March 1, 2018. https://www.thedailybeast.com/oath-cancels-show-starring-muslim-hat-er-pamela-gellers-instagram-star-daughters.

Points, perfectly referred to this style of reporting as "hall monitor journalism."

Hall monitor journalists patrol the internet looking for anything to be upset or offended by so they can drive outrage clicks to their articles or build their social media profiles. They are the adult version of college students who police their classmates for not using "inclusive" language or for donning a slightly edgy Halloween costume. The major difference is that journalists like Lorenz have the backing of extremely powerful corporate media outlets like the *New York Times* and the *Washington Post*.

"I think the way people use 'cancel culture' is this shorthand way of dismissing whatever accusations are against them," Lorenz once said in an interview with Katie Herzog.[200] "My general take on it is that it's very toxic but also necessary. We are in the correction phase right now and everyone is indiscriminately calling each other out, and that's because we're working to set new standards and norms as a society."

Lorenz was apoplectic when social media app Clubhouse rose to prominence during the pandemic. Clubhouse was a collection of unconstrained audio chat rooms where users could be thrown in with prominent venture capitalists, comedians, singers, and other famous people. No topic seemed to be off limits. Lorenz hated it because she could not control the conversations people were having.

In February 2021, Lorenz wrote an article for the *New York Times* complaining about the fact that people were having

---

[200] Herzog, Katie. "Cancel Culture: What Exactly Is This Thing?" The Stranger. https://www.thestranger.com/slog/2019/09/17/41416013/cancel-culture-what-exactly-is-this-thing.

"unfettered conversations" on the internet,[201] lining up squarely alongside the censorious Chinese Communist Party, which banned the app entirely.

How dare people say words online without getting Ms. Lorenz's prior approval!

"Clubhouse is also contending with rising complaints about harassment, misinformation and privacy," Lorenz wrote. "The growth has been accompanied by criticism that women and people of color are frequent targets of abuse and that discussions involving anti-Semitism, homophobia, racism and misogyny are on the rise."

Even before her piece in the *Times*, Lorenz was trying to woke scold her way around Clubhouse. Lorenz enjoyed large followings on TikTok, Twitter, and Instagram but struggled for relevance in this new space. In a desperate plea for attention and a grasp at some semblance of power, Lorenz started dropping into random Clubhouse spaces and whining about what was being said. Some of the biggest users on the app blocked Lorenz so she couldn't join the same rooms as them, which only seemed to infuriate her more. Lorenz created fake accounts to force her way into conversations where she was not wanted, and her old employer, *The Atlantic*, even published an article insisting that Clubhouse had a "blocking problem."[202]

201 Griffith, Erin, and Taylor Lorenz. "Clubhouse, a Tiny Audio Chat App, Breaks Through." *New York Times*, February 15, 2021. https://www. nytimes.com/2021/02/15/business/clubhouse.html.

202 Oremus, Will. "The Blue Check Mark's Evil Cousin." Atlantic Media Company, May 13, 2021. https://www.theatlantic.com/technology/archive/ 2021/05/clubhouse-has-blocking-problem/618867/.

In a particularly egregious attempt to snatch back some control, Lorenz falsely accused tech entrepreneur Marc Andreessen of using the word "retard" during a conversation on the app.[203]

"@PMarca just openly using the r-slur on Clubhouse tonight and not one other person in the room called him on it or saying anything," Lorenz tweeted.

It was a totally false claim. Andreessen was in a room with other techies who were talking about how the Reddit group r/WallStreetBets managed to band together and make GameStop a hot stock option. Felicia Horowitz, another user in the room, allegedly referred to the fact that r/WallStreetBets refers to itself as the "retard revolution."

Nait Jones, the moderator of the conversation, corrected Lorenz's account.

"Here's what actually happened," Jones said. "Felicia explained that the Redditors call themselves 'R-word revolution' but Marc never used that word, ever…and this is why people block because of this horse shit dishonesty."

Lorenz offered a nonapology apology, tweeting, "Many heard Marc's voice…because it was the male" and thanking Jones for "clarifying." Lorenz still managed to lecture the people who did use the r-word, even though it was being used in a completely contextually appropriate way and not as a "slur," as Lorenz claimed.

"I hope you can understand how some people in the room felt hearing it," she said, adding, "I hope everyone who used this word can think more carefully about why people in the audience were upset."

---

203 Takala, Rudy, and By. "NY Times Reporter Locks Twitter Account after Falsely Accusing Tech Entrepreneur of Using Slur." Mediaite, February 9, 2021. https://www.mediaite.com/news/ny-times-reporter-locks-twitter-account-after-falsely-accusing-tech-entrepreneur-of-using-a-slur/.

Lorenz then quickly locked her Twitter account to avoid being called out for her false accusation and to turn herself into the *real* victim.

Lorenz is an expert at lashing out at others but then playing victim when the microscope is turned on her. It's a tactic I saw frequently on campus. The most aggressive activists could malign your character with impunity, but if you dared respond, you were an oppressor and possibly even putting their lives in danger. Narcissists do this because it's a way to avoid accountability for their actions. Lorenz doesn't have the benefit of being a person of color, so she has to find other ways of pretending to be marginalized. Sometimes she attributes the backlash she receives to being a woman, but white women are also no longer considered victims thanks to the left's adoption of identity politics and "intersectionality." So, Lorenz and other reporters like her use a nifty little trick. They establish journalists themselves as an oppressed class, deeming them as something of a protected species and thus immune from all criticism.

It's an absurd concept, one that's divorced entirely from reality. Corporate media journalists are not victims because they are actually incredibly powerful—usually more powerful than the people they are covering. They have the ability to shape public debate, destroy people's lives, and affect the outcomes of elections. Journalists want all of this power with none of the responsibility, so they whine and cry online whenever their work is challenged.

Before Lorenz got in trouble for her Clubhouse shenanigans, she had already earned the ire of many in the tech space by going after Steph Korey, the former CEO of the travel brand Away. An article published in *The Verge* in December 2019 accused Korey of creating a toxic workplace culture, but many of the accusations were a bit flat.[204] In one case, employees were upset that they were busted for having a private company Slack room in which to complain about their colleagues, specifically "cis white men." The employees justified this by saying that they felt "marginalized" and were facing "microaggressions." Remember, Slack was the exact tool that staffers at the New York Times used to organize their revolts and bully their coworkers. Any manager worth his or her salt, at this point, would be very cautious about how employees use that platform.

Others quoted in the article alleged that Korey was generally a tough boss and sometimes quite snarky. How horrible!

Several months later, Korey posted a long message to her Instagram story about how internet journalism prioritizes salacious, click-worthy articles over good journalism. The perpetually aggrieved Lorenz decided to go after Korey on her Twitter account, calling her post an "incoherent" rant and accusing her of having "0 understanding" of journalism. When other venture capitalists and CEOs came to Korey's defense, suddenly Lorenz was the victim again. She insisted that she was being harassed publicly and privately for months, conveniently shifting attention away from the fact that she had attacked Korey for no particular reason.

Lorenz's dust-up with Silicon Valley seemed to only propel her career to new heights, as other journalists rallied to her defense and nauseatingly regaled her as one of the most talented writers they knew. Lorenz failed to live up to this high bar set for her, instead continuing to sink to the lowest gossip rag clickbait. In 2020, Lorenz ignited a family feud between Kellyanne Conway, her husband George, and their daughter Claudia after

---

204 Schiffer, Zoe. "Emotional Baggage." The Verge, December 5, 2019. https://www.theverge.com/2019/12/5/20995453/away-luggage-ceo-steph-korey-toxic-work-environment-travel-inclusion.

amplifying sixteen-year-old Claudia's TikTok's to her nearly two hundred thousand Twitter followers. Claudia was complaining in her TikTok videos about the fact that her mother works in the Trump White House, and Lorenz egged on the situation to the point that Claudia was making public allegations of abuse. Lorenz excused this clearly unethical behavior by describing her and the teenager as "mutuals" and arguing that Claudia expressed to her that she wanted more views on her videos.

I wrote about Lorenz's questionable ethics shortly after the Conway saga and was promptly blocked on Twitter. Lorenz continues to manipulate people into feeling sorry for her, crying about alleged harassment and bullying whenever convenient.

After building a career on smearing her perceived enemies, she had the gall to go on MSNBC and accuse her alleged online harassers of giving her "severe PTSD" and causing her to contemplate suicide. Just a few weeks later, Lorenz was seeking to "expose" another social media influencer who she decided was problematic, inevitably inviting the same type of online harassment she frequently complained about onto that individual.

On April 18, 2022, Governor Ron DeSantis' press secretary Christina Pushaw tweeted a screenshot of an email she received from Taylor Lorenz, who had recently moved to the *Washington Post*. Lorenz revealed that she was about to publish a story "exposing" the woman running the "Libs of TikTok" account and asked Pushaw to comment on her "relationship" with the account within an hour.

The "Libs of TikTok" (LOTT) Twitter account racked up hundreds of thousands of followers in the past couple of years by reposting videos from radical and deranged leftists on TikTok. The account owner stayed anonymous during this time, preferring to let the videos speak for themselves minus the occasional one- to two-sentence caption. The reposted TikToks ran the gamut from public school teachers questioning age-of-consent laws to teenagers faking mental disorders for attention. LOTT offered an inside glimpse of the perverse lives of the terminally online left, some of whom used positions of power to behave unethically.

The left hates to be exposed, so LOTT had to be intimidated into silence. The left needed to reveal her identity so that their agitators would know exactly where to direct their harassment, hate, and threats. What followed was a model example of how left-wing activism gets swept up and "reported" on by mainstream journalists. Lorenz used all of the tools of the cancel mob: character assassination, public shaming, and misrepresentation.

Allow me to introduce you to Travis Brown, a former Twitter employee and online researcher who runs a "Hate Speech Tracker." Brown receives financial support from the Prototype Fund, which is, in turn, funded by the German government. Brown claims to have "millions" of "far right" social media accounts archived under his tracker and has openly expressed support for Antifa, the violent left-wing group that burns cities and assaults people they claim are "fascists."[205] Targets of Brown's cancel campaigns say he obsessively stalked them, harassed them, and tried to destroy their careers over relatively minor ideological disagreements.[206]

"Unmasking bullies is good, whether they're an anonymous troll who harasses trans women in an obscure programming language community, or an anonymous hate brand with an audience of millions," Brown tweeted, failing to see that he is a bigger bully than anyone he is "unmasking."

---

[205] Twitter. https://twitter.com/travisbrown?lang=bg

[206] John A De Goes. "Supporting Martin Odersky & Other Scala Oss Developers." John A De Goes, November 19, 2021. https://degoes.net/articles/travis-brown-abuser.

Just two days before Lorenz reached out to Christina Pushaw for comment, Brown and another Antifa researcher posted a series of tweets revealing old usernames and tweets from the LOTT account.[207] The pair deduced that the account was owned by a New York-based woman named Chaya Raichik. Their doxxing was immediately amplified by other left-wing activists at Media Matters, including our old friend Ari Drennen. Remember him/her? Graph Massara, a night editor for *Politico*, liked several of the sleuth's tweets. Most importantly, Taylor Lorenz herself follows Travis Brown and liked several of his tweets about Raichik.

Even before Lorenz published her article revealing Raichik's identity, her use of the word "expose" in her email to Christina Pushaw confirmed that she had negative intentions. It was also problematic that she only gave Pushaw an hour to respond to the inquiry. It's a tactic journalists use to avoid giving a subject of a story an appropriate amount of time to comment, while still being able to technically say that they were offered that chance. Lorenz obviously wanted to write that Pushaw declined or failed to comment in time for publication.

As if it weren't bad enough that Lorenz was writing a doxxing piece based on evidence gathered by German government-funded Antifa radicals, Raichik shared that Lorenz had showed up at the homes of her relatives, even posting a photo showing the reporter masked-up on their doorstep. Lorenz, the *Washington Post*, and their friends across corporate media insisted that this was normal shoe leather reporting and compared Lorenz's actions to those of

---

[207] Brown, Travis. "Pro-Tip: If You Want to Run a Viral Moral Panic Account for the Worst People on Earth and Stay Anonymous, Maybe Start from Scratch Instead of Doing Whatever the Fuck This Is. https://T.co/Ojzuxgqdog Pic. twitter.com/imskpdjn4A." Twitter, April 16, 2022. https://twitter.com/travisbrown/status/1515218000001081346.

Woodward and Bernstein during Watergate.[208] Give me a break! Are we really comparing exposing one of the biggest presidential scandals of all time to knocking on doors in a mask because someone reposted a TikTok on the internet?

Despite public outcry, Lorenz's laughably biased piece dropped on April 19.[209] She revealed Raichik's full name and location and linked to a copy of her real estate license that included a full address. She also curiously mentioned that Raichik is an Orthodox Jew. The article tried to justify "exposing" Raichik, noting the far reach of the Libs of TikTok account, but never explained why her identity in particular was newsworthy or even interesting. As far as anyone could tell, Raichik was just a private citizen who started the account as a hobby. She had no secret connections to politicians or activist groups, outside of donations she wasn't being paid, and otherwise wasn't a public figure. So why was her name suddenly of public interest?

Lorenz tried to thread this needle by smearing Libs of TikTok and Raichik. She referred to the account as "anti-LGBTQ+" and "antitrans" and accused it of bringing unwarranted harassment on people for no reason other than their sexuality or gender identity. Several of the examples used to make this point were

---

[208] Thompson, Alex. "Showing up at People's Homes Is Standard Journalism That More Reporters Should Do Like Half of 'All the President's Men' Is Woodstein Showing up at People's Homes. Https://T.co/LqMyjlfdV3." Twitter, April 19, 2022. https://twitter.com/AlexThomp/status/1516406517729316866?ref_src=twsrc%5Etfw%7Ctwcamp%5Etweetembed%7Ctwterm%5E151640651 7729316866%7Ctwgr%5E%7Ctwcon%5Es1_&ref_url=https%3A%2F%2F-www.mediaite.com%2Fprint%2Ftaylor-lorenz-sparks-furious-uproar-for-re-vealing-brooklyn-realtor-as-creator-of-libs-of-tiktok-account%2F.

[209] Lorenz, Taylor. "Meet the Woman behind Libs of TikTok, Secretly Fueling the Right's Outrage Machine." *Washington Post*, May 11, 2022. https://www.washingtonpost.com/technology/2022/04/19/libs-of-tiktok-right-wing-media/.

deliberately misrepresented or described in a vague manner so as to make Libs of TikTok seem like a bully.

The opening paragraph of Lorenz's article claims that Libs of TikTok "posted a video of a woman teaching sex education to children in Kentucky, calling the woman in the video a 'predator.'" The real story is that the Kentucky woman was hosting a "Sexy" summer camp for teenagers that included lessons on "The Three P's: Pee, Poop, and Pleasure," "Sex on Drugs," and "Oversexualization and Policing of Blackness." Even worse, this same woman had posted a video encouraging toddlers to masturbate and "explore their bodies."[210]

Lorenz also fretted that "Tyler Wrynn, a former English teacher in Oklahoma, posted a video telling LGBTQ kids shunned by their parents that Wrynn was 'proud of them' and 'loved them' but was faced with harassment after his video was featured on Libs of TikTok. What did Wrynn actually say?

> *"If your parents don't love and accept you for who you are this Christmas, fuck them, I'm your parents now."*

Oh sure, that's who I want teaching children. Lorenz and the *Washington Post* know that there is no defense for this type of behavior, so they have to lie and allege that Raichik is just being mean to gay people.

Lorenz went beyond misrepresenting the content of the Libs of TikTok account. She also reached back into Raichik's personal history in an attempt at character assassination. Old tweets from Raichik show that she was present at the January 6, 2020, protest

---

[210] Poff, Jeremiah. "Kentucky Summer Camp Teaches Children to Masturbate and Have Sex on Drugs." Restoring America, March 9, 2022. https://www.washingtonexaminer.com/restoring-america/community-family/kentucky-summer-camp-teaches-children-to-masturbate-and-have-sex-on-drugs.

against election fraud in Washington, DC. Lorenz's allies in the media cried that Raichik was an "insurrectionist" who was subverting democracy, first through her appearance at the Capitol riot and again with her aggregative Twitter account. However, Raichik's tweets also reveal that she left the rally when it started to get violent. It is not a crime to attend a protest nor does it make someone a public figure worthy of being reported on in one of the most powerful newspapers in the country.

As if the bias wasn't evident yet, Lorenz also made sure to quote "experts" in her article—all of whom were from left-wing activist organizations. She included a quote from Drennen, the Media Matters director who was amplifying Brown's doxxing campaign days earlier, and Gillian Branstetter, a media strategist for the ACLU, who claimed Libs of TikTok was casting all transgender people as "villains." Media Matters must have been thrilled that Lorenz had done their dirty work for them. The week before Lorenz's piece dropped in the *Washington Post*, Media Matters had run something of an investigation complaining that Christina Pushaw had interacted with Libs of TikTok often.[211] In addition to quoting Drennen, Lorenz cited the Media Matters investigation.

I reached out to multiple editors at the *Washington Post* to ask them if Lorenz abided by their journalistic standards in the course of reporting on Libs of TikTok and Raichik. Specifically, I asked, how did Lorenz showing up at her family member's homes comport with the universally recognized journalistic principle of minimizing harm? The *Washington Post* eventually responded

---

[211] Gogarty, Written by Kayla, and Research contributions from Jeremy Tuthill. "Anti-LGBTQ Twitter Account 'Libs of TikTok' Seemingly Inspired Attacks from Florida Governor's Press Secretary." Media Matters for America. https://www.mediamatters.org/twitter/anti-lgbtq-twitter-account-libs-tik-tok-seemingly-inspired-attacks-florida-governors-press.

with a statement they published concurrently on their social media accounts:

"Taylor Lorenz is an accomplished and diligent journalist whose reporting methods comport entirely with the *Washington Post*'s professional standards," Cameron Barr, senior managing editor at the *Washington Post* said. "Chaya Raichik, in her management of the Libs of TikTok Twitter account and in media interviews, has had significant impact on public discourse and her identity had become public knowledge on social media. We did not publish or link to any details about her personal life."

This was a straight-up lie. We've already established that an early version of Lorenz's article did include a link to Raichik's real estate license. I followed up with the *Washington Post* on that point, and they told me this:

> *"We linked to publicly available professional information and ultimately deemed it unnecessary."*

The real estate license was only "publicly available" at that point, of course, because bad faith left-wing activists had started sharing Raichik's name on social media and the *Washington Post* chose to elevate their work. Alex Stamos, a tech expert at Stanford University, debunked the whole idea that Lorenz did not dox Libs of TikTok.[212]

"De-anonymizing somebody online in a major outlet is a form of doxxing, period. Even if done with public records. Even if done to somebody you dislike," Stamos said. "I have been

---

[212] Stamos, Alex. "'It Was in the Public Record. 'I Have Been Threatened by Extremist Groups Using Public Records. I Have Friends Who Have Been Swatted Using Public Records. the Act of Taking Somebody's Public Information and Pointing to It in a Charged Context Is the Doxxing." Twitter, April 19, 2022. https://twitter.com/alexstamos/status/1516400147755798531.

threatened by extremist groups using public records. I have friends who have been swatted using public records. The act of taking somebody's public information and pointing to it in a charged context is the doxxing."

At least, the *Washington Post* admitted that their "professional standards" are now pure garbage. I suppose it takes some guts to be honest about that.

Lorenz continued her own lies during an appearance on CNN's *Reliable Sources*, telling host Brian Stelter that the *Post* never included personal information about Raichik and arguing that exposing her was newsworthy because she could have been part of a foreign disinformation campaign. That's a delicious layer of irony since the information sourced for Lorenz's article was obtained with funding from the German government. Further, when Lorenz discovered that an average American citizen was running the account and *not* a foreign actor or secret paid political activist, shouldn't that have been her cue to stop digging? Even the *Daily Dot*, a publication that loves to smear conservatives whenever possible, declined to actually name Raichik in its piece about her account history published a day before the *Washington Post*'s article.[213]

Beyond trying to justify the article, Lorenz did what she does best—complained about the harassment she brought onto Raichik and her family being turned around on her.

Unsurprisingly, the rest of the mainstream media leaped to the *Washington Post*'s defense. Most hardly covered the actual substance of her reporting, instead focusing on right-wing attacks on her methods and insisting that Raichik's identity was

---

[213] Goforth, Claire. "Libs of TikTok-the Influential, Mystery Twitter Account Hailed by Mainstream Conservatives-Attended Jan. 6 Capitol Protest." The Daily Dot, April 20, 2022. https://www.dailydot.com/debug/libs-of-tiktok-attended-capitol-riot/.

newsworthy. Poynter, an organization that offers online courses in journalistic ethics and credentials fact-checking outlets, said Lorenz was "doing her job."[214] NBC News,[215] Rolling Stone,[216] CNN,[217] MSNBC[218] concurred.

It troubles me that I have spent such a large portion of this book on this loathsome individual, but Lorenz's rise in media and acceptance at corporate outlets is important because it is emblematic of a much deeper rot.

The corporate media is willing to openly use left-wing activism to guide its reporting. It abandons journalistic standards if they can be used to advance and control certain narratives. It is not actually interested in holding power to account but in wielding its own power to crush dissenting viewpoints from average American citizens. It does all of this not just because it is ideologically beholden to the left but also because it is terrified of people like Taylor Lorenz. As we saw earlier, Lorenz was one of the many bullies at the *Times* who got into private and public

---

[214] Jones, Tom. "Opinion: The Taylor Lorenz Controversy Should Not Be a Controversy at All." Poynter, April 22, 2022. https://www.poynter.org/newsletters/2022/what-happened-taylor-lorenz-libs-of-tiktok-controversy/.

[215] "Why the 'Doxxing' of 'Libs of TikTok' Creator Is Justified." NBCNews.com, April 21, 2022. https://www.nbcnews.com/think/opinion/doxxing-libs-tiktok-creator-justified-rcna25280.

[216] Bouza, Kat. "Taylor Lorenz Wrote about Libs of TikTok -- and Conservatives Are Having a Meltdown over It." *Rolling Stone*, April 19, 2022. https://www.rollingstone.com/culture/culture-news/libs-of-tiktok-expose-taylor-lorenz-1339595/.

[217] Bouza, Kat. "Taylor Lorenz Wrote about Libs of TikTok -- and Conservatives Are Having a Meltdown over It." *Rolling Stone*, April 19, 2022. https://www.rollingstone.com/culture/culture-news/libs-of-tiktok-expose-taylor-lorenz-1339595/.

[218] "The 'Libs of TikTok' Creator Has Been Unmasked. That's a Good Thing." MSNBC, April 20, 2022. https://www.msnbc.com/the-reidout/reidout-blog/libs-of-tiktok-creator-identified-rcna25036.

spats with her colleagues and, despite being a mere staff reporter, demanded changes to the paper's editorial content.

The corporate media implicitly understands that young, woke staffers can turn their progressive anger internally at any time. The same tactics that they use to expose people like Chaya Raichik can and will be used against them. The corporate media's major folly is believing that offering these young staffers some control over the editorial and cultural direction of their outlets will save them. It is the same mistake made by the college administrations who sought to quell protests by giving the campus left everything they wanted.

After crying—complete with audible sobs, shaking hands, and a trembling voice—on MSNBC to a sympathetic host about online harassment, Lorenz bashed the network, saying they "f–ked up royally."[219] Instead of doing some soul-searching about why a TV segment featuring an extremely privileged woman complaining about people being mean to her online evoked such a negative reaction from viewers, Lorenz blamed MSNBC for their edit of the interview.

"Instead of using me for clickbait NBC news [sic] needs to educate their journalists on how to cover these types of campaigns," Lorenz wrote. "Their segment lacks crucial context and only serves to fuel the right-wing smear campaign I've been dealing with for a year. The media must do better."

She reiterated in another message, "If your segment or story on 'online harassment' leads to even worse online harassment for your subjects, you f--ked up royally and should learn how to cover these things properly before ever talking about them again."

---

[219] Wulfsohn, Joseph A. "MSNBC Faces Backlash from Two Journalists Profiled in on-Air Segment about Online Harassment." Fox News, April 6, 2022. https://www.foxnews.com/media/msnbc-taylor-lorenz-kate-sosin-online-harassment.

Kate Sosin, who appeared on the segment with Lorenz, also complained publicly that the network had "misgendered" her by indirectly labeling her a "female journalist." Sosin reportedly uses "they/them" pronouns to refer to herself. Sosin is the same reporter for The 19th who had previously instructed *Politico* staff how to report more "inclusively" on transgender individuals.

No matter how much you offer them, it's never enough for the woke left.

CHAPTER 19

GETTING CANCELED

When I started writing this book, I had run afoul of the left-wing cancel mob many times but somehow managed to avoid facing serious social or professional consequences.

Yes, I was reviled by left-wing students at Georgetown, but outside of politics I had a very normal social life. I snuck into bars with my roommates, played too much beer pong at house parties, pulled all-nighters at the library with classmates, attended fraternity formals, and played goalie for the club field hockey team. After graduation, angry Twitter activists would come after me occasionally but never to the point that I thought my bosses would be angry with me.

The first time I really worried that my career was in jeopardy was when Media Matters came after me for my high school tweets. That incident taught me a lot about cancel culture, so I was mentally prepared the next time I found myself in the crosshairs.

In the fall of 2021, I signed a contract with a DC conservative talk radio station, WMAL, to co-host the morning drive-time radio show. The program was called "O'Connor & Company" and featured longtime radio host Larry O'Connor alongside a rotating group of three female co-hosts: myself, Julie Gunlock, and Patrice Onwuka. I co-hosted the show every Wednesday and Thursday. The station received a lot of great feedback about the new programming and invested a lot of money into having the four of us do a professional photo shoot for marketing materials. Within a few months, we ladies were receiving requests from local businesses to advertise for them on the program.

I first started guest hosting on WMAL in 2019 and was thrilled to finally have a permanent slot in the lineup. WMAL carried Rush Limbaugh, Mark Levin, Ben Shapiro, Dan Bongino, and other incredibly talented radio broadcasters and was listened to daily by very influential DC politicos. Having grown up in the area, it was an honor to be able to speak directly to the DMV and to interview top-notch guests, including senators and congressmen, Trump administration officials, best-selling authors, and more.

Unfortunately, this gig that my family and I were so proud of would come to an end just about five months after it started.

On March 1, 2022, I was keeping track of Biden's State of the Union address. I was actually out at bar trivia with friends, which is my typical Tuesday night ritual, but was staying updated via Twitter. I saw a photo of Vice President Kamala Harris's brown suit and was quite disturbed. Who the hell wears brown in DC? Specifically, that shade of brown? This fashion crime had to be called out.

I initially was going to tweet "Kamala looks like a poop emoji" but, ironically, advised by the trivia team that it could get me in trouble. I brainstormed something new:

> "Kamala looks like a UPS employee. What can brown do for you? Nothing good, apparently."

It certainly wasn't my most genius or original joke, but I thought it'd be good for a few retweets. The joke was fairly obvious, so I thought. "What can brown do for you" was a longtime UPS slogan—retired in 2010—that referred to the employees' signature brown uniforms. The answer, "nothing good, apparently," was a reference to the fact that Kamala has been an incredibly ineffective vice president, from bungling every assignment she's given, to botching public appearances and hemorrhaging staffers.

The tweet performed fairly well and got some chuckles. A few Twitter users even made some memes placing a UPS ballcap on Kamala's head and a UPS logo on the breast of her blazer. Her outfit was pretty universally panned, even by left-wing magazines that chastised her for not wearing yellow to complete the Ukrainian flag theme that inspired Speaker Nancy Pelosi's royal blue suit. Even Saturday Night Live made a dig at the fact that Kamala's suit blended into her leather chair, with Weekend Update anchor Michael Che joking, "Many of the members of Congress attending the State of the Union wore blue and yellow to show their support for Ukraine, while Kamala Harris wore all brown to do what she's done for the last year: Disappear into the background."

It wasn't until a few days later that my joke became a problem. We're going on a little aside here, so bear with me.

Halfway across the country, conservative students at the University of North Texas were gearing up for an event with Jeff Younger, a candidate for a state House seat. Younger was scheduled to speak on March 2 in favor of criminalizing sex transitions for minors. Younger had recently lost custody of his own son because his ex-wife was convinced that the child was actually a girl and needed medical intervention to "affirm" the child's gender.

I had started covering the story about a week earlier when Kelly Neidert, the chairwoman of the Young Conservatives of Texas (YCT) at the University of North Texas (UNT), tipped me off to some brewing contention.[220] Neidert was printing out flyers at the campus library for the event with the tagline "Criminalize Child Transitions" when a male student confronted her, calling her a "bitch" and a "fake-ass Christian." The video received 1.2 million views on Twitter and sparked death threats against Neidert and her family as well as a petition to have her expelled from campus, which got over twenty thousand signatures.[221] University President Neal Smatresk got involved, sending a campuswide email reluctantly affirming the YCT's right to free speech but chastising them for holding "intolerant views."

"I know the last several days may have felt particularly difficult for the transgender members of our community, due to the intolerant views of a handful of campus members," Smatresk wrote. "We have a variety of resources through our Division of Inclusion, Diversity, Equity and Access to support you during your time at UNT, and we hope to offer you a safe place to heal and grow your support system."

Smatresk also asserted that the "very existence" of students might be challenged "in ways that are incredibly hurtful," but urged them to use the "freedom to express yourself" to "[disempower]" their oppressors.

The situation reminded me so much of my experiences at Georgetown. You had a strong, conservative woman standing up

---

[220] "Opposing Child Gender Transitions Is 'Intolerant,' Says College President." The Spectator World, February 23, 2022. https://spectator-world.com/topic/university-north-texas-president-students-intolerant-child-gender-transitions/.

[221] "Sign the Petition." Change.org. https://www.change.org/p/the-university-of-north-texas-expel-kelly-neidert-for-harassment-towards-the-trans-community?redirect=false.

to a mob, a spineless administrator egging on the mob, and a mob that was still dissatisfied. I knew that Younger's speech was a powder keg ready to explode. Sure enough, dozens of protesters showed up on March 2, banging on desks, cursing, screaming about "transphobia," and chanting "fuck these fascists." The event got so volatile that police had to escort Neidert and Younger out of the building as hordes of protesters chased them and shouted threats. Neidert and a police officer were forced to take refuge in a janitor's closet at one point, but eventually both Neidert and Younger made it to police cars. The mob wasn't happy that the pair were getting away and attempted to surround and block the police cars.

According to Smatresk and video at the scene, the protesters banged on the cars and tried to impede their movement. The police flipped on their lights and sirens and inched forward to push the protesters out of the way.[222] One member of the mob can be seen quickly getting out of the car's way and then limping their way to the nearby grass. That individual was taken to the hospital, but no serious injuries were reported.

Left-wing activists and the media seized on this minor injury and ignored the violent behavior of the protesters and the fact that they were impeding emergency vehicles. Suddenly, the news that the police had bumped a protester while escorting the transphobic fascists off campus was the *real* story.

Arguably the loudest voice pushing this narrative was Steven Monacelli, a Texas-based freelance writer for *Rolling Stone*, the *Daily Beast*, and *Dallas Weekly*. Monacelli had been following the

---

[222] Lucinda Breeding-Gonzales Staff Writer. "UNT Police SUV Strikes Protester at Evening Event." *Denton Record-Chronicle*, March 3, 2022. https://dentonrc.com/education/higher_education/university_of_north_texas/unt-police-suv-strikes-protester-at-evening-event/article_2ea56f4d-7ce2-5fb6-9efe-a95bc9134e0f.html.

UNT story as long as I had and had something of an obsession with Neidert. He was constantly tweeting at and about her and cheering on the campus mob that sought to harass her off campus. Very normal journalistic behavior!

After the March 2 event with Jeff Younger, the *Daily Wire*'s Matt Walsh floated the idea of hosting his own speech at UNT about transgenderism. Monacelli declared that he would be the "new bullying candidate" for UNT students, and I called him a "creep" for being so hung up on a female college student.

"Did you see the bit about the cop car hitting the protester?" Monacelli asked me.

"Oh, I saw the video. Looks like your buddies surrounded and tried to impede an emergency vehicle with its sirens on that was repeatedly honking at them to move. It's no wonder you were fired from your reporting job with this level of misrepresentation," I wrote back.

Monacelli was getting ratioed, and he and his rabid left-wing followers didn't like that very much. They started trying to dig up dirt on me and settled on—you guessed it—the tweet about Kamala's State of the Union outfit. Monacelli posted a screenshot of the tweet multiple times and suggested that the "what can brown do for you" comment was not about Kamala's suit, but about her skin color.[223] His followers complied with this implicit request to cancel me, and started tweeting at and sending emails to my employers.

Monacelli graduated from Northwestern University in 2013 with a theater degree and was a contributor to the *Daily Northwestern*, where he wrote about "privilege" and "institutional"

---

[223] Monacelli, Steven. "Oh My Well Now We're Just Telling on Ourselves Now Aren't We Amber Pic.twitter.com/brxv6KIqRT." Twitter, March 5, 2022. https://twitter.com/stevanzetti/status/1499971516347387904.

and "internalized" racism.[224] He went on to work at Google for three years before diving head first into progressive activism and "journalism" in 2020. Monacelli was fired from his job at the *Dallas Observer* just a year later after falsely reporting that a series of flyers posted by a local social justice group urging white parents not to send their kids to college was a "false flag" operation by a right-wing organization.[225] Despite a track record of fake news, he's managed to contribute regularly to multiple news outlets and has even appeared on CNN to talk about "QAnon." The *Daily Beast* and *Rolling Stone* have published "reports" by him calling opposing medical gender transitions for minors "transphobia." He has excused harassment and threats toward conservative college students and has written that concerns over grooming in schools are "rooted in delusion." He's even posted threatening photos with a gun to his Twitter account. In short, Monacelli is your typical woke activist journalist, and the media is more than happy to give him a platform to spew nonsense.

I thought (and still think) his followers' attempts to cancel me over a joke about the vice president's outfit were ridiculous. After the previous attempt at cancellation over my high school tweets, I was determined to not be fearful of and apologetic to the woke mob. I mocked them by tweeting a list of my employers for their "cancellation convenience," quite sure that neither *The Spectator* nor WMAL would take their accusations of racism seriously.

The Spectator received one email from someone claiming to be canceling their subscription over my Kamala joke, but a quick

---

[224] DailyNorthwestern, and Steven Monacelli. "Letter to the Editor: The Invisibility of Racism and of Privilege." *The Daily Northwestern*, September 17, 2012. https://dailynorthwestern.com/2012/04/30/archive-manual/letter-to-the-editor-the-invisibility-of-racism-and-of-privilege/.

[225] OSD, Team. "Steven Monacelli out at Dallas Observer." The Other Side Dallas, August 4, 2021. https://othersidedallas.com/2021/08/03/steven-monacelli/.

search of our subscriber database proved they were lying. We called them out on Twitter, and within a day or two, the commotion had died down. I thought I was home free.

The following Wednesday, March 9, I co-hosted the morning radio show at WMAL per usual. We had our typical show meeting afterward, and my direct supervisor didn't mention the tweet or the backlash. Instead, I stayed a few minutes late to discuss an endorsement deal with a local wine company that was set to start the following week. Everything seemed totally normal.

However, that afternoon I received a phone call from an unknown DC number. It was Jeff Boden, the vice president of DC programming, and Kriston Fancellas, the vice president of Human Resources for Cumulus Media, WMAL's parent company. At this point, I thought maybe I would receive a warning to be more careful on social media. I was completely unprepared for what happened next.

Boden and Fancellas informed me that they had been made aware of a tweet I sent about the vice president and that the company does not condone racism. The tweet, and the follow-up where I joked about being canceled, were in violation of Cumulus Media's social media policy. As such, I was terminated effective immediately.

To recap, I made a throwaway joke about Kamala Harris wearing a brown suit. Radical activists who believe children should transition to another gender, possibly leaving them with osteoporosis, brain damage, and infertility, reframed the joke as racist so they could get me in trouble. Cumulus, which owns numerous conservative talk radio stations around the country, complied.

I was upset, obviously, but mostly furious. It wasn't surprising to me when campus administrators and already liberal media outlets caved to the woke mob. They at least had some ideological overlap. But a billion-dollar media conglomerate that for years hosted Rush Limbaugh, Mark Levin, Ben Shapiro, and other conservative heavy hitters? That didn't make much sense to me.

Over the next month, other WMAL hosts worked behind the scenes to try to get me back on the air. They held multiple meetings with corporate executives but were unable to make any progress. During one meeting, executives actually admitted that they weren't sure my tweet about Kamala was actually racist. All that mattered, they said, was that it had the perception of being racist. What a dangerous standard. Pretty much every conservative talk radio host is accused of racism with shocking regularity. As discussed before, left-wing activist organizations like Media Matters literally pay people to listen to conservative programming, to manipulate and misrepresent our words, and to launch boycotts to get us off the air. If a media company just fired their talent every time this happens, these activists would be able to single handedly destroy conservative media with a few well-placed articles.

Nonetheless, my ousting seemed to be final, so I started planning next steps. My first moves were to get a written termination letter so that Cumulus could not lie about why they fired me as well as additional copies of company policies and my contract. I reached out to my union representative, who offered…nothing. I spoke to two lawyers to see if I could file a wrongful termination lawsuit or at least scare Cumulus into giving me some severance. Both advised that because I was an at-will employee and because the social media policy included a vague clause about avoiding "public discredit" to the company, I had no legal recourse.

By this point, listeners were already asking why I wasn't on the air. My instinct was to blast Cumulus and WMAL publicly for what they did to me, but I considered if being seen as a troublemaker or someone who speaks negatively about past employers could hurt my career. That path seemed selfish and wrong to me. After years of my life fighting back against people who wanted to silence me, why stop now? For a few extra dollars in the bank? No way.

I ended up calling up a valued mentor who cemented my decision. When I asked him if I should be worried about burning bridges, he said emphatically, "There are no bridges anymore!"

How true. Wokeness had infected every part of society: major corporations, Hollywood, social media, the government, and, as reported in this book, the media. Now, the owners of conservative outlets were allowing this disease to spread too. What would we have left if we were all governed by the fascistic rules of progressives? We don't have freedom if a young woman from a working-class background cannot criticize the most powerful woman in the country because she comes from a "marginalized" group. We don't have freedom if we cannot call the chemical castration of children "abuse." We don't have freedom if we are all terrified of speaking freely on the most important issues of our time because of the potential to be fired, deplatformed, debanked, or otherwise shunned from participating in society. I may sound a bit dramatic over losing a part-time radio gig, but censorship in all its forms is an existential threat to our country. Think about it this way: there would be no America if our founders did not exercise their God-given right to speak against tyranny.

I couldn't save the *New York Times*, the *Washington Post*, *Politico*, or Disney, but maybe I could affect change in my little corner of the industry.

On April 4, almost a month after I was fired, I published an article with the *Spectator* explaining what happened to me.[226]

---

[226] "I Was Fired for a Joke about Kamala Harris's Outfit." The Spectator World, April 5, 2022. https://spectatorworld.com/topic/fired-joke-kamala-harris-outfit-wmal-cumulus-cancel-culture/.

The outpouring of support was immediate and overwhelming. My story was picked up by the *Daily Mail*, the *New York Post*, Mediaite, Fox News, the *Daily Caller*, *The Hill*, the *American Spectator*, and more. I was a guest on over thirty television and radio programs that week, including *Inside Edition* and *Tucker Carlson Tonight*.

I told Tucker that Cumulus Media's biggest mistake was that "they thought I was going to roll over and shut up about this."

Cancel culture thrives on compliance and silence. That is how mobs are effective. Companies comply because they erroneously believe they can appease the mob and protect themselves from further reputational damage. They do not understand that they are incentivizing additional cancellations. The targets of the cancel campaigns stay silent because they fear becoming unemployable or are unaware that they are helping to perpetuate the very system that destroyed them.

I wanted to flip the script. I wanted to make it more painful for Cumulus Media to fire their employees than to stand up for them. I wanted to show them that conservatives, when we fight back, have far more power than they could've ever imagined. If corporations aren't going to abide by principles—and they won't, because they are soulless—then we need to meet them with even greater force than the woke mobs. That is the only way they will stop giving in.

Naturally, after publicly tarring and feathering Cumulus Media and its executives for two weeks, I was not offered my job back. But I am told that they were completely blindsided by the amount of angry emails, tweets, Facebook posts, and phone calls from conservatives they received. Good. Almost two weeks after I went public, Reuters reported that media titan Jeff Warshaw offered $1.2 billion to acquire Cumulus Media.[227] I don't know much about Warshaw, but hopefully he can better support a culture of free speech for my many friends who still work at Cumulus-owned radio stations.

We never learned who actually made the decision to fire me, but in retrospect, I am not surprised that it happened.

CEO Mary Berner was brought in to Cumulus in 2015 and bragged about how she fixed the media conglomerate's "dysfunctional," "toxic," and "lousy" culture.[228]

I'm sure there were positive changes to be made, but all I saw when I was brought on in the fall of 2021 was useless bureaucracy and an outsized focus on corporate buzzwords like "equity" and "inclusion." New employees had to take hours of diversity and sexual harassment training, despite numerous studies showing that diversity trainings are useless or even counterproductive. I was stunned one day when I logged onto our corporate database and saw that Berner was offering employees a $2,000 bonus if they referred new employees who "increased the company's diversity" (paraphrased). Even if a particular white candidate was more qualified for a position at Cumulus, employees were being financially incentivized to recommend a minority candidate instead. Is that not discrimination?

The cavern between the values we espoused on the radio and those of our parent company was most prevalent in the vaccine mandate implemented in the summer of 2021, before I was officially brought on. Talented board operators, producers, and hosts

---

[227] Person, and Dawn Chmielewski Greg Roumeliotis. "Exclusive Warshaw-Led Consortium in $1.2 Bln Bid for Cumulus Media -Sources." Reuters, April 15, 2022. https://www.reuters.com/business/media-telecom/exclusive-warshaw-led-consortium-12-bln-bid-cumulus-media-sources-2022-04-14/.

[228] Berner, Mary. "How We Fixed Our Toxic Culture: The 'Culture Fix Playbook." ChiefExecutive.net, September 21, 2017. https://chiefexecutive.net/toxic-culture/.

were forced out of Cumulus over their refusal to let a company make their medical decisions for them. Former employees have told me that they were warned not to speak negatively about the vaccines on the air.

I wish I had taken all of these warning signs more seriously when I was hired for "O'Connor & Company." I had faith that my friends at WMAL would be able to protect me from Cumulus.

However, after digging into the politics of the company executives after my firing, I understand now that I probably never stood a chance. Cumulus didn't just give in to the leftist mob because they are cowards. They gave in because they are leftists themselves.

CEO Mary Berner, who earned more than $6.5 million in total compensation in 2021[229] on the backs of conservative talent, is a Democratic donor—and apparently a soulless corporate heathen. A well-placed source tells me that at an event with Cumulus investors a couple of years ago, Berner bragged about how she would "throw anyone under the bus if it meant protecting shareholders." So much for getting rid of that "toxic" workplace culture!

According to FEC records,[230] Berner gave $1,000 each to Democratic candidates Sara Gideon and Cal Cunningham in 2020. In 2019, she gave $1,000 to Amy Klobuchar. Between 2017 and 2018, she donated $280 to ActBlue, a left-wing fundraising company.

Her biggest donation was in 2018 when she gave a whopping $20,500 to the Human Rights Campaign's Equality Votes PAC. The Human Rights Campaign (HRC) is the largest LGBTQ+

---

[229] Sec.gov. https://www.sec.gov/Archives/edgar/data/1058623/000139843222 000015/a51570.htm#a07

[230] "Browse Individual Contributions." FEC.gov. Accessed September 8, 2022. https://www.fec.gov/data/receipts/individual-contributions/? contributor_name=mary%2Bberner.

advocacy organization in the nation, and the Equality Votes PAC is its political advocacy arm. The HRC believes that biological men should be allowed to play women's sports, declared the Florida Parental Rights in Education bill to be "anti-LGBTQ+," and claim that puberty blockers for children are "fully reversible" and "medically necessary" for transgender children. Of course Berner and Cumulus took the side of the trans activists looking to can me.

The trend continues among the rest of the Cumulus board of directors. All of them, except for Berner, were named to the board in 2018 after Cumulus emerged from bankruptcy.

Most disturbingly, a longtime Media Matters director by the name of Tom Castro joined the board in 2018. Castro has been with Media Matters since 2013. My former *Daily Caller* colleague Andrew Kerr reported in the summer of 2021,[231] shortly before I joined WMAL, that Media Matters had curiously pulled back on coverage of Cumulus Media. Media Matters mentioned Cumulus at least 160 times before Castro joined the board in 2018, and just three times since then. Even when writing about comments made on air by Cumulus radio hosts, Media Matters placed blame for these statements on the host's other employers, like Fox News. They also declined to push boycotts of Cumulus advertisers, even though they organized one such boycott against Rush Limbaugh's show in 2012.

It's unclear if Castro was appointed to the Cumulus board so he could assist them in taming Media Matters' aggressive coverage of its hosts, but his biography on the Cumulus Media website curiously does not list his affiliation with the left-wing activist group.

---

[231] Kerr, Andrew. "Media Matters Gives Pass to Major Radio Network with Overlapping Board Membership." The Daily Caller, June 16, 2021. https://dailycaller.com/2021/06/15/media-matters-mark-levin-rush-limbaugh/.

Matthew Blank, the interim CEO of AMC and another Cumulus board member, gave at least $120,000 to Democrats and their affiliated PACS between 2012 and 2021, including thousands of dollars to Kamala Harris.[232] He is an especially big fan of Andrew Cuomo and Chuck Schumer.

Joan Gillman gave more than $18,000 to Democrats since 2016,[233] including multiple donations to the presidential campaigns of Hillary Clinton in 2016 and Joe Biden in 2020.

Board member David Baum gave $8,000 to Democratic candidates between 2018 and 2021.[234]

Brian Kushner was not as prolific as his colleagues, giving only $250 to a Democratic candidate way back in 2002.[235]

Andy Hobson, the chairman of the board, appears to be more split politically, giving tens of thousands to Mitt Romney and the Republican National Committee ahead of the 2021 election, but also peppering Democrats with smaller donations in the hundreds or thousands of dollars in the mid-2000s.[236]

That means of the seven current Cumulus board members, six give their money exclusively to Democrats. Is it any wonder why they were so quick to listen to the mob?

---

[232] "Donor Lookup." OpenSecrets. https://www.opensecrets.org/donor-lookup/results?name=matthew%2Bblank&order=desc&page=1&sort=D.

[233] "Donor Lookup." OpenSecrets. https://www.opensecrets.org/donor-lookup/results?name=joan%2Bgillman&order=desc&sort=D.

[234] "Browse Individual Contributions." FEC.gov. https://www.fec.gov/data/receipts/individual-contributions/?contributor_name=BAUM%2C%2B-DAVID&contributor_employer=the%2Bgolf%2Bchannel&max_date=12%2F31%2F2022.

[235] "Donor Lookup." OpenSecrets. https://www.opensecrets.org/donor-lookup/results?name=brian%2Bkushner.

[236] "Donor Lookup." OpenSecrets. https://www.opensecrets.org/donor-lookup/results?name=andrew%2Bhobson&order=desc&sort=D.

CHAPTER 20

THE WOKE DESTRUCTION

Have you ever heard of the black-eyed children? The story of the black-eyed children is an urban legend that originated in Abilene, Texas. According to the story, the black-eyed children show up at people's homes, knock on the door, and demand to be let inside. The children are said to spark an intense feeling of dread in those who encounter them. But they cannot enter unless they are invited. What happens if you let in the black-eyed children? Well, some say it's like bringing the devil himself into your home.

Think of the woke millennials like the black-eyed children. They can only go where they are invited, but they will wreak havoc on whoever gives them the tiniest opening.

Former President Donald Trump put it more simply: "Everything woke turns to shit."

The millennial takeover of the media is backfiring spectacularly. The same publications that seek to cancel people who challenge the liberal orthodoxy have to fire the little woke reporters who fired off racist tweets in their activist days.

Alexi McCammond promised when she was appointed as editor of *Teen Vogue* that she would be focusing on diversity and inclusion efforts. However, shortly after the announcement, she was forced to resign[237] when colleagues complained about decade-old tweets that were derogatory toward Asians and used homophobic slurs. Sarah Jeong lasted only a year on the *New York Times* editorial board after conservatives discovered that she had tweeted about being cruel to "old white men," expressed anger at "white people marking up the internet with their opinions like dogs pissing on fire hydrants," and asserted that white people's propensity to burn in the sun makes them "only fit to live underground like groveling goblins."

I was the first to report that Jeong also suggested it was okay to throw rocks and Molotov cocktails at police officers and often tweeted about how she wanted to "kill all men."[238]

Too bad, so sad. Media companies accelerated their downfall by filling their newsrooms with young, activism-minded journalists and then dropped their standards further to allow them to insert their woke nonsense into news stories. They started covering stories about offensive Halloween costumes and left-wing protest politics that were of little interest to the average American. Stories that readers actually care about are twisted to benefit the left as much as possible. When the stories can't be merely twisted, consumers are fed outright lies and news outlets refuse corrections. Anyone who doesn't comply with the new millennial regime is smeared by the powerful corporate media ecosystem.

---

[237] Robertson, Katie. "Teen Vogue Editor Resigns after Fury over Racist Tweets." *New York Times*, March 18, 2021. https://www.nytimes.com/2021/03/18/business/media/teen-vogue-editor-alexi-mccammond.html.

[238] Athey, Amber. "Nyt's Sarah Jeong Also Sent Anti-Cop, Anti-Men Tweets." *The Daily Caller*, August 3, 2018. https://dailycaller.com/2018/08/03/nyt-sarah-jeong-cop-men-tweets/.

This isn't how the media is supposed to operate in a democratic republic. This is how the media operates when it is run by mini Bolsheviks whose college years taught them that censorship, intimidation, and shame are the tools of power.

Actions have consequences, however, and the American public is wholly rejecting the millennial model for the media.

The same news outlets seeking redemption after getting the 2016 election so wrong are less trusted than ever. The Edelman Trust Barometer, an annual measure of trust in major institutions, revealed the extent of the crisis of confidence in the media.[239] In 2021, it reported that 56 percent of Americans believed journalists intentionally try to mislead them by saying things they know are not true. Fifty-nine percent believed that most news organizations are more interested in supporting certain political ideologies than informing the public, and 61 percent believe the media is doing a bad job at being objective and nonpartisan.

Corporate media arrogantly thought that demand for their services was inelastic. That no matter how much they lied to and gaslit the American people, viewers and readers would keep coming back for more.

At CNN, where Brianna Keilar and Brian Stelter threw around the term "white rage" and reporters dismissed Hunter Biden's laptop as "Russian disinformation," management foolishly believed they could draw millions of people to a new streaming service. CNN's parent company, WarnerMedia, invested $300 million[240] in CNN+ only for the platform to spectacularly col-

---

[239] Meek, Andy. "Fewer Americans than Ever before Trust the Mainstream Media." *Forbes*, December 10, 2021. https://www.forbes.com/sites/andy-meek/2021/02/20/fewer-americans-than-ever-before-trust-the-main-stream-media/?sh=66f3988b282a.

[240] Koblin, John, and Michael. "Inside the Implosion of CNN+." *New York Times*, April 24, 2022. https://www.nytimes.com/2022/04/24/business/media/cnn-plus-discovery-warner.html.

lapse. Within just a couple of weeks of its debut, WarnerMedia announced they'd be shutting down the service and laying off all of the employees involved. Executives had somehow identified twenty-nine million "CNN superfans"[241] who they believed would carry CNN+, even though CNN's primetime news programs can barely draw over half a million viewers.

In the first quarter of 2022, Netflix, which drew public outrage for sexualizing children in the film "Cuties" and recently added another title about a man getting pregnant, hemorrhaged millions of subscribers. It was the first time the streaming giant had lost subscribers in ten years.

Spotify recently declined to renew a multimillion-dollar podcast deal with the Obamas. Barack and Michelle Obama declined to appear more frequently on episodes, instead wanting to give airtime to "new, young voices," but couldn't draw enough listeners to make the exclusive deal worthwhile.

Jon Stewart once found great success with *The Daily Show* by mocking the absurdity of politics and bringing a satirical take to the news. It was the Democrat party line but it was funny. Stewart's new show, *The Problem with Jon Stewart*, instead fully leaned into wokeness. Stewart offered viewers exhausting lectures about "white resentment" and dreamed about "finger snapping" for guests who accused "white men" of racism.[242] By the show's fifth episode, viewership was down 78 percent from the pilot. Just 40,000 people were watching.

---

[241] Enjeti, Saagar. "How Delusional Are the People inside CNN? They Believed There Are 30 Million 'CNN Superfans' Who Would Pay for Their Product Pic.twitter.com/fwcv6xpnmf." Twitter, April 26, 2022. https://twitter.com/esaagar/status/1518977456216150016.

[242] Gillespie, Brandon. "Jon Stewart under Fire for Displaying 'Super-Woke' Views in Moments with Cory Booker, Andrew Sullivan." Fox News, April 7, 2022. https://www.foxnews.com/media/jon-stewart-under-fire-super-woke-views-moments-cory-booker-andrew-sullivan.

The media's leftward lurch has made it more out-of-touch with the American public than ever. That's reflected in more Americans abandoning legacy media and choosing to consume content from right-leaning and independent outlets.

The media is doing a great job of destroying its own credibility, but conservatives owe it to themselves to wreck them even more. We spent years assuring ourselves that the college "snowflakes" would disappear quietly into the night, only to watch them seize control and use it to bludgeon us. Our atonement for this grave error needs to involve learning how we can fight back and strip the corporate media of its remaining power.

My experience with Cumulus Media and WMAL confirmed for me that conservatives cannot be successful operating under the same corporate structure as left-wing media. Corporations are simply too responsive to external pressures to be reliable investors in conservative thought.

Even corporations that were once reliably apolitical cannot be trusted to abide by principles of free speech and diversity of thought thanks to the rise of ESGs. ESG stands for "environmental, social, and corporate governance" and is essentially a kind of social responsibility score for corporations. The ESG score presupposes that shareholders in a company can get a greater return on investment if the company adopts a certain moral framework. There is no regulatory agency that decides an ESG score for a company. Various institutions, including financial companies, asset managers, and stock brokers determine a company's ESG using public data, but the scoring methods—and thus results—can differ wildly.

I would be remiss if I didn't point out that this sounds awfully similar to the reasons environmental activists on college campuses give to encourage their schools to divest from fossil fuels and other "immoral" industries. Another case of campus politics being exported to the real world.

Each year, more and more investors are adopting ESGs as part of their calculation in determining whether or not to invest in a business. It doesn't sound bad on its face for companies to behave morally, but ESGs have become Trojan horses for a left-wing political agenda.[243] Because ESGs are so subjective, they can encourage companies to take positions on controversial legislation, accepting certain views on climate change, or offering specific trainings on sexual harassment, gender, and diversity. Consumers and investors can no longer simply vote with their wallets, because corporations are all encouraged to operate with the same set of—usually left-wing!—principles.

Launching boycotts against companies like Disney, Coca-Cola, and Nike, is a great first step in combating the woke take-over, but conservatives must recognize that corporations are not operating solely on financial incentives.

That being said, conservatives can be incredibly power-ful when we are willing to use some of the left's tactics against them. Flooding companies with emails, social media harass-ment campaigns, negative PR, and canceling subscriptions are effective tactics. That's why the left is so successful. After Disney responded to pressure from its woke employees to speak out against Florida's Parental Rights in Education bill, conservatives rallied and dropped Disney's stock to its lowest level in two years.

Historically, conservatives are not great at boycotts. We tend to purchase products or content because we enjoy it and we com-partmentalize the politics of the creator. This is a natural coping

---

[243] Morrison, Richard. "Conservatives Waking up: 'Responsible Investing' Could Mean Left-Wing Control." *National Review*, September 3, 2021. https://www.nationalreview.com/2021/09/conservatives-waking-up-re-sponsible-investing-could-mean-left-wing-control/.

mechanism because so many industries that used to be more apolitical, particularly sports and Hollywood, have gone irrevocably woke and there are few good alternatives. Data from Morning Consult suggests that brand boycotters tend to be wealthy, liberal, and well-educated.[244] Conservatives are more likely to latch on to a "Buycott." Rather than encouraging conservatives to pull their money from certain companies, a Buycott suggests they actively spend money at competitors that better align with their values. But this is only successful if the alternative product is actually...well, good and the strategy is especially challenging when it comes to the entertainment industry, where conservative artists are exceedingly difficult to find.

"I love conservative movies, but it's rare that the people who make them are trained in making them," Amanda Milius, a filmmaker, screenwriter, and John Milius's daughter, wrote in the *Spectator*. "As it turns out, there is a technique and rules that one ought to abide by. They actually make the movie better."

Sometimes, taking on the woke media is simply a matter of will power. Conservatives have to be willing to stand up the mob, even if it means a temporary sacrifice.

I'm not recommending that a working-class American who relies on their job to feed their family quit their job or cause a scene. But for those of us with a platform and the financial flexibility to speak out, what's your excuse? I lost 40 percent of my income leaving WMAL. I probably could have kept my mouth shut and started pitching myself to other radio stations, but I thought that my story was too important to keep bottled up. Cumulus needed to be held responsible, even in a small way,

---

[244] "Wealthy, Liberal and Well-Educated: Some of the Traits of a Brand Boycotter." Morning Consult, July 6, 2022. https://morningconsult.com/2019/09/18/wealthy-liberal-and-well-educated-some-of-the-traits-of-a-brand-boycotter/.

for what they had done, and other employees with the company needed to be warned about what could happen to them.

The truth, anyway, is that the public is so fed up with cancel culture that they love when people fight back. Conservatives who stand up for themselves usually end up better off because other patriots want to support people who speak unapologetically for our values. I used the extra ten hours a week I gained to launch my own podcast, *Unfit to Print*, a show that's completely independent of corporate media. I gained nearly forty thousand new followers on social media. Alex Epstein, who fought the *Washington Post*, was given free earned media for his book *Fossil Future*. Libs of TikTok gained hundreds of thousands of followers on Twitter, finally cracking one million, and announced an official partnership with the *Babylon Bee*.

The worst thing you can do when the mob comes after you is apologize.

Apologizing shows weakness, and the mob thrives on weakness. When they spot blood in the water, they will strike even harder.

CBS, of all places, had the right idea when they hired former Trump Chief of Staff Mick Mulvaney to be an on-air contributor. CBS staffers said they were "embarrassed" by the staffing decision because of Mulvaney's defense of Trump and his negative comments about the news media. But since those initial stories about backlash in March, there has been no further reporting on the issue nor any change to Mulvaney's status at the network. That suggests CBS didn't entertain the staff complaints and rightfully allowed the situation to blow over. Well done.

I saw firsthand the perils of caving to the woke mob in October 2018 when the Young Americans for Liberty (YAL) at American University invited me to speak on campus about a topic of my choice. It had been a little over two years since I left

Georgetown, and I was looking forward to using my platform to share conservative ideas to new audiences of young people.

The former YAL members who were involved in the following situation don't like it when I talk about it, because I suppose it's a bit embarrassing for them. But, again, this is my book and I get to do what I want.

My speech was set to take place around the same time as the Brett Kavanaugh hearings in front of the Senate Judiciary Committee, and we had learned a lot of information that would cast doubt on Christine Blasey Ford's claims of sexual assault. I decided to title my speech "No, Don't Believe All Women" and talk about the importance of due process when adjudicating sexual assault cases. I knew the title would probably rile some liberal students, but isn't that just good marketing? If I am going to volunteer to speak at an event for free, I'm at least going to make sure it has good attendance.

After the event went public, left-wing students immediately announced a protest against my "misogynistic" speech. YAL cowered and suggested changing the name of the speech, which I warned would get them nowhere. They changed it anyway, without my permission, to "Your Due Process." Boring!

Changing the name, of course, didn't do anything to quell anger from student activists. They still planned to protest. I appeared on Fox News to talk about the ridiculousness of the protest and sent some tweets promoting the event. The speech was very well attended and fairly respectful despite the group of protesters holding signs and chanting outside. My favorite part was when the protesters started chanting "Believe All Women" as I spoke about how Emmett Till was lynched for allegedly physically accosting a white woman in a store.

The YAL members told me that they were happy with how the event unfolded, and yet the club's leadership bashed me in a quote given to the student newspaper.

The article referred to the event as "controversial" and cited the Southern Poverty Law Center to suggest I worked for a news outlet with a "white nationalist problem."[245] The authors of the article, Aneeta Mathur-Ashton and Nazli Togrul, did not bother to reach out to me for comment. They now work for the *Washington Post* and Reuters. Surprise, surprise.

As for YAL, they told the reporters that I was "provocative" and "inflammatory" and that I had not promoted a civil discourse. This was patently false, as I stayed for a nice Q&A session with students, some of whom were incredibly disrespectful to me. YAL had already changed the name of my speech, and now they were throwing me under the bus in some bizarre attempt at damage control. This de facto apology didn't endear the club to the left-wing activists, who would despise them no matter what, and it had the unfortunate side effect of betraying the individual who did them a favor by speaking for free and putting on a well-attended event with tons of earned media.

I will truly never understand conservatives—or libertarians—who think they can win over people who hate them if they capitulate on their core beliefs. It is a self-degrading losing battle. A 2021 *Axios* poll found that 71 percent of college Democrats wouldn't go on a date with someone who voted for a Republican presidential candidate. Nearly 40 percent said they wouldn't even

---

[245] Nazli Togrul", "Aneeta Mathur-Ashton. "Young Americans for Liberty Chapter Hosts Controversial Event with Daily Caller Editor." The Eagle, October 30, 2018. https://www.theeagleonline.com/article/2018/10/young-americans-for-liberty-amber-athey.

be friends with someone who had done so.[246] A 2018 poll of adult Democrats found that 61 percent think Republicans are bigoted, racist, and sexist.[247] Have some self-respect, conservatives, and tell these people to buzz off!

Even when conservatives aren't trying to win the left over, they're often using their language.

Although I am glad that conservatives are making great efforts to expose the radical race-based teachings in our public schools, for example, we've made an unnecessary error by labeling it all "Critical Race Theory" (CRT). The left responds by insisting that CRT is a "theory taught in law schools," and conservatives are stuck explaining how the principles of CRT are being applied to grade school curricula. Instead of making it so complicated, we should just call it what it is. Racism. Don't use the term "post-birth" or "partial birth" abortion. It's infanticide. People who vote in favor of killing babies are not "pro-choice," they are pro-abortion. Arguing on someone else's terms and accepting their flawed premises is not how you win a debate.

This is especially true when you are up against the fundamentally dishonest woke crowd. We need to stop sanitizing our language for fear of being too harsh. The right successfully did this during the backlash over the Parental Rights in Education bill. Conservatives correctly and forcefully noted that if the left wants to teach sexually inappropriate topics to kindergartners, they are in favor of grooming. Leave it to the left to defend themselves. We don't need to do it for them.

---

[246] Rothschild, Neal. "Young Democrats More Likely to Despise the Other Party." *Axios*, December 8, 2021. https://www.axios.com/poll-political-polarization-students-a31e9888-9987-4715-9a2e-b5c448ed3e5a.html.

[247] Hart, Kim. "Poll: Majority of Democrats Think Republicans Are 'Racist,' 'Bigoted' or 'Sexist.'" *Axios*, November 12, 2018. https://www.axios.com/poll-democrats-and-republicans-hate-each-other-racist-ignorant-evil-99ae7afc-5a51-42be-8ee2-3959e43ce320.html.

One of the quickest ways Republicans in power can make the corporate media irrelevant is to stop engaging with them. Don't give them interviews, offer them scoops, leak information to them, or even entertain their existence. When they reach out to you with a bad faith request for comment, blast them publicly to all of your followers. Christina Pushaw, Saagar Enjeti, and Alex Epstein did this brilliantly to the *Washington Post*, and it neutered the hit pieces before they ever ran.

Republicans routinely complain about biased media coverage but continue to play the game. Many of them secretly want mainstream acceptance and relevance or foolishly believe they can outsmart the reporters trying to do them damage. The Trump administration was the worst offender. Trump publicly called the *New York Times* the "Failing *New York Times*" but would then call up Maggie Haberman to give her stories. He would give exclusive sit-down interviews to NBC News and CBS and speak to *Washington Post* reporters for their books, then complain when the coverage wasn't fair. His communications team would grant background interviews to reporters from the worst outlets and then come running to conservative and independent media to clean up the mess when they were inevitably given the fake news treatment. It was one of the most frustrating things to witness as a reporter who actually tried to be impartial. They were constantly rewarding the worst kind of behavior from journalists.

Compare how Trump handled the hostile press to how Florida Governor Ron DeSantis does it. DeSantis does not give interviews to reporters who hate him. He does not give the benefit of the doubt to outlets who have previously taken his comments out of context or asked biased questions at pressers.

After the *Washington Post* doxxed Libs of TikTok, another reporter reached out to press secretary Christina Pushaw asking to profile her. How did she respond? She told them to go pound sand.

"Wielding the power of a national newspaper to intimidate a private citizen for the thoughtcrime of posting TikTok videos… is not journalism," she wrote to the reporter. "I do not trust that a newspaper that elevates this sociopathic behavior will cover me fairly."

DeSantis avoids unnecessary PR damage and leaves partisan outlets begging for scraps. Losing access is a great incentive for the media to clean up its act.

Finally, conservatives have to dispel the notion that we can "infiltrate" the corporate media in the same way as the woke millennials. For decades, nonprofit organizations have trained young conservative journalists and then sent them off to work at mainstream publications in the hopes that they'd be able to change the culture. Instead, many of those conservatives were neutered by their editors or, when faced with the groupthink of a liberal newsroom, abandoned their conservative principles.

Eliana Johnson, who reported at *Politico* and was a CNN contributor, described this dynamic after CNN nixed her contract and she became editor-in-chief of the *Washington Free Beacon*.

"I worked at Politico. Your social circle becomes the *Politico* reporters, the *Times* reporters, the [Washington] *Post* reporters, these people are all talking to each other and that's part of what I found sort of unsatisfying," Johnson said. "You're not talking to persuadables or really making a difference."

She added that "covering things about wokeism gone too far" didn't fit in at liberal outlets, even though they had all had their own run-ins with backlash from younger staff.

There's no doubt that conservatives have a lot of work to do, but there's reason for hope. Shortly before I finished writing this book, I watched a stunning display of real journalistic talent at the University of Chicago.

Young reporters with the *Chicago Thinker*, a right-leaning student publication, sparked a national media conversation by merely asking thoughtful and challenging questions during a "Disinformation" conference being held at their school.[248] The students recognized that the media uses the term "disinformation" to root out information that they don't like. One student asked *The Atlantic*'s Anne Applebaum about the corporate media's suppression of the Hunter Biden laptop story, which was confirmed true, and earned the stunning admission that Applebaum didn't find the story "interesting." Another reporter asked CNN's Brian Stelter about his network's history with fake news, citing several specific examples, to which Stelter accused him of repeating a "popular right-wing narrative."

The Atlantic's editor-in-chief, Jeffrey Goldberg, was livid that his event was hijacked by these sharp youngsters. He used the best defense he had, calling the *Chicago Thinker*'s questions—you guessed it, "disinformation."

Thanks to a few well-placed questions, a small group of conservative students managed to embarrass and upend an entire corporate media parade. If they can do that, then there's no reason the tens of millions of patriotic, freedom-loving Americans can't take back our country from the dishonest, gaslighting, woke media.

Let's get to it.

---

[248] "*The Chicago Thinker* Staged a Media Regime Takedown This Week-Here's How We Did It." *The Chicago Thinker*, August 15, 2022. https://thechicagothinker.com/the-chicago-thinker-staged-a-media-regime-takedown-this-week-heres-how-we-did-it/.

ACKNOWLEDGMENTS

First, allow me to thank God. Through his grace I somehow made it through the worst year of my life and came out on the other side with my first book in hand.

I'd like to thank my family, of course, for learning very quickly that they should stop asking me how my book was coming along. Jonathan, for his love and endless patience in enduring all of the canceled date nights and midnight brainstorming sessions. My wonderful friends, who accompanied me for a cocktail or a round of golf when I just needed to get out of the house. ATHOS PR, including my agent Jonathan Bronitsky and Alexei Woltornist, for taking a chance on a first-time author. *The Spectator* for giving me the time I needed to finish my manuscript and my colleagues for picking up my slack. Lastly, my sweet cat Bentley who lovingly draped himself across my lap during my late-night writing sessions.